JOB

A Man of Heroic Endurance

Books in the Great Lives from God's Word series

David
A Man of Passion and Destiny

Esther
A Woman of Strength and Dignity

Joseph
A Man of Integrity and Forgiveness

Moses
A Man of Selfless Dedication

Elijah
A Man of Heroism and Humility

Paul
A Man of Grace and Grit

Job
A Man of Heroic Endurance

Fascinating Stories of Forgotten Lives
Rediscovering Some Old Testament Characters

Jesus
The Greatest Life of All

Great Days with the Great Lives
Daily Insight from Great Lives of the Bible

A Man of Heroic Endurance

JOB

Profiles in Character from

CHARLES R. SWINDOLL

THOMAS NELSON
Since 1798

NASHVILLE   DALLAS   MEXICO CITY   RIO DE JANEIRO

Published in Nashville, Tennessee, by Thomas Nelson. Thomas Nelson is a registered
trademark of Thomas Nelson, Inc.

Thomas Nelson, Inc., titles may be purchased in bulk for educational, business,
fund-raising, or sales promotional use. For information, please e-mail
SpecialMarkets@ThomasNelson.com.

All Scripture quotations in this book, except those noted otherwise, are from the *New American Standard
Bible* (NASB) © 1960, 1962, 1963, 1971, 1973, 1975, 1977, and 1995 by the Lockman Foundation, and are
used by permission.

Other Scripture quotations are from the following sources:

The Living Bible (TLB), © 1971 by Tyndale House Publishers,
Wheaton, Ill. Used by permission.

Holy Bible, *New Living Translation* (NLT) (Wheaton, Ill.: Tyndale House Publishers, 1996). Used by
permission.

The Message (MSG), © by Eugene H. Peterson,
1993, 1994, 1995, 1996. Used by permission of
NavPress Publishing Group.

Swindoll, Charles R.
   Job: a man of heroic endurance : profiles in character from Charles R. Swindoll.
   p. cm.
                                    ISBN: 978-1-4002-0250-8 (TP)
                                    ISBN: 978-0-8499-1389-1 (HC)
   1. Job (Biblical figure).   2. Bible. O.T. Job—Criticism, interpretation, etc.
   I. Title.
BS580.J5.S95   2004
223'.1092–dc22

                                                                2003021465

Printed and bound in the United States of America

HB 11.27.2023

DEDICATION

This book is dedicated to all in the family of God

who are going through times of great suffering

and have been devastated by the pain

you have had to endure.

Like Job, you have been unable to understand why.

Like Job, you have not deserved the affliction,

but the pain continues.

Like Job, you have prayed for answers

and waited for God to bring relief.

Neither has occurred.

Like Job, you keep praying and waiting.

Like Job, you sometimes wonder, "Where is God?"

He remains silent and seems aloof.

Nevertheless, you faithfully endure.

Because of that, like Job, you will someday be greatly rewarded.

You have my highest admiration.

CONTENTS

INTRODUCTION

Job: A Man of Heroic Endurance

The scarcity of heroes has troubled me for years. I am not alone. Friends I have, others I meet, and authors I read agree that the ranks of heroes have gotten remarkably thin. Whether it is because the cynics of this age take delight in highlighting the most insignificant flaws of the famous or because those whom we once admired from a distance failed to pass the more exacting litmus tests of close examination or because the public has simply wearied of the fallen-hero syndrome, even the idea of calling someone our hero has come into disfavor in today's culture. A malaise of fear over finding some hidden fact that discredits the one being admired has robbed the trust once placed in others.

Nevertheless, I am still convinced we need heroes. The imperfections of humanity notwithstanding, our hearts hunger to be stimulated by examples of great character being modeled in everyday life. We are fortified by exemplary lives, especially those who have earned the right to be respected by their character, sacrifice, patience, and ability to press on in spite of hardship, injustice, pain, and failure. Our heroes do not have to be perfect. They must, however be courageous, authentic, clear-minded, and determined to endure no matter the sacrifice or cost. We need heroes of integrity and consistency, admirable men and women we can admire, not because they exemplify a quick burst of bravery, but because they represent the stuff of greatness and stay at it to the end. Finishing strong is a vital part of standing tall. By having that "great cloud of witnesses" urging us on, we're better able to endure.

Peter Gibbon, in his splendid work, *A Call to Heroism*, agrees:

> I cannot imagine a world without heroes, a world without genius and nobility, without exalted enterprise, high purpose, and transcendent courage, without risk and suffering. It would be gray and flat and dull. Who would show us the way or set the mark? Who would inspire us and console us? Who would energize us and keep us from the darkness?[1]

Realizing the ever-present importance of models of greatness we can trust, back around the turn of the century I began writing a series of books based on the lives of selected men and women whose biographies appear in the pages of the Bible. I called the series Great Lives from God's Word. During the past four years I have released six volumes. The response has been wonderfully gratifying. If you have journeyed with me through these profiles in character, you will remember the lives we have examined together:

David: A Man of Passion and Destiny
Esther: A Woman of Strength and Dignity
Joseph: A Man of Integrity and Forgiveness
Moses: A Man of Selfless Dedication
Elijah: A Man of Heroism and Humility
Paul: A Man of Grace and Grit

During the past year I have discovered another hero tucked away in the biblical text. He was neither hidden nor obscure, but I had never realized how significant he was until I began a thorough investigation of who he was and what he endured. He appears rather boldly in the ancient book that bears his name, but since most of his story is so full of pain and loss, humiliation and hardship as he suffers through a debilitating illness and a heated, lengthy debate with several of his friends, most of us have not taken the time to examine his life in depth. A quick glance at his circumstances leaves the reader heartbroken and confused. In most minds, Job is a pathetic study in tragedy—little more than a helpless victim of unfair treatment rather than a man of enormous endurance.

On the contrary, a careful examination of the man's life—especially his response to the painful experiences that assaulted his once peaceful and God-honoring existence—will convince us that this is another hero with character qualities worth emulating.

Before we begin our journey into Job's world, I need to pause and express my gratitude to those in my world who have helped birth the seventh volume in this current biographical series. First and foremost, it was Michael Hyatt, Executive Vice President and Group Publisher of Thomas Nelson Publishers, who quietly yet confidently encouraged me to pick up my pen and put my thoughts into print. Mike and my longtime friend, David Moberg with the W Publishing Group, have continued to believe in this project and have provided great encouragement to me during the writing of this particular work.

Carol Spencer, my executive assistant, has faithfully, patiently, and efficiently turned my handwritten pages into a well-crafted manuscript that met my publisher's demands and deadlines. Though broadly experienced in the business world, she had never undertaken this sort of project. Nevertheless, she happily accepted the challenges with a captivating smile and an energetic will, fitting the many extra hours it required into her already-busy schedule. Thanks to Carol, especially, you are holding this book in your hands today. And with Carol, I must thank Mary Hollingsworth and her splendid staff for their keen-eyed diligence and attention to detail in editing the final copy and putting the finishing touches on the manuscript before it was released to the printer.

There is one other group of people who deserve special mention. I'm refer-ring to the congregation of Stonebriar Community Church in Frisco, Texas. It is not only my privilege to serve as the founding pastor of this fine flock, but I should mention that they were the ones who first heard the results of my work in the text of Job during most of the Sunday mornings throughout the year 2002. They exemplified great patience as we kept returning to the numerous and sometimes tedious chapters of the Book of Job week after week. I'm not saying they began to weary under the load, but I can testify that when the day arrived when I was able to announce we were coming to an end of our study of Job, the place exploded with spontaneous, loud applause! May God abun-dantly reward them for their endurance.

Finally, I want to thank Cynthia, my wife of forty-eight years and devoted partner in ministry. Even though I have been glued to this desk all these months completing this book—and have been sustaining a schedule similar to this since I first began writing far back in 1975—not once have I heard her com-plain. On the contrary, she has remained supportive and encouraging, willing to sacrifice her own plans and preferences in order to help me accomplish the task at hand. My love and gratitude for her know no bounds.

And now it's time for us to travel far back in time and meet the man in the land of Uz who will soon emerge from print on an ancient page into a modern-day hero in your heart. My hope is that you will come to realize in a personal way the truth of what Paul once wrote regarding the Old Testa-ment Scriptures;

Even if it was written in Scripture long ago, you can be sure it's writ-ten for us. God wants the combination of his steady, constant calling and warm, personal counsel in Scripture to come to characterize us, keeping us alert for whatever he will do next.

—Romans 15:4, MSG

With that in mind, it may be God's desire to prepare you for some of the same things Job endured. Since that is a very real possibility, I'd suggest you pay close attention to everything you are about to read. Who knows what God will do next?

—Chuck Swindoll
Dallas, Texas

CHAPTER ONE

Setting the Stage for Disaster

L ife is difficult. That blunt, three-word statement is an accurate appraisal of our existence on this planet. When the writer of the biblical book named Job picked up his stylus to write his story, he could have begun with a similar-sounding and equally blunt sentence, "Life is unfair."

No one could argue the point that life is punctuated with hardship, heartaches, and headaches. Most of us have learned to face the reality that life is difficult. But *unfair?* Something kicks in, deep within most of us, making it almost intolerable for us to accept and cope with what's unfair. Our drive for justice overrides our patience with pain. A couple of examples come to mind.

You're born and reared in Canada, and you're on ice skates as far back as you can remember. Throughout your growing-up years, while skating along the ice, you are dreaming of someday making it to the Olympics. Skating is difficult. You fall more times than you can remember, but in every fall you learn another lesson, and every year you perfect your technique. Ultimately, you learn to skate very well. You get a special teacher and you find a skating partner, who is also from your homeland. The two of you skate toward your mutual dream of being at the Salt Lake City 2002 Winter Olympics.

Finally, your moment comes. As your names are announced, you slide smoothly and gracefully onto the ice. Your dream has come true. You perform your routine to perfection—better than you've ever done it. And you know in your hearts as you finish that it was a gold-medal performance. Both of you are ecstatic . . . until you see the scores. Your heart sinks. As you read those numbers you realize that you'll get the silver medal and another couple less qualified than you will win the gold. At that moment, life is difficult. In a few hours time, however, you will find out that the judging was skewed, that the competition was fixed. And in fact, one of the judges would later be removed. You didn't know that at the time you saw the score. When you find all that out, difficult is changed to unfair, and that's a whole different subject. Once you learn that the judging was deliberately unfair, you can't tolerate the thought of accepting the silver medal.

My second example doesn't have as good an ending. You're a single parent living 1,200 miles from a job offer that comes to you from Houston. So you give serious thought to moving you and your three children (who are all under the age of fifteen) down south so that you might get a much better job working for a lot more money in a company that is really moving ahead. You make the move as you begin working for Enron. You find yourself fulfilled and stretched. Things are really looking up. You're doing so well you decide to invest in the company's stock. The money is good, your future is bright, and the news is out that this is the blue-chip company to be a part of. They're even naming the new stadium in Houston after the Enron Corporation. Then one day you overhear some troubling comments at the water fountain.

The scuttlebutt around the office isn't encouraging. You doubt it, you question it, and in fact you put it out of your mind because, after all, your entire retirement funds are there, your health benefits are there, and your financial security is there. Suddenly, almost before you can blink, you get a pink slip, and it's all over. You lose everything. It's not your fault—you were doing a good job. You moved for all the right reasons, and now there's the threat of losing your house. Life is difficult as you ponder telling the kids.

A couple of days later you're showering and you notice a small lump under your left breast. Your stomach turns. You can't believe it. Two days later the biopsy reveals that you have an aggressive malignancy. Oh, I failed to mention, three years ago your husband ran off with his much younger and attractive assistant and, by the way, they're doing great. Both of them have new cars, secure, well-paying jobs, and no kids. And you? You're going to move in with your aging parents, neither of whom is all that healthy, and their little home has only three bedrooms. One day the full load hits you: Life is not just difficult, it's downright *unfair*.

Welcome to Job's world.

Without realizing it, you have just walked onto Job's turf. (And to think some people believe the Bible is irrelevant!) Not only is Job's story relevant, it represents one of the oldest and best pieces of literature in all of time. Some would date it back to the days of Genesis. In light of Job's old age, it falls in the category of being written during the days of the patriarchs. Martin Luther once used these two words when referring to Job: *magnificent* and *sublime*. The nineteenth century Scottish essayist, Thomas Carlyle, wrote, "There is nothing written, I think, in the Bible or out of it, of equal literary merit."[1] Victor Hugo, the French poet and author, concluded that Job is perhaps the greatest masterpiece of the human mind.

Eugene Peterson, one of our contemporary writers, in his paraphrase of The Old Testament, says this in his introduction of Job:

> It is not only because Job suffered that he is important to us. It is because he suffered in the same ways that we suffer—in the vital areas of family, personal health, and material things. Job is also important to us because he searchingly questioned and boldly protested his suffering. Indeed, he went "to the top" with his questions.
>
> It is not the suffering that troubles us. It is undeserved suffering.
>
> Almost all of us in our years of growing up have the experience of disobeying our parents and getting punished for it. When that discipline was connected with wrongdoing, it had a certain sense of justice to it: *When we do wrong, we get punished.*

One of the surprises as we get older, however, is that we come to see that there is no real correlation between the amount of wrong we commit and the amount of pain we experience. An even larger surprise is that very often there is something quite the opposite: We do right and get knocked down. We do the best we are capable of doing, and just as we are reaching out to receive our reward we are hit from the blind side and sent reeling.[2]

A QUICK AND DIRTY ANALYSIS

Those words describe precisely what happened with Job. Life was not simply difficult, it became absolutely unfair. You may not know about Job's agony. It's easy to think that a story this old is familiar to everyone, but it may be new to you. So, allow me a few lines to offer a quick and dirty analysis.

Job was a man of unparalleled and genuine piety. He was also a man of well-deserved prosperity. He was a godly gentleman, extremely wealthy, a fine husband, and a faithful father. In a quick and brutal sweep of back-to-back calamities, Job was reduced to a twisted mass of brokenness and grief. The extraordinary accumulation of disasters that hit him would have been enough to finish off any one of us living today.

Job is left bankrupt, homeless, helpless, and childless. He's left standing beside the ten fresh graves of his now-dead children on a windswept hill. His wife is heaving deep sobs of grief as she kneels beside him, having just heard him say, "Whether our God gives to us or takes everything from us, we will follow Him." She leans over and secretly whispers, "Just curse God and die." Pause and ponder their grief—and remember the man had done nothing to deserve such unbearable pain.

I have a friend who is also in ministry. When I e-mailed him recently, I mentioned my plans to write a book about Job, calling him "A Man of Heroic Endurance." He quickly responded and warned me about taking on such subjects. "You never know what happens when you get into stories like Job's," he wrote. "How often you become a participant in the story that you're writing." Sort of put a chill up my back. To keep me from becoming grim, he added this touch of humor: "I have a friend who was driving across Texas late one night searching for a radio station to keep him company. Finally, he tuned into a country preacher who was beginning a series on Job. The preacher had titled his radio message, 'I Can't Eat by Day, I Can't Sleep by Night, and the Woman I Love Don't Treat Me Right.' "[3] Not bad. That's Job in less than twenty words. Only difference is there's nothing funny in the real account. Unfair suffering is never funny.

Misery and mystery are added to the insult and injury of Job's real-life disasters. As he sits there covered with skin ulcers that have begun erupting with pus, swelling his body with fever and giving him a maddening itch that will not cease, he looks up into the faces of three friends who arrive on the scene. They sit and stare at the man for seven days and nights without uttering a word. Just imagine. First, they don't recognize him, which tells you something of the extent of his swelling and the sores that covered his body. The sight causes them to be at a loss for words for a full week. Unfortunately, they didn't remain silent. When they finally did speak, they had nothing to say but blame, accusation, and insult. "You're getting what you deserve." Though they shaped their cutting remarks in much more philosophical terms, they proved unmerciful. His pain only intensified.

His misery turns to mystery with God's silence. If the words of his so-called friends are hard to hear, the silence of God becomes downright intolerable. Not until the thirty-eighth chapter of the book does God finally break the silence, however long that took. If it were just a few months, try to imagine. You've become the object of your alleged friends' accusations, and the heavens are brass as you plead for answers from the Almighty, who remains mysteriously mute. Nothing comes to you by way of comfort. It's all so unfair; you've done nothing to deserve such anguish. So much for openers.

LET'S GO BACK AND START OVER

The story begins with the remarkable résumé of a fine man. Job may become our hero of endurance, but let's remember he's only a man. He's not superman. He's not an angel in a human's body. He's just a man. "There was a man in the land of Uz, whose name was Job; and that man was blameless" (Job 1:1). It doesn't mean perfect; it means he did not compromise with moral evil. He was a man whose business dealings were handled with integrity. He kept his word. He dealt fairly with others. As a result, he was respected by those around him, whether within or outside the family. He was upright. He held God in respect, and he consistently eschewed evil. He was a man with character. And speaking of his family, Job was blessed with seven sons and three daughters. By the time Job's story gets told, all ten are grown. His was a life at its zenith.

By now he had amassed a remarkable number of possessions. Among them were 7,000 sheep. Much of the wool from the animals would have been sold. The portion held back could be woven into fabric that would be made into warm clothing for the cold winter days. The family's food would be provided from these animals and acres of crops. There were also 3,000 camels. I would imagine Job "ran a trucking business" for the caravans that went from east to west. No doubt, his camels were for hire. And those camels became his personal transportation. There were 1,000 oxen, yoked together in pairs to plow the fertile fields, preparing the soil for planting the seed that was later harvested for an abundance of food. And then we're told there were 500 female donkeys. In that ancient era, female donkeys provided the delicacy of the day—donkey milk.

Over and above all that was a happy, healthy family of ten adult children living nearby. No diapers to change. No baths to give. No carpools. No big meals to prepare. No lunches for school. No boys with big tattoos, driving sleek chariots, showing up and honking out front for the daughters. No teenaged daughters with nose rings and pierced belly buttons running around the house. All that's now behind Job and his wife. Job's got it made, and amazingly, no one was criticizing because there's nothing about him to criticize. Job had it made.

The late J. Vernon McGee wrote this about Job: "This man lived in the lap of luxury. The last part of verse 3 would indicate to us that he was Howard Hughes, John D. Rockefeller, Henry Ford, and the oil men of Texas all rolled into one."[4] When I read that, the thought struck me that he wrote those words far back in the 1970s. Let's face it, by the economic collapse in the late 1980s, the closest Texas oilmen got to money was when they pumped gas at the Texaco station on the corner. Today we might say he was Bill Gates, Donald Trump, and Ross Perot all wrapped up in one. Job was healthy, wealthy, good, and godly, but he was not out of touch. You will notice he did have his concerns.

> His sons used to go and hold a feast in the house of each one on his day, and they would send and invite their three sisters to eat and drink with them.
>
> It came about, when the days of feasting had completed their cycle, that Job would send and consecrate them, rising up early in the morning and offering burnt offerings *according* to the number of them all; for Job said, "Perhaps my sons have sinned and cursed God in their hearts." Thus Job did continually.
>
> Job 1:4–5

By offering up ten burnt offerings in the name of each young adult, he was concerned that in their hearts there may have been a hint of disobedience or perhaps one of them told an off-colored story during their frequent get-togethers. Job is diligent deep within—spiritually sensitive not only regarding his life, but for the walk and talk of his children. Praying man. Pure man. Priestly man. Faithful man. What a man!

Francis Andersen writes clarifying words in his fine work on Job.

> We need not suppose that they spent all their time in roistering and did no work. There is no hint of drunkenness or licence or laziness. Job expresses no anxiety on this score, although he is aware of the danger that they might slip into profanity. These delightful family gatherings are part of the atmosphere of well-being that begins the story. They are a mark of good fortune, or rather of God's blessing. . . .
>
> The finishing touch to this happy scene is the godly parent making doubly sure that all is well.[5]

I say again, what a man!

THE SCENE CHANGES

At the end of verse 5 there must have been a pause. If this were a novel, you would turn the page and move into the next chapter of the story. If this were a film, it would be a slow fadeout. You would sit in darkness for a few seconds, then a bright scene would appear telling you that you were in another setting at another time. If this were a stage play, the curtains would close at the end of verse 5. The audience would be given a few moments to stretch and stand, then sit back down for the opening of the curtains after the stagehand changed the scenery from earth to heaven. But no such markings appear in the Bible. You simply move from verse 5 to verse 6. Verses 1 to 5 are full of good news, wonderful blessing, business integrity, purity of heart, faithfulness of life. The man is spiritually mature, domestically diligent, and professionally respected.

As he sleeps, another scene opens to us that Job knows nothing about. Similar things happen in our lives as well. When we're not aware of it, God is carrying out a plan that would amaze us and, on occasion, shock us. He is permitting things to get under way that we would have never expected. Without Job's knowledge, something is happening in the heavenlies. We are transported from planet Earth to the third heaven to witness its occurrence.

Ponder the difference between the opening lines of Job 1:1 and Job 1:6: "There was a man . . . there was a day." There was a man who lived on this earth. There was a day in the throne room of God. We are lifted from earth's familiar setting to the unfamiliar scene of God's presence in heaven. The only ones comfortable there would be the seraphim who filled the presence of the living God with the movement of their wings. They are the ever-present attendants of the Almighty, called in verse 6, "the sons of God."

As the Lord God looks about, He sees His angelic servants who have come to present themselves before Him. And why not? They're accountable to Him. They do His bidding as they carry out His will.

Present among them is an intruder. There is one who is not among the elect angels. He is identified in the Hebrew text *"the Satan." HAA-SahTahn.* (Every time the name Satan appears in the first two chapters of Job, it is *HAA-SahTahn,* meaning *the SahTahn, "The Satan.").*

What does it mean? *SahTahn* is a Hebrew verb. Most often Hebrew words originate with the verb form. *SahTahn* means, "to be an adversary, to resist." Therefore, in noun form it is often rendered, the Adversary or the Accuser. Satan accuses God's people day and night. Suddenly the Accuser appears among the other angels.

Pause and remember Satan is not a little imp with a red body, carrying a pitchfork and sitting on one of your shoulders whispering ugly little nothings in your ear. That's a medieval caricature that Satan would love for you to believe. He is the most attractive, brilliant, powerful archangel that God ever created. He has not lost his brilliance. He has not lost his power. He has certainly not lost his appealing beauty. He is also insidious. Satan's favorite method of working is behind the scenes. Because he is invisible does not mean he is not real. As we will see a little later, he has personality. And he is engaged in a relentless commitment to destroying God's people and opposing God's plan. It is this insidious Adversary we find standing in the heavenlies among the group of faithful angelic servants.

AN INSIDIOUS PLAN SUGGESTED BY SATAN

Beginning at verse 7 down through verse 12, we have a dialogue that is most interesting. You won't find it anywhere else in the Bible. The Lord God sees the intruder and speaks to him. "From where do you come?" (Job 1:7). Please don't misread that. Being omniscient (all-knowing), God knows everything. His question could be rendered, "Tell me what you've been about. What's been going on?"

Satan's answer is brief and seems impudent. "From roaming about on the earth and walking around on it" (Job 1:7). The Adversary has access to this planet as well as the heavenlies. He moves all about earth as do his demonic forces. He has random access to wherever he wishes to go. The earthly elements that hold us in check do not affect him. Being supernatural, he can move instantly from Asia to America. He could leave Australia and be at the North Pole in a split second. When Satan says, "I've been roaming about on the earth," he means that, literally.

The Lord then asks, "Have you considered My servant Job?" (Job 1:8). What a wonderful title God gave Job! "My servant." He may have been considered the "greatest of all the men of the east" (Job 1:3), but the wonderful fact about Job is that he was God's servant. Though well known far and wide, he was no celebrity in God's eyes. There was no pride in the man's heart. God's evaluation is impressive: "For there is no one like him on the earth, a blameless and upright man, fearing God and turning away from evil" (Job 1:8).

Hearing the word *evil*, the source of evil responds, "Does Job fear God for nothing?" (Job 1:9). In our words, "Look, God, talk about kid glove treatment! The man gets penthouse perks." The Accuser continues, "Have you not made a hedge about him and his house and all that he has?" (Job 1:10).

Consider the categories. "You have protected his body from illness. You have protected his family from harm. And, You have protected his possessions from destruction. He has it made on every side. The divine wall around this man's life is nothing short of enviable. You have not only protected him, You have blessed the work of his hands. His possessions, as his fame, have increased in the land." The Accuser is claiming divine favoritism. I mean— the audacity of that! "You have built a thick hedge around him. You have blessed him like no other. Who wouldn't worship You?"

Here we witness the Accuser's personality. We know that he has an *intellect* because he converses with the Lord. We see that Satan has *emotions* because he is antagonistic toward Job. He also has *volition* because he purposes to destroy Job in hopes of disgracing God. Satan's great hope is to level Job. "But put forth Your hand now and touch *all* that he has; he will surely curse You to Your face" (Job 1:11, italics mine). "You bring him down to the dirt like the rest of those humans have to live their lives, and You'll see what he's made of. He'll turn on You in a heartbeat!"

It's a clever plan. It is also unfair. Job does not deserve even the suggestion of mistreatment. Job has walked with God, certainly in his adult years. He is now the best of the best, "greatest of all the men of the east." On top of all that, he is a servant of God. But none of that impresses Satan. Evil suspicions prompt his insidious plot: "You want to know what he's really made of, remove all that indulged treatment and pervasive protection. Strip away the veneer of the man's comfort, and You'll see right away, he'll turn on You. 'He will surely curse You to Your face'" (Job 1:11). Satan's prediction. "Instead of treating him like an overindulged child, why don't you treat him like anybody else on earth? Let him know what it's like to suffer the death of a child. Let him go through the loss of all those possessions. Let all that hit him full force, and You'll see what Job's made of." His point is clear: Job is worshiping God because of what he gets out of it, not because the Lord is truly first in his life.

God has heard enough: "The LORD said to Satan, 'Behold, *all* that he has is in your power'" (Job 1:12, italics mine). Don't read any further for a moment. That's a terribly frightening thought. Read the Lord's words once again, only slower.

Look at the permission slip He hands Satan. "All that he has is yours to deal with." He adds a caveat, "only do not put forth your hand on him" (Job 1:12). "Don't you touch his life. Don't touch his body or his soul or his mind. You can remove his possessions and you can attack his family, but leave the man, himself, alone."

Satan departed from the presence of the Lord with a sinister grin. Keep in mind, Job knew nothing of that dialogue.

FOUR PRINCIPLES THAT REMAIN TRUE TO THIS DAY

That's enough for one sitting. We'll return to Satan's plan in the next chapter. Let's pause here and give some thought to how all this relates to our world today. Four principles emerge that seem relevant.

Principle one: There is an enemy we encounter we cannot see . . . but he is real. We have a supernatural enemy, and we encounter him or one of his emissaries regularly. And never doubt it—all of that is real. He hopes that his deceptive strategy will play tricks on your mind and will weaken you and ultimately bring you down. The Accuser's desire is to ruin your testimony as he destroys your life. In the process, if it means ruining your family relationships, he'll go there. If it takes tempting you to secretly cut a few corners in your business which you would not have done in earlier days, he'll go there. Whatever it takes to bring you down, he will try. Because we have an enemy we cannot see does not mean he is not real.

Principle two: There are trials we endure we do not deserve, but they are permitted. You read that correctly. Life includes trials that we do not deserve, but they must, nevertheless, be endured. At the beginning of this chapter I mentioned a woman who did not deserve to work for a company that turned against the very principles she thought they believed in. She did not deserve losing her retirement or getting cancer. After all, she was a hardworking, single mother trying to raise three kids under the age of fifteen. She may not have been dealt a fair shake in life, but it was all permitted. The same can be said about you. In the mystery of God's unfathomable will, we can never explain or fully understand. Do not try to grasp each thread of His profound plan. If you resist my counsel here, you'll become increasingly more confused, ultimately resentful, and finally bitter. At that point, Satan will have won the day. Accept it. Endure the trial that has been permitted by God. Nothing touches your life that has not first passed through the hands of God. He is in full control and because He is, He has the sovereign right to permit trials that we do not deserve.

Principle three: There is a plan we explore we will not understand, but it is best. Though each segment of it may not be fair or pleasant, it works together for good. The disease Job later endured wasn't good in and of itself. Hardly! But it worked together for good. Our perspective is dreadfully limited. We see in the pinpoint of time, but God's view is panoramic. God's big-picture, cosmic plan is at work now, and He doesn't feel the need (nor is He obligated) to explain it to us. If He tried, our answer would be like the confused teenager listening to his calculus teacher, "What?" You wouldn't get it, nor would I. Just remember, the Father knows what is best for His children. Rest in that realization.

Principle four: There are consequences we experience, we could not anticipate, but they are necessary. I don't know where you find yourself today, but I would be willing to wager that most of you reading this book are going through something that is unfair. Chances are good that you simply don't deserve what's happening. The consequences may have started to get to you. You didn't anticipate any of this. You didn't think it would come to this, but it has. Trust me here. What has happened is a necessary part of your spiritual growth. Yes, *necessary.* I've finally begun to accept that reality after all these years of my life.

As I close this chapter, I want to address you who have moved onto Job's turf. If nothing else, it has prepared you to pay closer attention to the message woven through this book. You've seen only a glimpse of how things started. The story doesn't end with Satan's departing from the presence of the Lord. There's a whole lot more to Job's story. And I need to repeat what I said at the beginning: the more it unfolds, the more you will realize that life is not only difficult, it is unfair.

The silence of God's voice will make you wonder if He is even there. And the absence of God's presence will make you wonder if He even cares. He is. And He does.

CHAPTER TWO

Reeling and Recovering from Devastating News

S ome events hit with such ferocity they leave mental shrapnel embedded in our brains. The mention of the dates reminds us not only of the atrocity, but also where we were at the time and how we reacted when the news struck with full force.

- December 7, 1941, Pearl Harbor, Oahu
- November 22, 1963, Dallas, Texas
- September 11, 2001, New York, Washington, D.C., and a Pennsylvania countryside

If you've lived as long as I have, those three dates live in infamy. I can tell you exactly where I was, what I was doing, and how I felt. The most recent, of course, is the most vivid.

A carefully coordinated strategy planned and performed by terrorists resulted in the murder of thousands of innocent lives as those acts of devastation were carried out. The twin towers that once added their elegance to the New York City skyline are now conspicuous by their absence; an entire wing of the Pentagon was destroyed; and a peaceful site near a wooded section in southwest Pennsylvania was changed forever. In the wake of that third horrendous event, a name has emerged. Many others were heroic, but the story of this particular individual stands out in bold relief.

He is Todd Beamer, faithful husband and devoted father of two, with his wife, Lisa, who was carrying their third child. The events of Todd's life that fateful morning are familiar to most of us. While on the hijacked plane, he called GTE Communications Center in Oakbrook, Illinois, and spoke with one of the supervisors, Lisa Jefferson. In that conversation there was a mixture of calm, carefully guarded words, tears, and a hint of panic. Finally, Todd asked her to pray the Lord's Prayer with him. After that prayer, Todd's last words were firm: "Are you guys ready? Let's roll!" And indeed they did. They diverted United Airlines Flight 93 from being a missile that would kill many more than those on board. Ultimately, thanks to Todd and his fellow passengers, the aircraft was kept from accomplishing a far greater devastating objective as it crashed into a meadow in Pennsylvania.

Todd Beamer was just a passenger on the plane. He was not trained to fight terrorists. He never dreamed he would or could do such a thing. But he and the others did. Without ever giving thought to such, Todd Beamer became heroic.[1] As I heard of the report, the words from the nineteenth century poet, Henry Wadsworth Longfellow, came to mind:

> The heights by great men reached and kept
> Were not attained by sudden flight,
> But they, while their companions slept
> Were toiling upward in the night.[2]

I've never known anyone who deliberately set out to be heroic. You may have never thought of it, but the way you and I will be remembered by some who have watched us going through certain trials will be, from their perspective, an heroic accomplishment.

Travel back with me many centuries to a date the sands of time have now erased. To a place few could locate on a map. To a setting that seems almost idyllic. To a man who had no clue what extremes he would be called upon to endure. Even though this man was also a good husband and a devoted, faithful father, a businessman with great integrity, he would live to see all that change in a back-to-back sweep of devastating events. Interestingly, Job would be remembered—not for being healthy, wealthy, and wise—but for his heroic level of endurance after losing everything.

Centuries later, when another biblical character mentioned Job, he wrote "You have heard of the endurance of Job" (James 5:11). Using the Greek term, *hupomone,* James was saying, in effect, "You have heard of the man who stood fast, enduring under the load." Job's losses hit him like a two-ton pallet of bricks. Going through one blow after another, after another, after another, the man steadfastly endured. His name has become a byword for heroic endurance.

How many patients facing radical surgery have taken comfort from the life of Job? How many grieving, shattered parents, laying their son or daughter to rest have turned to Job for reassurance? How many who have endured a failing business venture have remembered Job and found the strength to go on?

Job's heartbreaking losses are intensified because they occurred without a hint of warning. That alone was enough to send the average person reeling. It's easy to overlook the abrupt swiftness of the blows that hit him because we knew they were coming . . . and why. Having been informed of this strange "cosmic agreement" between the Sustainer of Life and the Adversary, the shock factor is diminished. While we knew the unusual nature of the deal that was struck, Job knew nothing. In fact, he may have never been told all the details of the plot. But responding with the strength of character he had cultivated over years of trusting his God and walking with Him, the loss of everything did not cause Job to curse God and turn against Him. But it must have been terribly confusing.

I think Philip Yancey's take on all this is worth considering.

It helps to think of the Book of Job as a mystery play, a "whodunit" detective story. Before the play itself begins, we in the audience get a sneak preview, as if we have showed up early for a press conference in which the director explains his work (chapters 1–2). He relates the plot and describes the main characters, then tells us in advance who did what in the play, and why. In fact, he solves every mystery in the play except one: how will the main character respond? Will Job trust God or deny Him?

Later, when the curtain rises, we see only the actors on stage. Confined within the play, they have no knowledge of what the director has told us in the sneak preview. We know the answer to the "whodunit" questions, but the star detective, Job, does not. He spends all his time on stage trying to discover what we already know. He scratches himself with shards of pottery and asks, "Why me? What did I do wrong? What is God trying to tell me?"

To the audience, Job's questions should be mere intellectual exercises, for we learned the answers in the prologue, the first two chapters. What did Job do wrong? Nothing. He represents the very best of the species. Didn't God himself call Job "blameless and upright, a man who fears God and shuns evil?" Why, then, is Job suffering? Not for punishment. Far from it—he has been selected as the principal player in a great contest of the heavens.[3]

Remember, Job knew nothing of what had transpired in God's presence. All he knew is this: One day things were delightful, and the next day they were dreadful. Throughout his life he had been strong and healthy, and in a flash he was in anguishing, debilitating pain. There was no rhyme or reason. Not knowing why was the maddening part.

I have found in life that when we don't know why we are suffering, the suffering is harder. If I could pinpoint the cause, if I could determine the sin that brought on all this pain, I could deal with it, confess it, and maybe the suffering will end—or at least ease up. But when there's no cause, no sin, no one to blame, no source to identify, the absence of anything tangible leaves us hanging.

SETTING THE STAGE

Our hero, Job, is about to go there. But before that happens, let's pause long enough to rehearse and enter into the original setting.

Then the LORD said to Satan, "Behold, all that he has is in your power, only do not put forth your hand on him." So Satan departed from the presence of the LORD.

Now on the day when his sons and his daughters were eating and drinking wine in their oldest brother's house, a messenger came to Job and said, "The oxen were plowing and the donkeys feeding beside them, and the Sabeans attacked and took them. They also slew the servants with the edge of the sword, and I alone have escaped to tell you."

While he was still speaking, another also came and said, "The fire of God fell from heaven and burned up the sheep and the servants and consumed them, and I alone have escaped to tell you."

While he was still speaking, another also came and said, "The Chaldeans formed three bands and made a raid on the camels and took them and slew the servants with the edge of the sword, and I alone have escaped to tell you."

While he was still speaking, another also came and said, "Your sons and daughters were eating and drinking wine in their oldest brother's house, and behold a great wind came from across the wilderness and struck the four corners of the house, and it fell on the young people and they died, and I alone have escaped to tell you."

Job 1:12–19

I suggest you pretend you've never read this before. That'll help. Please notice the turning point of the biblical account: "So Satan departed" (v. 12). He wasted no time: "Now it happened" (v. 13). Stop right there. The entire dialogue between God and Satan was inaudible. I've already mentioned it was not known by Job. We learn that all Job's grown children have gone over to Job Junior's home for a relaxing time together. They're eating together and having a great time with each other. Job, being the good father that he is, not super-pious but genuinely concerned, is praying for them. Maybe one of them had begun to drift, or something could be said that would cause another to respond inappropriately in such a way it would damage the relationship that he or she has with the Lord. As we would expect, Job resorts to prayer. He goes to his knees, all alone, in his own home.

At the same time, if you were to look out Job's window, you would see the oxen plowing the field, preparing the soil for the next crop. It's a sunny afternoon, soft clouds floating in the distance. There are sheep grazing on the field, and donkeys feeding nearby. The camels are being loaded up for the next journey on the long caravan trail. All the field hands are hard at it, handling the animals they know by name. Over in the oldest son's house, a couple of miles away, the brothers and sisters are having a blast telling family stories and laughing over a few recent events. If you listen closely through the door at the home of Mr. and Mrs. Job, you could hear the prayers of a good father as he names one child after another. This father doesn't have the foggiest idea of what he's about to face. But in the cosmic realm, "Satan departed . . . and now it happened."

SHOCK-AND-AWE NEWS . . . DEVASTATING GRIEF

Suddenly there's a loud banging at the door of the big house. Once he opens that door, Job's life will never be the same. It's like the chilling phone call you would get in the middle of the night or the unexpected rap at your front door . . . an unannounced visit from someone wearing a uniform.

The messenger bursts in without being invited. He's winded and sobbing. With uncontrollable passion he blurts out, "The oxen . . . our oxen were plowing and the donkeys were feeding beside them, and those people from Shebea . . . they *attacked us!* We've talked about the possibility of their coming; they've done it . . . they've assaulted us, master . . . and they took those animals, all the animals— and they've cut your servants to ribbons. I'm the only one who escaped!"

While he was still speaking, another messenger plunges into the scene. Without hesitation he screamed: "There was this bolt of lightning, it was like fire that came down from heaven and in an instant it consumed all of the sheep and all of the field hands who take care of the sheep . . . and I'm the only one who made it out alive!"

Another pushes him aside as he grabs Job by his sleeve, "Master, you wouldn't believe it, but three raids from the Chaldeans have hit that area where we were preparing the camels for the next trip . . . they have taken all your camels away, and before leaving they murdered every one of your servants. I alone am left."

As Job stumbles to the side to regain his balance, surely he must have thought, "At least I've got my kids." Interrupting that thought, another workman plunges in, fighting back the tears. "Master Job, your sons and your daughters . . . *they're all gone!* There was this fierce tornado that swept through the wilderness, throwing wooden carts and animal carcasses into the air, and, Master, it kept coming with this deafening roar, it came right over the house of your oldest son, and the place exploded—and all of your children . . . were . . . killed."

Force yourself to pause and picture the scene. Just imagine . . .

I have half a shelf of books on Job in my library. One of them is a treasured volume containing a few wonderful works of art. As I thumbed through the book, I happened upon two woodcut prints by Gustave Doré circa 1860. The artist depicts two scenes that the Scriptures leave for the reader to imagine. Both are titled "Job Hearing of His Ruin." One of them shows the anguishing man with his forearm and open palm stretched across his eyes. His mouth is open as he grieves. You can almost hear the news that everything is gone—including all the kids. Everything. Everyone. The second scene shows a man who has fallen flat on his face, barefoot, alone with his hand across the back of his head.[4] The longer I stare and feel Job's devastating grief, the more I see.

Those who have seen the film, *Saving Private Ryan,* will not soon forget a very moving scene. There's a country house at the end of a long dusty road. The mother is at the kitchen sink fixing supper. While working, she looks up. To her surprise, she sees an olive-drab sedan coming along that winding road toward her. She stops and stares. The closer it gets, the more obvious it is—this is an official vehicle. There are four stars in her window. Terrified, she clutches her apron to her face. Kindly but firmly, one of the army officers begins, "We regret to inform you, Mrs. Ryan . . ." As she hears of the death of three of her four sons, she drops to her knees in unbearable anguish. The theater audience sits in absolute silence as they absorb the mother's grief. At that point the plot is set in motion for searching for and saving Private Ryan to preserve the family name.

There is a magnificent swell of national pride and gratitude in the loss of one's sons in a war to preserve the liberty of the United States of America. There is nobility and respect in placing those precious remains in a grave, knowing they died for all the right reasons. Mrs. Ryan could at least draw strength from knowing her sons paid the ultimate price out of love for their country's freedom. The lonely sound of "Taps" echoes with dignity.

But Job lost all of his precious children in a freak storm out of nowhere, for no apparent reason. And for the first time in thirty-five, maybe forty years, Job and his wife are childless. Furthermore, God hid from that father and mother the meaning of this confusing quagmire. He provided no explanation. Offered no comfort. The silence of heaven became more devastating than the shocking news on earth.

Upon reading the biblical account, when you arrive at the end of that heart-wrenching episode where four trembling messengers have poured out their souls and Job has absorbed the full brunt of their tragic reports, you have to pause and let the grief seep in. Talk about the classic opportunity to allow your emotions to run free—this is it! This is life at its lowest ebb—the absolute end of the trail. The only one taking delight in the scene is the supernatural creature who caused it to happen. Satan and his demonic hosts are on the edge of their seats in the invisible evil empire, watching anxiously, anticipating the venom that is certain to burst from that father's lips. "He can't endure this without cursing his God, spoiled man that he is. We've taken it all, and he's left with nothing to hold on to. Just wait; we'll see the real Job now!"

A REMARKABLE RESPONSE

Then Job arose and tore his robe and shaved his head, and he fell to the ground and worshiped. He said,

Naked I came from my mother's womb,
And naked I shall return there.
The LORD gave and the LORD has taken away.

> Blessed be the name of the LORD.
> Through all this Job did not sin nor did he blame God.
>
> Job 1:20–22

Focus first on the opening word. We do not know how much time passed between Job's hearing the news and responding to it. Could have been all the rest of the afternoon he lay there. He could have stumbled outside to look in the distance and to see with his own eyes the remains of the house, now a shambles, holding the bodies of his children. Job may not have responded until after the burials, as he stood beside ten fresh graves. After enduring such brutal blows, words serve little purpose. The man was shattered, deep within, having lost it all. The great Scottish preacher of yesteryear, Alexander Whyte, put it well, "Job's sorrows came not in a single spy, but in battalions."[5]

Perhaps the man lay under the stars until he was wet from the dew. Finally, he spoke. And when he did, what a remarkable response! Verse 20 is comprised of nine words in the Hebrew text. These words describe what Job did, before the text goes on to tell us what Job said. Five of the nine words are verbs. The English Bible I use (New American Standard Version) has 19 words in verse 20, but still, 5 of them are verbs. When you read your Bible, always pay close attention to the verbs. They move you through the action of a narrative, helping you vicariously enter the event.

First, Job peeled himself off the ground. He "arose."

The next verb tells us of something strange. He "tore his robe." The word translated *robe* is a term describing a garment that fits over the body loosely, like an outer gown one would wear, that goes down below the knees. This is not the undertunic; this is the outer robe that kept him warm at night. Job reached to his neck, and, not finding a seam, but seizing a worn part of the fabric, he rips it, and in the ripping of the robe he is announcing his horrible grief. It was the action of a man in anguish. It's used several times in the Old Testament to portray utter grief.

And then we read the third verb. He "shaved his head." The hair is always pictured in the Scriptures as the glory of an individual, an expression of his worth. The shaving of the head, therefore, is symbolic of the loss of personal glory. And to carry his grief to its lowest depth, his fourth action is to fall to the ground. But, let's understand, this was not a collapse of grief, but for another purpose entirely. It is this that portrays the heroism of Job's endurance. He doesn't wallow and wail . . . he worships. The Hebrew verb means "to fall prostrate in utter submission and worship." I dare say most of us have never worshiped like that! I mean with your face on the ground, lying down, full-length. This was considered in ancient days the sincerest expression of obeisance and submission to the Creator-God.

Before moving on, I'd like to suggest you try this sometime. Palms down, facedown, knees and toes touching the ground, body fully extended, as you pour out your heart in worship. It's the position Job deliberately took. Complete and humble submission.

By now, the only one cursing is Satan. He hated it! He resented Job's response! Of all things, the man still worships his God—the One who would allow these catastrophes to happen. There wouldn't be one in millions on this earth who would do so, but Job did exactly that. The wicked spirits sat with their mouths wide open as it were, as they watched a man who responded to all of his adversities with adoration; who concluded all of his woes with worship. No blame. No bitterness. No cursing. No clinched fist raised to the heavens screaming, "How dare you do this to me, after I've walked with you all these years!" None of that.

Instead, "Naked I came from my mother's womb, and naked I shall return there. Blessed be the Name of the LORD." That says it all. At birth we all arrived naked. At death we will all leave naked, as we're prepared for burial. We have nothing as we are birthed; we have nothing as we depart. So everything we have in between is provided for us by the Giver of Life. All we have is skin-wrapped bones, organs, nerves, and muscles, along with a soul for which we must give account before our God. Job has already taken care of that. It's as if he is saying, "The One who gave me life and has put everything on loan to me during my lifetime has chosen (and has every right) to take everything away. I won't take anything with me anyway. Blessed be His name for loaning it to me while I had it. And blessed be His name for choosing to remove it."

Get that down nice and clearly. Get it, affluent Americans as we are. Get it when you stroll through your house and see all those wonderful belong-ings. Get it when you open the door and slip behind the steering wheel of your car. It's all on loan, every bit of it. Get it when the business falls and fails. It, too, was on loan. When the stocks rise, all that profit is on loan.

Face it squarely. You and I arrived in a tiny naked body (and a not a great looking one at that!). And what will we have when we depart? A naked body plus a lot of wrinkles. You take nothing because you brought nothing! Which means you own nothing. What a grand revelation. Are you ready to accept it? You don't even own your children. They're God's children, on loan for you to take care of, rear, nurture, love, discipline, encourage, affirm, and then release.

This is a good place to consider a statement Paul wrote in his letter to his younger friend, Timothy. "For we have brought nothing into the world, so we cannot take anything out of it either. If we have food and covering, with these we shall be content" (1 Timothy 6:7–8). Put that not only in the margin of your Bible alongside Job 1:21, better still, tuck it in a permanent crease in your brain. We brought nothing in. We take nothing out. In the meantime, everything is on loan.

As financial consultant Ron Blue, a longtime friend of mine, taught me years ago, "God owns it all." Yes, I know your name is on the title, I know. It won't be when you're gone. So, God has the final say in it. I know you built that place where you live and you're mighty proud of it. That's okay—nothing wrong with that. Nothing wrong with having a nice place to live. Nothing wrong with having things in it. Nothing wrong with driv-ing a fine car (or an old car!). My point? Job's point? It's never about stuff. The problem comes when the possessions own us—when the car drives us. Get this straight: Stuff never owned Job. The man endured heroically be-cause he'd learned to live heroically.

Without realizing it, Job is saying, "In your face, Lucifer. I never set my affections on these things in the first place. And when it came to the kids, I've understood from the day we had our first child until we had our last, they're all God's. He is the One who gave them all, and He is the One who has the right to take them all whenever He wants them all back."

That explains how Job could say in all sincerity, "Blessed be the name of the Lord." And why the biblical narrative adds, "Through all this Job did not sin nor did he blame God" (Job 2:21–22). Since he never considered himself sole owner, Job had little struggle releasing the Lord's property. When you understand that everything you have is on loan, you are better prepared to release it when the owner wants it back.

My dear friend and one of my mentors in the early years of my ministry was Ray Stedman, pastor of Peninsula Bible Church. Ray once told me he traveled to a site for a week-long series of ministry-related meetings. He had forgotten there was a very nice evening dinner he was to attend where he was scheduled to speak. When he packed, he failed to include a nice suit. He realized it toward the afternoon when the hour was getting late. Since his motel was located near a funeral home, he thought, for just one evening, the funeral director might be willing to loan him a suit—one that would later be used on a cadaver. He told me he went over and bargained with the director to use the suit for that one night. Then he said, "That evening, as I was addressing all the people, I did what I usually do . . . I reached up to put my hand in my pocket. I couldn't. Right then I learned that cadaver suits have no pockets."[6]

We enter the world with our tiny fists clenched, screaming, but we always leave the world with hands open on our silent chests. Naked in, naked out. And in the interlude, "Lord God, blessed be Your name for loaning me everything I'm able to enjoy."

"Through all this Job did not sin." Isn't that wonderful? "Nor did he blame God." Why blame God?

As one man has written, "God has given him a rehearsal for death. All things belong to God, absolutely, to be given as a gift, not claim, to be taken back without wrong. There is no talk of human 'rights.' The Lord is the sovereign owner of all, and Job rejoices in this wonderful fact."[7]

With 20/20 perspective, Job lifted himself off the ground, looked around at all that had changed, then put his arm around his grieving wife, held her close, and whispered, "God gave, and for some unrevealed reason, He chose to take back. He owns it all, sweetheart."

This entire chapter could have been written in three words. I believe they represent the reason Job became a man of heroic endurance: *Hold everything loosely.*

Are you doing that?

CHAPTER THREE

Satan vs. Job . . . Round Two

The curtain rises for act one, scene two. We've been here before.

Again there was a day when the sons of God came to present themselves before the LORD, and Satan also came among them to present himself before the LORD. The LORD said to Satan, "Where have you come from?" Then Satan answered the LORD and said, "From roaming about on the earth and walking around on it." The LORD said to Satan, "Have you considered My servant Job? For there is no one like him on the earth, a blameless and upright man fearing God and turning away from evil. And he still holds fast his integrity, although you incited Me against him to ruin him without cause."

Satan answered the LORD and said, "Skin for skin! Yes, all that a man has he will give for his life. However, put forth Your hand now, and touch his bone and his flesh; he will curse You to Your face."

So the LORD said to Satan, "Behold, he is in your power, only spare his life."

Then Satan went out from the presence of the LORD and smote

Job with sore boils from the sole of his foot to the crown of his head. And he took a potsherd to scrape himself while he was sitting among the ashes.

Then his wife said to him, "Do you still hold fast your integrity? Curse God and die!"

But he said to her, "You speak as one of the foolish women speaks. Shall we indeed accept good from God and not accept adversity?"

In all this Job did not sin with his lips.

Job 2:1–10

When bad things happen they often happen to the wrong person.

Johnny Gunther was a handsome boy of sixteen when the shadow of brain cancer fell across his life. He majored in math and chemistry at Deerfield Academy and was a straight-A student. During the fourteen months after the diagnosis, he endured two operations. Even after his second operation, he passed the grueling entrance examinations for Columbia University. Two weeks after being accepted to Columbia, young Johnny Gunther died.

The character of this brave young man was revealed following the first surgery. The doctors explained the life-threatening seriousness of the boy's condition to Johnny's parents, John and Frances Gunther. "What should we tell Johnny about his condition?" they asked the surgeon.

"He's so bright and so curious about all that's happening to him," the surgeon replied. "He really wants to know everything that's happening to him, so I think we should be honest with him."

The Gunthers agreed.

The surgeon went to Johnny alone in his hospital room and explained to him the seriousness of his brain tumor. The boy listened attentively throughout the explanation, then asked, "Doctor, how shall we break it to my parents?"[1]

When bad things happen, they often happen to the wrong person. And when that occurs, we're always left with that haunting word, "Why?"

28

Why did such a terrible thing as brain cancer invade Johnny Gunther's young and promising life?

That question is being asked in every major hospital around our nation today. Furthermore, every large community in every city has within it a home or two where that same question is still being asked without an answer.

Somewhere in all of this, there is room for the story of Job. For, as we have learned, a better man never lived in his day. He was not only a good man, he was a godly man. He was not only a faithful husband, he was a loving and devoted father. He was a good employer. His hard work and integrity had led to a prosperous lifestyle during the later years of his life. With plenty of land, an abundance of food, and sufficient livestock and camels to fund Job's dreams, it looked as though his entire future would be a downhill slide.

And then, the bottom of his life dropped out. Seemingly, senseless tragedy invaded the life of one who didn't deserve it. And he and his wife were left to pick up the pieces. He'd lost most of his servants, all but four. He'd lost all means of making a living. And he'd lost all ten of his grown children. To make matters worse, there was more to come. He had no idea that additional unfair and undeserved suffering lay ahead. Unexpected, it would level him. He dropped in bed the night before having no idea he'd never be the same in twenty-four hours.

Just like those workers in New York City on the tenth of September 2001. They left work late in the evening after a busy day in the World Trade Center already thinking about tomorrow. Putting their notes on their PDAs, they were making plans for the next day, completing their to-do list for 9/11. Many of them returned to their offices early the next morning to begin their work. A little before 8:00 a.m. they had no idea that American Airlines flight 11 was heading directly for their office in the North Tower. Suddenly it *struck*. It was so surprising and unexpected, not even those in the South Tower knew of it and, for sure, had no idea that the terrorist plan was running its course for that tower, to be struck by United Flight 175 only eighteen minutes later. New Yorkers couldn't believe it—no one could believe it! It was beyond belief. Why them? Why that? Why now? Job's thoughts exactly, when all of his oxen and donkeys and camels and servants, and finally all ten of his children were *gone*. Seriously, what would have been *your* response?

Eugene Peterson gives us Job's response in the paraphrase of *The Message*.

> Job got to his feet, ripped his robe, shaved his head, then fell to the
> ground and worshiped:
>> Naked I came from my mother's womb,
>> naked I'll return to the womb of the earth.
>> God gives, God takes.
>> God's name be ever blessed.
>> Not once through all this did Job sin; not once did he blame
>> God.
>
> Job 1:20–22, MSG

I would imagine in the struggle of that first fitful night trying to sleep after burying all ten children with his own hands, laying alongside his grieving wife who had also endured the loss, much of what had happened was still a blur There was more to come. Much more. He couldn't have imagined it any more than those in the Pentagon who were already busily engaged in dealing with the details of the Northeastern Atlantic shoreline and the New York Harbor, where the terrorists had struck. Our military personnel had no idea they were next. A third plane on another evil mission would soon plunge into the very side of the building where some were already working on the atrocity that had just happened in New York.

I have spoken to some of those officers who were in the building at that time. One admitted to his own embarrassment, "It never dawned on most of us that the Pentagon was next." We may never know for sure if the third plane was seeking to locate the White House, and because of the foliage of mid-September, couldn't do so. Whatever, the pilot in his maddening plan to crash the plane, spotted this five-sided building and tore a hole 200 feet wide due to a double explosion—first from the plane itself crashing into the building and then the igniting of the fuel that sent fire down the wide hallway.

As with Job, it just wasn't fair! At least, it wasn't fair from our perspective. The man had modeled genuine integrity. He had blest his Father, in fact, he had worshiped Him, and Satan couldn't stand it.

The Adversary lost round one.

ANOTHER AUDIENCE WITH THE ADVERSARY

The second chapter begins round two. It starts scene two as ominously as scene one in the first chapter. "Again, there was a day" (v. 1). Satan likes to hit us with a double blast. The first one comes as a complete surprise; the second one hits with a stunning shock. As before, Satan had a plan when he stood before the Lord God.

> The LORD said to Satan, "Where have you come from?" Then Satan answered the LORD and said, "From roaming about on the earth and walking around on it." The LORD said to Satan, "Have you consid-ered My servant Job? For there is no one like him on the earth, a blameless and upright man fearing God and turning away from evil. And he still holds fast his integrity, although you incited Me against him to ruin him without cause."
>
> Job 2:2–3

See the word *ruin?* The Hebrew word means, "to swallow." It is in the verb stem that *intensifies* the term. And when used in that sense it's the idea of a barb. The idea of scraping away, or even gagging, if you will. "You urged me to scrape away at him without cause." Satan, not one to be outclassed, answered impudently, as if to say, "Absolutely! Skin for skin! Yes, all that a man has he will give to protect his own life. But You've still got that hedge around him. He still receives penthouse treatment. He may not be able to make a living with all his animals and buildings gone, but he's still got his health. He no longer has his children, but the couple can still have more. Allow me to go further. Give me the freedom to break him down at the deepest level by taking away his health, and he will curse You to Your face." I think the Adversary said this out of irritating anger. He exists in an attitude of murderous rage. His prediction is repeated: "He will curse You to Your face."

Read the Lord's response thoughtfully: "So the LORD said to Satan, 'Behold, he is in your power, only spare his life'" (Job 2:6). *Can you imagine that?* Can you imagine *your name* connected to such an agreement? "All right, Lucifer, go after him, just don't kill him." God again set the boundary, "Preserve his life, but he's fair game." As stunned as those at the World Trade Center and the Pentagon were, Job would soon face the shock of his life.

Yawning awake the next morning, Job felt unusually sore and feverish. Why?

ROUND TWO: LET THE SUFFERING INTENSIFY

"Then Satan went out from the presence of the LORD and smote Job with sore boils from the sole of his foot to the crown of his head" (Job 2:7). He felt the sting of pain under his arm, and then he felt a swelling at his neck. Another couple of sores were inside his mouth. Small red spots appeared across his forehead, even up in his scalp. And of all things, his feet were so swollen he couldn't get his sandals on. Before noon his fever began to rage. By now he'd lost his appetite. It was like he was coming apart. He said something about it to his wife. She looked closer and noticed something like a rash breaking out. He asked her to check his back. She observed, "There are swollen marks all over." In the biblical account they are called "sore boils."

Medical doctors have been curious about this particular ailment for years. In my research I've found numerous comments made about the disease. One said it was smallpox. Another one, elephantiasis. Another, chronic eczema. Another leprosy. One suggested psoriasis. Another pityriasis. Another keratosis. One identifies in medical terms, pemphigus foliaceus. Not surprisingly, several suggested it was melanoma, an aggressive form of skin cancer.

Satan had wasted no time. He "went out . . . and smote Job." Hit him while he was down. What Job first thought was sore muscles from the burying of his ten children, he now realized was now much more serious, especially when he spotted the growing number of skin ulcers. His heart sank as he realized he had a disease that would only add pain to his misery.

I have carefully examined each chapter of Job and taken note of all the references to the symptoms that accompanied this ailment. This is a summary of what he suffered:

- Inflamed, ulcerous sores   Job 2:7
- Persistent itching   Job 2:8
- Degenerative changes in facial skin,
  disfiguration   Job 2:12
- Loss of appetite   Job 3:24
- Fears and depression   Job 3:25
- Purulent sores that burst open, scab over,
  crack, and ooze with pus   Job 7:5
- Worms that form in the sores themselves   Job 7:5
- Difficulty in breathing   Job 9:18
- A darkening of the eyelid   Job 16:16
- Foul breath   Job 19:17
- Loss of weight   Job 19:20;
                                                    33:21
- Excruciating, continual pain   Job 30:27
- High fever with chills and discoloring
  of skin as well as anxiety and diarrhea   Job 30:30

In addition, Job endured delirium, sleeplessness, and the rejection of friends (Job 7:3; 29:2). All of which lasted for months. In short, Job became the personification of misery.

We should remember that this resulted in Job's being rejected, isolated, and relocated to the city dump, as we would call it today. It was the place where they burned garbage and rubbish and human excrement from the city. That became his place of existence.

Warren Wiersbe describes the dreadful setting:

> There the city garbage was deposited and burned, and there the city's rejects lived, begging alms from whomever passed by. At the ash heap, dogs fought over something to eat, and the city's dung was brought and burned. The city's leading citizen was now living in abject poverty and

shame. All that he humanly had left were his wife and three friends, and even they turned against him.[2]

Complete confusion, total isolation, unbearable pain, no hope of change, sitting in filthy surroundings, removed from all the comforts of home. In short, Job became "Ground Zero" in human form.

There came a day when all of this overwhelmed Mrs. Job. She could bear it no longer. At the end of her rope, she came to him for a visit. Sitting beside him, she leaned over and asked, "Do you still hold fast your integrity?" Quickly return to an earlier scene when God had said to Satan, "Have you noticed My servant Job? He still holds fast his integrity." Unknowingly she put her finger on the single quality in Job's life that God used in answering Satan. Her question called into question his need to maintain that any longer. And then she uses Satan's line when she says to her husband, "Curse God!" Satan was never closer to a smile than at that moment as he and his minions gathered near, staring, waiting, hoping. Surely they were urging, "Say it, Job. *Say It!* Go ahead—curse your God!" Everything hung on Job's response to his wife.

A PLEA FOR UNDERSTANDING

I want to confess that for too long in my ministry I took unfair advantage of Job's wife, especially since she was not present to defend herself. I think it was probably due to immaturity on my part. Furthermore, I hadn't been married long enough to know better than to say those things. I cannot leave this one snapshot of Mrs. Job in the story without clarifying the record in her defense. I want to suggest four reasons she would respond in this way:

First, she, too, had lost ten children. Until you or I have lost all our children, let's guard against saying anything critical of anyone who is in that depth of grief. Who knows what we would do in the horrible backwash of such a loss? I suggest it was in the weakening struggle of her grief that she blurted this out.

Second, she, too, had suffered the loss of their wealth and possessions. As every wife, whose husband has reached a high level of financial security could testify, there are benefits, perks, and pleasures that bring great satisfaction with that lifestyle. Those many possessions that were destroyed were her possessions too. Those were also her livestock, that was her home. Suddenly she, too, was reduced to the same level as he economically.

Third, for years she had enjoyed being the wife of "the greatest of all the men of the east" (Job 1:3). There's honor with that. There are also great moments of public acknowledgement and inner joy in that. She is no longer the leading lady of the community. She's now the pathetic wife of a broken man whose world has collapsed, who now sits alone in abject poverty, covered with sores.

Fourth, she's lost her companion. She no longer has her beloved to enjoy in the quiet give-and-take of conversation. There are no longer any gratifying, private moments of romance and lovemaking. The woman has no hope that this will ever change. We need to cut her some slack.

Isn't it a little easier to understand how she could suggest, "Job, darling, let's just pull the plug? Don't go on. You can't keep living like this, I can't stand it. Curse God and let Him take you home to be with Him." I think so. She's reached her limit and is willing to let him go. I'm not justifying the woman's reasoning as much as trying to understand it.

Now, with that said, let me offer a couple of "on the other hand" practical comments to you who are wives. (Just think of it as a little counsel from Mars to Venus, if that will help.) I want to suggest something wives should consider *always* doing and *never* doing.

First, the always. *Always guard your words when your husband is going through terribly hard times.* I want to confess something about us men. Mainly, I want you to remember: Going through sustained hard times weakens most men. For some reason, hardship seems to strengthen women; we admire you for that. But we men are weakened when times of affliction hit and stay. In our weakened condition we lose our objectivity, sometimes our stability. Our discernment is also skewed. Our determination lags. We become vulnerable, and most men don't know how to handle themselves in a vulnerable state of mind. You women do very well with vulnerability; we men do not. And we become—hard as it is to admit this—afraid. When men become afraid, strange things happen inside us. We don't understand ourselves. We entertain alien thoughts we would otherwise never consider. So in light of all of this—hear me—we need your clear perspective, wisdom, and spiritual strength. Most of all, we need you to pray for us as you've never prayed. We need not only your prayers, we need your emotional support. We need you to take the initiative and step up.

We need your words of confidence and encouragement. We even find it hard to say, "I need you right now." My wife could tell you that she lived with me for our first ten years in marriage before she ever thought I needed her. I finally admitted it and learned how to say it. In the lonely hours of a man's great trial nobody's words mean more to him than his wife's words. That is one of the God-given reasons you and your partner were called to be together. When we husbands lose our way, you wives help us find our way back.

Now, the never. *Never suggest that we compromise our integrity, even if it would provide temporary relief.* Please, never go there. We may be so weak we'll believe you and act on your tempting suggestion. Understand, when we are weakened we become fragile within. We are easily seduced by words that offer relief, because most men consider relief the most important thing when times are hard. That's why many a man undergoing an intense time of testing will begin an affair. I'm certainly not justifying that, I'm just saying that's an option some will choose at their lowest ebb.

God had said to Satan, "He holds fast his integrity." And she, of all things, asked him, "Why do you want to keep doing that?" He needed her to say, "Job, whatever you do, stand fast! I'll go with you wherever we need to go. I'll endure whatever we have to endure. But don't compromise your integrity. Let's walk with God through this, together."

HOW JOB RESPONDED

Now Job's response is magnificent. "You speak as one of the foolish women speaks" (Job 2:10). Hats off to the old patriarch! In his weakened condition, sitting there in the misery of all those sores, not knowing if any of that would ever change, he stood firm—he even reproved her. He said, in effect, "I need to correct the course of this conversation. We're not going there."

He went further than stating a reproof; he asked an excellent question. "Shall we indeed accept good from God and not accept adversity?" (Job 2:10). His insight was rare, not only back then, but today. What *magnificent* theology! How seldom such a statement emerges from our secular system.

Rather, we hear responses like, "What kind of a God is that who will treat you this unfairly after you have lived so devotedly? Why in the world would you continue to stand fast when this so-called loving God treats you like that?"

Job's counsel was different: "Shall we indeed accept good from God and not accept adversity?" The Hebrew sentence reads, "The good shall we accept from God and the trouble shall we not accept?" emphasizing the good and the trouble. It's a rhetorical question, not asked to be answered but asked for the purpose of making the listener think it through. Job is thinking these thoughts: Doesn't He have the right? Isn't He the Potter? Aren't we the clay? Isn't He the Shepherd and we the sheep? Isn't He the Master and we the servant? Isn't that the way it works?

Robert Alden in his fine work on Job writes very practically:

> This is a hard lesson for some believers to learn, especially if they feel they have been promised health and wealth or have misunderstood that God's wonderful plan for their lives involves only pleasantness and not trouble. Believers on this side of the cross have many more examples from both the Bible and church history of God's people who have suffered. Job was much more in the dark. Yet out of that darkness his strong belief in the sovereignty of God shown forth all the more brilliantly.[3]

Somehow he already knew that the clay does not ask the potter, "What are you making?" And so he says, in effect, "No, no, no, sweetheart. Let's not do that. We serve a God who has the right to do whatever He does and is never obligated to explain it or ask permission. Stop and consider—should we think that good things are all we receive? Is that the kind of God we serve?

He's no heavenly servant of ours who waits for the snap of our fingers, is He? He is our Lord and our Master God! We need to remember that the God we serve has a game plan that is beyond our comprehension, hard times like this notwithstanding."

And I love this last line, "In all this Job did not sin with his lips"(v. 10). There's absolute trust there. And faith. "Sweetheart, we can't explain any of this, so let's wait and watch God work. We would never have expected what happened. Both our hearts are broken over the loss. We've lost everything. Well—not everything. We've still got each other. Our God has a plan that is unfolding even though we cannot understand it right now."

A FITTING CONCLUSION

I began this chapter by referring to a teenager named Johnny Gunther; I close it by referring to you. And I want to offer you three timeless principles we can glean from Job's experience thus far, along with a little advice that may be helpful for you . . . if not now, soon.

First, since our lives are full of trials, we need to remember there are always more to come. Job later admits, "For man is born for trouble, as sparks fly upward" (Job 5:7). He is absolutely correct. Trials are inevitable, so don't be surprised. Be aware that the Adversary is on the loose. Be alert wherever you are, since one place was hit, no place is immune. Who knows what may be next? Here's the advice: *Don't be surprised.* Peter wrote in 1 Peter 4:12: "Beloved, do not be surprised at the fiery ordeal among you, which comes upon you for your testing, as though some strange thing were happening to you." Don't think trials are strange. They are the rule, not the exception.

Second, since our world is fallen, we need to understand that those who love us may give us wrong advice. During these many years of my life I have received wrong advice on several occasions from people who truly love me. They were sincere, but wrong. They didn't *mean* to be wrong, but they were. Here's the advice: *Don't be fooled.* Just because he is your husband and advises you of such-and-such doesn't mean that advice is correct and wise. Just because he or she is your partner in business and is giving you advice doesn't mean it is sound advice. Square whatever you hear with the principles of God's Word. That is our standard and our unerring guide. With loving tact, Job had to say, "You speak as one of the foolish women. Sweetheart, I love you, but I can't go there."

Third, since our God is sovereign, we must prepare ourselves for blessing and adversity. Because He is God, He's unpredictable. My advice here? *Don't be disillusioned.* Because our God is sovereign, we must prepare ourselves for blessing *and* adversity. Include the last two words.

In my research for this book I came across the writings of Dr. Frances I. Andersen, a medical doctor and archaeologist, biblical scholar and author from Australia. In reading his comments on this segment of Job's story, his words sort of jumped off the page and landed right in front of me. They are worth special attention.

> Job finds nothing wrong with what has happened to him. . . . It is equally right for God to give gifts and to retrieve them (round one); it is equally right for God to send *good* or *evil* (round two). *Receive* is a good active word, implying cooperation with Providence, not mere submission. Such positive faith is the magic stone that transmutes all to gold; for when the bad as well as the good is received at the *hand of God,* every experience of life becomes an occasion of blessing. But the cost is high. It is easier to lower your view of God than to raise your faith to such a height.[4]

Some theologians have done that these days. Their theory is called Open Theism. In brief, here is the sum and substance of that theory. Because bad things are happening to good people, then God, because He is good, did not know they were going to happen and therefore would never have allowed such to occur. He would not cause such a thing. And so, depending on how we respond, God determines what He will do next.

Let me clarify here, that is heresy. Omniscience doesn't learn. Omniscience doesn't discover. You'll never hear these words in God's throne room: "Why, I didn't know that! Can you even imagine such a thing, Gabriel? Look!" No. The psalmist makes it clear, "But our God is in the heavens; He does whatever He pleases" (Psalm 115:3).

Our God has no obligation to explain Himself. Our God does not have to step into a hospital room and say, "Now let me offer five reasons this has happened to your son." Understand, our God is full of compassion, but His plan is beyond our comprehension.

"For My thoughts are not your thoughts, neither are your ways My ways," declares the LORD. "For as the heavens are higher than the earth, so are My ways higher than your ways, and My thoughts than your thoughts" (Isaiah 55:8–9). And so we say, with Job: "O, God, I trust You. I don't know why I'm going through this. If there's something I can learn, wonderful. If there's something someone else can learn, great. Just get me through it. Just hold me close. Deepen me. Change me."

Job asked, "Shall we accept good from God and not accept adversity?" Because he knew that God is God, someday He will make it clear. That's one of the reasons I believe heaven will be such a delightful place. When we step into His presence for the first time we will be given the panoramic view, and then (and not *until* then) we will respond, "So that's the reason! Now I get it!"

"It is easier to lower your view of God than to raise your faith to such a height," writes a perceptive author. He then adds, "We shall watch the struggle as Job's faith is strained every way by temptations to see the cause of his misfortune in something less than God."[5] God is totally and completely and absolutely in charge. If He wipes out every member of your family, He is in charge. If He ends your business in abysmal bankruptcy, He is in charge. If the x-ray returns and it couldn't be worse, He is in charge. Please accept and submit to that teaching. How magnificent it is to find those who trust Him to the very end of this vale of suffering saying, "And may His name be praised. I don't understand it. Can't explain it. Nevertheless, may His name be praised." That is worship at its highest level.

May God enable us to raise our faith to such heights rather than lower our view of Him.

CHAPTER FOUR

Job's Advice to Husbands and Friends

Examining the life of Job is like crawling into a crucible. For the next few moments think about that word *crucible*. At the core of the term is the Latin word, *crux*, which means "cross," used as a synonym for torture. We still use the word in that way, like when we refer to "A cross one must bear." Our English term *excruciating* bears a similar resemblance. In Job's case, his crucible would mean his pit of agony. Webster defines *crucible*, "a severe test; a place or situation in which concentrated forces interact to cause change or development." Study that definition before you rush on. Go back and read it again, slower this time.

Job's crucible was brought about by two severe attacks from Satan, both permitted by God. Round one—he was attacked in the area of his possessions and his family. His means of earning a living and sustaining a comfortable lifestyle were suddenly removed.

Round two came on the heels of the first, before the grieving father could catch his breath. Satan was determined to hear Job curse his God, so he attacked him in the one area that remained—his health. Not only did he take it away by covering him from his scalp to his soles with sore boils that oozed and cracked and turned his skin black, the awful disease created a maddening itch, high fever, and swelling so severe he hardly resembled himself. The misery is staggering to imagine.

The nineteenth century Scottish divine, Alexander Whyte, put it best in these few words: "Till Christ came, no soul was ever made such a battleground between heaven and earth as Job's soul was made."[1] Job's crucible was a battleground. Keep in mind, we know what Job did not know. We know why it happened, and we know how it came about. He knew neither. All he knew was one day he was a model of health and strength, a man of prosperity and integrity with a full quiver of children and happy, wholesome relationships with his circle of friends and workmen, only to lose it all in a matter of hours. Rather than reacting in panic and anger, the man heroically endures. In fact, since his day, Job has come to be known, not as the model of *suffering* but as the model *of endurance.*

I remind you of what is written of him in the middle of the first century, "You have heard of the endurance of Job" (James 5:11). Job endured the crucible; he didn't fight it or attempt to escape from it. The only ones he had left when all the dust settled was a wife and a small circle of friends from whom he received no affirmation. No encouragement. No comfort. No soothing words of compassion. No embrace of affection. They only added stink to his stack. Nevertheless, Job endured.

A professor of history once said, "If Columbus had turned back, no one would have blamed him but nobody would have remembered him either."[2] The single reason we remember Job with such admiration is because he endured.

Not only did he endure the afflictions I've described, he also endured the words of a grieving, shortsighted wife. As we shall see, he also endured the accusations of friends who took upon themselves the role of judge and jury. If you have gone through your own crucible, chances are good you know what it is like in the midst of pain to have people turn against you. What pain that brings! But, returning to the definition, that's when the crucible causes change and development. As a result of enduring pain, we change from being mere sufferers to wise counselors and valuable comforters.

I was walking the hallways of our church staff offices recently, and I stopped by my son Chuck's office. He serves as the chief audio engineer at Stonebriar Community Church. As you'd guess, his desk is piled high with specs, catalogues, technical gear, CDs, and various equipment. I couldn't help but notice a piece of paper he had taped to the wall above his desk. It was a quotation he had lifted from John Eldredge's book, *Wild at Heart.* The statement read: "I don't trust a man who hasn't suffered . . . "[3]

Looking at the statement, I realized the most valuable counsel I have received in my life has never come from a novice. It's come from those who bore the scars of the crucible. "As diamonds are made by pressure and pearls formed by irritation, so greatness is forged by adversity."[4] Sound advice comes from veterans of pain.

ADVICE FROM JOB

Since that is true, this would be a good time to get some advice from Job. Later on, we will examine the counsel and advice others gave to him, but I think one should first consider what Job's counsel might be to us. A man who is enduring such anguish certainly has some helpful things to say to all of us. None of it directly, understand, but drawn indirectly by inference from the final few verses of the second chapter of Job.

In my previous chapter, I suggested a couple of pieces of advice for wives. Allow me a few moments of repetition, just to jog your memory.

Advice to Wives

First, always guard your words when your husband is going through a hard time. This good advice is not only for ladies with husbands, this is for single women who have men you're close to and, perhaps, work alongside. Men can become vulnerable and, in fact, gullible during difficult times. It would be regrettable if you thoughtlessly dumped out words that would not be wise. Job's wife, in fact, did that . . . thankfully Job did not agree with her counsel.

Second, never suggest to us that we should compromise our integrity. Don't ever go there. Even if it would bring us instant relief or temporary gratification. Integrity is a tough enough virtue to sustain without the temptation to compromise it. Gauge your words, ladies. And I'm addressing this to the ladies because—believe it—your words do mean more than we act like they do. More often than not, wives' words are wiser words than we give you credit for, which is unfortunate. So when you do speak, never suggest solutions that could weaken our integrity. Keep in mind, ladies, there's nothing more important (aside from a relationship with Christ), than one's moral and ethical integrity.

Advice to Husbands

Now, let me write a few practical words to you who are husbands. Thanks to Job's example, here are four pieces of advice we would do well to hear and heed, men.

First, listen well and always tell your wife the truth. I'm impressed that Job listened to the words of his wife. He pondered them, he considered them, he turned them over in his mind. He neither misunderstood nor ignored her. He heard what she said, and he didn't interrupt her as she said it. That places Job in a unique category among husbands, quite frankly.

Men, I've found that most of us are not hard of hearing; we're hard of *listening.* Our wives frequently have the most important things to say that we will hear that day, but for some strange reason, we have formed the habit of mentally turning off their counsel.

We say to ourselves, "Oh, boy, I've sat through this before; I know where she's going here." Wait, wait, wait! Probably Job and his wife have had a few spats; it's a marriage, isn't it? I would imagine they had a reasonably good marriage. That's the best any couple can hope for. At critical times in a marriage, wives will have the kernel of truth that we need to hear, but we will miss it if we are not careful. If we operate from habit by reacting in an impatient manner, we will fail to pay attention. (We'll look like we are, but the truth is we're not listening).

Let me add here—when we do respond, always tell her the truth. Which means, if what she says is wise and squares with what you know to be truth—if it is helpful—then say so. And thank her. If it is not, say *that*. Job disagreed and said so. His response after hearing her was, "You speak as one of the foolish women speaks."

As one author analyzes the scene:

She sees death as the only good remaining for Job. He should pray to God (lit. 'bless') to be allowed to die, or even *curse God* in order to die, an indirect way of committing suicide.

Whatever lay behind her words, Job rejects them with fury. But he does not call her 'wicked', merely *foolish,* that is, lacking in discernment. She thinks God has treated Job badly, and deserves a curse; Job finds nothing wrong with what has happened to him. At this point, Job's trial enters a new phase, the most trying of all. Instead of helping, the words of his wife and of his friends cause him more pain and put him under more pressure than all the other things that have happened to him so far.[5]

Job detected in his wife a snag of bitterness, some disillusionment, so he said to her, in effect, "This is advice I cannot and I will not act on. This isn't wise. This is wrong counsel and I refuse to accept it."

In the four decades I've been dealing with folks who are married, I find one of the most difficult things to get couples to do is *say the truth* to each other. Admit when we've done wrong rather than skirt it or rationalize around it or excuse it—just say, "I was wrong." Or, if we hear our mate say something that we know is not wise or we detect a questionable motive, we tend not to say the hard thing. How much better to respond, "You know, honey, I realize you've got my good at heart, but I honestly have to say, I don't agree with it. I think it is unwise for you to suggest that." In the long haul, your marriage will be healthier if you will allow truth to prevail. Especially if it's truth spoken in love. Listen well, and always speak the truth.

Second, teach her what you have learned about God. Clearly that's what Job did. Notice how he did it: He asked a question. "Shall we indeed accept good from God and not accept adversity?" As I mentioned in the previous chapter, his statement communicated great theology! Job had learned this about his Lord over the years he had walked with Him. Therefore, he explains, "You and I have to understand that our God is not a God who provides only health and wealth. He is our sovereign Master . . . Lord over whatever occurs in our home, in our lives, including what I'm going through. Our loss and my condition are no surprise to God. This is His will for us; He's having His way in all of this. For some unrevealed reason He has permitted it and we need to remember, while we can't explain it, He is still sovereign over this as well." Job used their circumstances to teach his wife about God.

I've not met a godly woman who has ever said to me, "I really am not interested in what my husband has to say about spiritual things." Godly women are teachable. They say, without hesitation, "I'd rather learn truth from my husband than anybody I know." Difficult circumstances, painful though they are, provide great opportunities for instruction in righteousness. Affliction, hardship, and sickness can draw couples—in fact, entire families—closer. As the Lord teaches us things about Himself during the crucible, let's be faithful to pass them on to our mates as well as our children.

Consider Job's situation. Here's a man covered with sore boils, in such anguish he can hardly sleep. And yet he's communicating this spiritual insight about the Father's will that his wife needed to hear . . . learn. If he could do that, so can we. Let's take the time to share with her some of the things we're learning in the crucible. But let's do so with gentleness and grace. Again, like Job, who simply asked the question, "Shall we accept good from God and not accept adversity?" Gentle, gracious words are always preferred.

Third, model verbal purity. "In all this Job did not sin with his lips." Because we've lived with our wives over the years and have become extremely comfortable around them, we tend to be unguarded in our words. Wives usually get the brunt of our worst words. Since this is true, let's agree today that we will restrain ourselves from verbal impurity. Job did not make a blasphemous statement. He did not curse God. Furthermore, he didn't curse her. As we read earlier, Job didn't call her "wicked," but "foolish."

Be careful how you talk to your wife, my friend. Love her, don't scold her. If you must disagree, do so with tenderness. I can recall a particular pastor at the door of the church, when his wife simply asked, "Shall we have lunch at a restaurant or do you want to eat at home?" The man turned and rebuked her publicly! The man unloaded on her a piece of his mind he couldn't afford to lose. Amazingly, she didn't react, but my heart went out to her. As several of us witnessed the embarrassing and inappropriate comments made by this well-known preacher, we were all uncomfortable. I learned a lot about that preacher that day. Job may have been a public figure, but he didn't throw his weight around. It makes no difference how well known or how important you are, or how long you've been married, or how much money you make or how big your company is—or your church is; no man has the right to talk down to his wife. She is your partner—your *equal*. Furthermore, she knows a lot of stuff on you. Someday she may write your long-awaited, unauthorized biography!

Fourth, accept her completely; love her unconditionally. A wife thrives in a context of love and acceptance. She is who she is. God has made her into the woman she has become. And may I remind you, she is the wife you chose. She has become the woman that God is making her into, and that calls for complete acceptance and unconditional love on your part. Ideally, that combination results in a deep commitment. Both of you are in this relationship for the long haul. You're there to stay. And no amount of hardship, difficulty, test, or trial will separate you. In fact, it can pull you closer. Tragically, many a marriage is bound together by very thin, fragile threads. As tests come—from the in-laws or the children, perhaps a difficulty at birth that leads to birth defects in a child, or trials and tests in the business or financial realm . . . whatever, deliberately pull together and determine to hang in there. Tell her how much she means to you. Talk to her about her value in your life—how much she represents to you. When the crucible heats up, too many guys look for ways to get out.

Maybe we need a brief break here. I've been pretty serious, so let me have a little fun with you. I have a close friend who sent me a funny story about a couple who'd been married a long time. The wife awakens in the middle of the night and discovers her husband has gotten out of bed. She gets worried about him, so she puts on her robe and slippers and walks downstairs to look for him. The guy is sitting all by himself at the kitchen table with a hot cup of coffee. He's staring at the wall, blinking through tears. She says, "What's the matter, dear?" He shakes his head but doesn't say a word. So she asks, "Why are you down here at this time of night? What's going on?" He looks up from the cup of coffee, glances at her, then says, "You remember twenty years ago when we were dating and you were only sixteen?" She says, "Yeah, of course I remember." He pauses. Words don't come easily. "Well," he says, "remember when your father saw us in the car and we were smooching and he got so mad he walked out to the car and stuck a pistol in my face and he said, 'Any boy who kisses my daughter like that is going to *marry* her! Either you marry her or I'm sending you to jail for the next twenty years.' Remember that?" She said, "Yeah, I remember that." He wipes another tear away and he says, "I just realized *I would have gotten out today.*" Now, that's a bad husband![6]

Okay, enough frivolity. Time to get back to the crucible.

THE ORIGINAL THREE AMIGOS

It isn't long after all this calamity before the word gets out to most of Job's friends. Understand, the man had many friends, not just those who showed up one day. All those friends got word that Job had come upon hard times, tragic times. But only a few decided to make a trip to be with him. We don't know much about these men, really, very little. We're not even sure where they lived originally. They're simply called "Job's three friends."

"Now when Job's three friends hear of all this adversity that had come upon him, they came each one from his own place" (Job 2:11). The biblical narrative names them for us—Eliphaz, Bildad, Zophar.

Just to inform you ahead of time, much later in the biblical account (chapter 32) we will meet a fourth friend—younger than these three. His name is Elihu. When Elihu finally steps into the story, he says he's younger and he admits that he's shy. So he stays in the shadows for quite some time. Three cycles of dialogue occur between Job and these three original friends as Elihu stays quiet. The first three are anything but quiet as they unload the truck of criticism and guilt, shame and blame on their friend. We'll hear from them shortly, but not Elihu. He patiently waits for them to have their say before he speaks.

The three older friends were closer to Job's age. They were probably wealthy sheiks who had the time and the money to leave their homes and be gone from their businesses in order to visit Job. Maybe the men had met Job in the business world. Perhaps they were part of the enterprise that had been Job's in better times. We don't know how they had formed their friendship, we're never told. The point is, each one came from a different place to spend time in the crucible with their friend.

The story unfolds, "They made an appointment together to come to sympathize with him and comfort him" (Job 2:11). I repeat, always pay attention to the verbs when you're reading through the Scriptures. These action words tie together the movement of the story. In this case, the men came for two reasons: to sympathize and to comfort. Keep that in mind. It will be easy to forget it.

Before this book ends, a lot of unattractive and unpleasant things are going to be said by these friends. Matter of fact, the longer they stayed, the worse things got. The more argumentative, and the more judgmental, and the more intense the dialogue.

Advice to Friends

But before we get to all that, these men should be commended for coming. While all of Job's other friends and acquaintances simply heard and stayed where they were, these friends at least showed up. Good for them! Their coming and their stated reason for coming gives us a choice opportunity to appraise true friendships. Earlier we considered Job's advice to husbands. Now would be a good time to focus on a few characteristics of true friends.

First, friends care enough to come without being asked to come. No one sent a message saying to Eliphaz and Bildad and Zophar, "Would you please come and bring a little sympathy and comfort for Job? The man is dying in this crucible of anguish and pain." That wasn't necessary, because real friends show up when someone they love is really hurting. Friends don't need an official invitation. Spontaneously, they come.

Remember the New Testament story of Lazarus when he got so sick? His sisters, Martha and Mary, let Jesus know about that. "The one whom you love is sick." That's all they said. They didn't ask Him to come. And when He doesn't come (which is another story), they're offended. But He could have said, "You never asked me to come." No, not really. You don't *ask* a friend. If a friend of yours has a heart attack and you find out he's taken to a hospital across town, it isn't long before you're there. You don't wait for an invitation. No one's ever invited to a funeral. We say we go because we're paying our last respects. On our own initiative, we attend out of respect. In the same way, these men cared about and loved Job, so they came alongside.

Second, friends respond with sympathy and comfort. Sympathy includes identifying with the sufferer. Friends do that. They enter into his or her crucible, for the purpose of feeling the anguish and being personally touched by the pain. Comfort is attempting to ease the pain by helping to make the sorrow lighter. You run errands for them. You take care of the kids. You provide a meal. You assist wherever you need to assist because you want to comfort them.

John Hartley writes insightfully,

> On learning of Job's affliction, three beloved *friends* . . . Eliphaz, Bildad, and Zophar, *agreed together* to travel to Uz in order *to console* Job. The term for friends has a wide range of meanings, including an intimate counselor . . . a close friend . . . a party in a legal dispute. Friends often solemnized their relationship with a covenant, promising to care for each other under all kinds of circumstances. The relationship between Job and his three friends gives every evidence of being based on a covenant. . . . Such a relationship was characterized by loyal love. . . . Motivated by love and their commitment, these men came *to console and to comfort* Job. The word *to console* . . . means literally "to shake the head or to rock the body back and forth" as a sign of shared grief. *To comfort* . . . is to attempt to ease the deepest pain caused by a tragedy or death . . . With the noblest intentions, these three earnestly desired to help Job bear his sorrow.[7]

Isn't that intriguing? Maybe while you were in school you had an unwritten pact with a small group of friends. You got so close, you said to each other, "No matter what, wherever we find ourselves in the future, we all want each other to know we're going to be there for one another, especially when you're in need."

That may have been the way it was with Job and these men. They never wrote it out and signed on the dotted line, but it's true. These men had that kind of closeness and so, naturally, they came to give sympathy and comfort.

Third, friends openly express the depth of their feelings. Friends have ways of doing that, don't they? It's not uncommon to see a friend standing nearby in the hospital room fighting back the tears. It's not unusual for the friend to express deep feelings. Casual acquaintances don't usually do that; genuine friends make their feelings known.

Truth be told, these men were initially *shocked* when they saw what they saw. They didn't even recognize Job! They probably first went to his old home site, where they had been before. The place didn't even look familiar. Everything around it was destroyed. There was nothing stirring. It was ghostly silent; all they could see were the gravestones on the hillside. And somebody nearby says, "Oh, Job? He left sometime ago. I think he's staying out at the city dump." Another shock.

When they arrived, even before they got up close, they could tell the difference immediately. Their friend had no hair, his robe was torn, and he is sitting there with dung burning near him, a pack of wild dogs not far away, and stinking, rotten garbage everywhere. They stood and stared in disbelief. That's when their feelings came out. "Man, look at this." And "they threw dust over their heads toward the sky" (an ancient expression of grief) as they cried. That implies they were down near the dust. The narrative states, "they sat down on the ground" (v. 13). That's what friends do. They don't worry about getting dirty or messy.

This brings me to my fourth principle. *Friends aren't turned off by distasteful sights.* On the contrary, they come alongside and they get as close as possible. Friends are not offended because the room has a foul smell. Friends don't turn away because the one they've come to be with has been reduced to the shell of his former self, weighing half of what he used to weigh.

Friends see beyond all of that. They don't walk away because the bottom has dropped out of your life and you're at wits' end. On the contrary, that draws them in. These men literally raised their voices and sobbed as they sat down on the ground with Job. They demonstrated the depth of their anguish by staying seven days and seven nights without uttering a word.

Fifth, friends understand, so they say very little. I love the way Warren Wiersbe writes of this:

> The best way to help people who are hurting is just to be with them
> saying little or nothing, and letting them know you care. Don't try to
> explain everything; explanations never heal a broken heart. If his friends
> had listened to him, accepted his feelings, and not argued with him,
> they would have helped him greatly; but they chose to be prosecuting
> attorneys instead of witnesses.[8]

Job's friends stayed because they had every reason to be near him. The
kind of anguish this man's going through, he may have died at any moment, for all they knew. So they stayed by his side with their lips sealed. It
was what happened *after* those seven days that fouled things up. The longer
they stayed the worse things became.

The moment we find ourselves in trouble of any kind—sick in the
hospital, bereaved by a friend's death, dismissed from a job or relationship,
depressed or bewildered—people start showing up telling us exactly what
is wrong with us and what we must do to get better. Sufferers attract fixers
the way road kills attract vultures. At first we are impressed that they bother
with us and amazed at their facility with answers. They know so much!
How did they get to be such experts in living?

More often than not, these people use the Word of God frequently and
loosely. They are full of spiritual diagnosis and prescription. It all sounds
so hopeful. But then we begin to wonder, "Why is it that for all their
apparent compassion we feel worse instead of better after they've said their
piece?"

The Book of Job is not only a witness to the dignity of suffering and
God's presence in our suffering but is also our primary biblical protest
against religion that has been reduced to explanations or "answers." Many
of the answers that Job's so-called friends give him are technically true. But
it is the "technical" part that ruins them. They are answers without personal relationship, intellect without intimacy. The answers are slapped onto
Job's ravaged life like labels on a specimen bottle. Job rages against this
secularized wisdom that has lost touch with the living realities of God.[9]

The late (and I might add great) Joe Bayly and his wife, Mary Lou, lost
three of their children. They lost one son following surgery when he was

only eighteen days old. They also lost the second boy at age five because of leukemia. They then lost a third son at eighteen years after a sledding accident, because of complications related to his hemophilia.

Joe writes in a wonderful book, *The View from a Hearse,* (which has been changed in title to *The Last Thing We Talk About*):

> I was sitting, torn by grief. Someone came and talked to me of God's dealings, of why it happened, of hope beyond the grave. He talked constantly, he said things I knew were true.
>
> I was unmoved, except I wished he'd go away. He finally did.
>
> Another came and sat beside me. He didn't talk. He didn't ask leading questions. He just sat beside me for an hour and more, listened when I said something, answered briefly, prayed simply, left.
>
> I was moved. I was comforted. I hated to see him go.[10]

Friends have done it right when those in the crucible hate to see you go.

We must leave Job in his misery for now. We're mere onlookers. Had we lived in his day, there is no way we could say, "I know how you feel." You don't. I don't. We can't even imagine. But we do care. Our presence and our tears say much more than our words.

Words have a hollow ring in a crucible.

CHAPTER FIVE

The Mournful Wail of a Miserable Man

Great people who accomplish great things often come from tragic beginnings. When you do an in-depth study of those great lives, you find, more often than not, they were birthed from wombs of woe.

I was reminded of that recently when Cynthia and I attended a banquet sponsored by Dallas Seminary. To my unexpected delight, our fine chaplain, Bill Bryan, who has been at the school for many years, told us of his background. It was not only surprising, it was shocking. Anyone who is acquainted with Bill knows that he is a fun-loving, joyful man. In addition, he is an accomplished musician on the trumpet, and he loves to sing as he serves as the "pastor" of the campus. His personality is contagious. When you are around Bill Bryan, you are encouraged by his joyful spirit. All of us would think his life must have been easygoing and fun-loving, relaxed and secure from the start. Chaplain Bill *always* turns your attention to the bright side of things. His cup seems always half full, never half empty. But that's not the way things started for him.

His life had a tragic beginning. His father suffered deep depression for many years. Bill's story of sadness goes back to when his dad's depression took him through a dark emotional tunnel. Back in those days, any kind of emotional or mental struggle was rarely brought out of the closet; there was very little known to do for people who suffered in this way.

Bill said he remembered going week after week to the medical arts building in Springfield, Missouri, where they would take the elevator to the sixth floor. He would sit and wait with his mother as his father was going through his sessions with a psychiatrist. As a little boy he didn't understand what was happening. He just knew his dad wasn't happy—didn't have any peace. He was troubled. His life was bleak and barren.

On one such occasion, Bill recalls his father being escorted out of the room and asked to stay with Bill (who was only four at the time) while the mother was asked to step into the private office of the physician. Since his father's depression was only getting worse, they were making plans to admit him to what was then called an "insane asylum." Unfortunately, you could hear those words through the walls, and the father overheard their conversation. In fact, the comment was made that they didn't know if the man would ever get out. Bill said, "I remember as my mother walked out with the doctors (there were several) that my dad picked me up and held me close and said, 'I love you son.' He then put me down on the floor, turned and ran, jumping through the sixth-story window as the glass shattered, and he fell to his death." A friend of the family found little Bill wandering around alone on the first floor of the building and cared for him until the rest of the family could be found.

These are the last memories Bill had of his father.

From that time on Bill was primarily cared for by his grandparents and his aunt as his mother attempted to recover from the terrible tragedy. This pattern went on for years. All of us who know this joyful servant of God would have never expected a man like the congenial Chaplain Bill Bryan to have emerged from such a sad, sorrowful beginning.[1]

I'm now reading a fine book by Benjamin and Roz Zander. At the time of writing *The Art of Possibility,* Benjamin Zander was the conductor of the Boston Philharmonic. In this intriguing volume Zander tells the fascinating story behind Mahler's now-famous Ninth Symphony. Gustav Mahler lived in the last part of the nineteenth and the early part of the twentieth centuries. Mahler, of Bohemian roots, became a composer and conductor, ultimately the director of the Imperial Opera in Vienna for ten years—a wonderful, privileged position that called for a wide range of skills. Not surprisingly, this particular symphony is known to contain just about everything! Those who are serious about classical music are students of Mahler's Ninth. There is a richness and a depth of orchestration, harmonies, melodies, and countermelodies that make it unique. We would think that the genius who wrote such orchestration would have lived a pampered life. It must have been a magnificent thing to have such training.

"But the fact is," says Zander, "Gustav Mahler's childhood was marked by tragedy. He lost seven brothers and sisters as he was a child growing up." He then adds, "The coffin became a regular piece of furniture in their house."

Mahler's father was a cruel and brutal alcoholic. His mother was a weak, vulnerable invalid who existed at the mercy of her husband's blows. Mahler survived those tragic years. As an adult, he married and had a lovely daughter whom he adored and therefore lavished his affection on her. He lost the daughter at age four, and he never fully recovered from his grief. On top of all that, because he was Jewish, he was forced to quit his work as director of the Vienna Opera House. Shortly thereafter he was told that he had a bad heart and didn't have long to live. Remarkably, in the midst of all that sadness, grief, and discouragement, Gustav Mahler composed his magnificent Ninth Symphony.

Benjamin Zander rounds out the story, "Mahler wasn't sad all the time. He was a great lover of nature and a powerful swimmer . . . he had a magnificent laugh and a huge love of life, and all this is in the music, too, as well as sadness and anger about his illness and the brutality of his father and the vulnerability of his invalid mother. In fact, Mahler thought he should put everything in life in his symphonies."[2] He wrote a tenth symphony that was never finished. While Mahler's life sadly ended in premature death, his music lives on to thrill the hearts of music lovers the world over.

Is it any wonder that the man Job has brought comfort for centuries to those crushed by pain? Is it a surprise that those who go through times of deep and dark depression finally turn to Job's story, the man who gives new meaning to misery? When you read Job, you connect with the man's misery, especially if you have known such depths yourself. None but the aching heart can feel such anguish.

JOB IN RAW REALITY

Now I need to warn you ahead of time, in case you haven't already anticipated it, this will not be a pleasant chapter. This is not easy writing. I don't know of a person who has ever said to me that Job 3 is his or her favorite chapter in the Bible. I don't even know anyone who has ever memorized a verse out of Job 3. It's one of those chapters in the man's life that make you shake your head, sigh, and turn quickly to the next scene. It's here the scabs are pulled from the sores as the pus of reality runs down Job's life.

If his story were made into a movie and you and your family had rented it for tonight, when you came to this part of the story you'd fast-forward; you wouldn't want your children to watch. It's not only unedited, it's raw and borderline heretical!

Some of it is downright offensive. You don't want to think a man as great as Job in chapters 1 and 2 is the same man you meet in chapter 3. You just don't want to believe it. Why? Partly because we have this skewed idea that anybody who walks this closely with God lives happily ever after. After all, "God loves you and has a *wonderful* plan for your life." Right? If you didn't know better, you could think you might sprout wings before your conversion is a week old and start to soar through life.

We need to understand that God's "wonderful plan" is wonderful from *His* perspective, not yours and mine. To us, "wonderful" means comfortable, healthy, all bills paid, no debt, never sick, happily married with two well-behaved children, a fulfilling, well-paying job, and the anticipation of nothing but blessing and success and prosperity forever. That's "wonderful" to us. But God's wonderful plan is not like that.

Job brings us back to reality—God's kind of reality. Remember his question, the one he asked his wife? "Shall we accept good from God and not accept adversity?" And remember that closing line? "In all this Job did not sin with his lips" (Job 2:10).

The same man soon steps into a whole new frame of reference. That's why Job 3 makes us uneasy. We don't want our hero to think or talk like he does here. He doesn't seem like he's a man of God anymore. He even has the audacity to say at the end, "I am not at ease. I am not quiet. I am not at rest. I am in *turmoil.*" What has happened? We are given entrance into a dark side of Job's life that is as real as any of our lives today, but the difference is, Job lets it all out. Thankfully, he reminds us even the godly can be depressed.

One of my favorite chapters in one of my favorite books, *Lectures to My Students,* is titled "The Minister's Fainting Fits." The author is Charles Haddon Spurgeon, a man enormously gifted and at the same time, painfully real. In it he admits to major bouts with depression. He openly declares he is not always vigorous and wise and ready. He's not always courageous and happy. In fact, he states openly,

> Before any great achievement, some measure of the same depression is very usual. . . . Such was my experience when I first became a pastor in London. My success appalled me; and the thought of the career which it seemed to open up, so far from elating me, cast me into the lowest depths, out of which I uttered my *miserere* and found no room for a *gloria in excelsis.* Who was I that I should continue to lead so great a multitude? I would betake me to my village obscurity, or emigrate to America and find a solitary nest in the backwoods, where I might be sufficient for the things which would be demanded of me. . . . This depression comes over me whenever the Lord is preparing a larger blessing for my ministry; the cloud is black before it breaks, and overshadows before it yields its deluge of mercy. Depression has now become to me as a prophet in rough clothing.[3]

And so with me. Maybe not as deep as some, but I have gone through troubling tunnels of depression at times. Interestingly, at the very same time when others would think I might be caught up in pride (of all things), I have experienced such struggles. I have wondered if I should even stay at it.

But I've never known the kind of pit Job fell into. If Job were in the hospital today, he would have a No Visitors sign hanging on the door.

But he cannot run and hide. Job hangs out here for all to see. We all have our unguarded moments. We all have times when we reach the end of our tether. When the clouds of doom eclipse the sun of hope. Our view is blocked and out gushes how we *really feel.* But, thankfully, no one is there to hear. But with Job there were three friends who sat and stared, listening to every word. That's when they began to collect their judgmental thoughts so they could set him straight as soon as they got a chance to talk, or should I say *preach?*

A QUICK ANALYSIS AND AN OUTLINE

Allow me a couple of technical comments in this section of the biblical text as we get underway. *First,* at this point in the Hebrew Scriptures, poetry replaces prose. In the prologue, chapters 1 and 2 of the book of Job are written in prose just as they appear in your Bible. This narrative style is common. A novel, for example, is written in prose. The same would apply to a magazine article or a newspaper column. But when you get to the third chapter of Job in the Hebrew text, you begin to read poetry. Therefore, the style changes from narrative to meter. It remains like that all the way through the sixth verse of chapter 42. The greater part of the biblical book is poetry. This explains why the book of Job falls in the poetry category of the Bible.

Now, you remember from your English literature classes that poetry is frequently full of allegory and wonderful word pictures and the repetition of similar thoughts. This occurs as the writer of the poetry turns thoughts over in his mind and revisits them from different angles. No good student of poetry tries to make every line "walk on all fours." Some things you leave "said," and you say with a shrug, "It's poetry." Because of my lifelong love for poetry, I've memorized lines from some of my favorite poems. When I quote them to myself I often think, though I've quoted those lines many times, I don't really know the full depth of what the poet was getting at. Don't be afraid to admit that on occasion as you read through Job, you're reading poetry. So please, give yourself the freedom to say when you come to certain things that seem convoluted and too knotty to unravel, "I just don't know. I'm not sure what he had in mind." (You can let yourself off the hook by simply saying, "It's poetry.")

Here's a *second* thought to remember: Job's outburst is not mainly due to his physical suffering. It's more emotional—prompted by his losing touch with God. His grief and bankruptcy and painful sores don't cause him to say what he says here in Job 3. Obviously, his pain plays a role in it, but that's not the underlying cause. It isn't because he can't sleep at night. These are not nocturnal meanderings that come because he's restless. He is at the bottom of his emotional barrel because he's lost his best Friend. For many years God seemed intimate. As his business grew and the camel caravans multiplied, and bumper crops were harvested and the profit began to pour in, blessing him and his family with enormous prosperity, he and God remained on close speaking terms. They walked hand in hand . . . until that awful day when everything broke loose. As we've seen, he lost everything—all of the animals, their home, all ten adult children, and finally, his health. That was terrible, but this isn't what depressed him.

His real darkness came when the heavens became brass. When God no longer walked with him in the cool of the evening. When God no longer spoke to him and reassured him with words like, "My son, let me explain what this is all about. Satan came and he dared Me to do this, claiming that you would curse Me. I knew you'd never do that. Furthermore, I want you to know, I'm right here with you through all of this." Job knew none of that. Matter of fact, he knew nothing of the *why*, only *what*. He's just living in the consequences of those horrific events. And worst of all, God is silent, and He seems absent.

The man has now reached the end of his rope. You've been there. This is the day you slam the door shut. This is the day you say to those close to you, "Leave me alone!" This is the day in his life when he cannot find his Friend.

Robert Alden writes:

> The third chapter of Job must be one of the most depressing chapters in the Bible. While some might be as depressed as Job was and use

these verses to give vent to their feelings, few sermons are made from this chapter, few verses are claimed as promises, and few are remembered for the warmth of their sentiment. It is the lowest of several low points in the book.[4]

WORDS OF A BROKEN MAN

Here's a simple (and depressing!) outline for Job 3:

- Job regrets his birth. (Job 3:1–10)
- Job wishes he'd died at birth. (Job 3:11–19)
- Job now longs to die. (Job 3:20–26)

"Afterward Job opened his mouth and cursed the *day of his birth*" (Job 3:1).

Because you have patiently read through my opening comments, you're not quite as shocked as the novice would be who suddenly stumbles upon this opening line. How easy to think, "Aha, there you go. Satan said he would curse God, now he does it." Look closer. He is not cursing God, he is cursing the day of his birth. There's a major difference. Between the words, "Why was I ever born?" and "I no longer believe in You, God," Job is saying, "I am so totally and completely alone. I regret that I ever drew breath. I regret that I was ever conceived in the my mother's womb."

Let's not move too quickly. The very first word gives us pause: "Afterward." Stop and do a quick flashback. The man is sitting at the city dump, head shaved, wife wringing her hands, three friends sitting and staring in silence for seven days and nights, and no hope from above. *After* all that he opened his mouth and out came, "I wish I had never been born." That's not all he said. Read for yourself:

> And Job said,
> "Let the day perish on which I was to be born,
> And the night *which* said, 'A boy is conceived.'
> May that day be darkness;
> Let not God above care for it,
> Nor light shine on it.

Let darkness and black gloom claim it;
Let a cloud settle on it;
Let the blackness of the day terrify it.
As for that night, let darkness seize it;
Let it not rejoice among the days of the year;
Let it not come into the number of the months.
Behold, let that night be barren;
Let no joyful shout enter it.
Let those curse it who curse the day,
Who are prepared to rouse Leviathan.
Let the stars of its twilight be darkened;
Let it wait for light but have none,
Neither let it see the breaking dawn;
Because it did not shut the opening of my *mother's* womb,
Or hide trouble from my eyes."

Job 3:2–10

If you like marking your Bible, you will have a field day with the words, *let* and *may,* which appear repeatedly in verses 3 through 9. Technically, these words are known as *jussives* in Hebrew syntax. Think of them as "wish verbs." They represent what Job is wishing—may this happen, may that happen, let this take place, let that take place. Let these things occur. Let those things occur. It's poetry, remember?

Verse 3: "Let the day perish."

Verse 4: "May that day be darkness. Let not God above care for it."

Verse 5: "Let darkness and black gloom claim it; let a cloud settle on it; let the blackness of the day terrify it."

Verse 6: "Let it not rejoice among the days of the year; let it not come into the number of the months." (Take it off the calendar, forget my birth date.) "Let that night be barren. Let no joyful shout enter it. Let those curse it who curse the day."

Verse 9: "Let the stars of its twilight be darkened."

Job is wishing all that had happened.

For goodness sake, why would Job say such things? He's depressed! "I want nothing to do with this thing called life." Interestingly, suicide doesn't enter his mind. Never an attempt, never a word about it, since it was so foreign to the life of the faithful.

I thought it was interesting while working through this mournful wail to see what he says in verse 3. Not only does he regret the day of his birth, he regrets his conception. "Let the day perish on which I was to be born." And in good poetic fashion he goes back nine months earlier, "And the night which said, 'A boy is conceived.'"

In our day of easy and frequent abortions, isn't it interesting that he does not call the conception of the fetus "tissue." Or a mass of protoplasm. He calls the microscopic multiplication of living cells "a boy" because life begins at conception. As soon as the sperm enters the egg—life! Conception was applauded by those in the patriarchal era. "A boy! A boy! We are going to have a boy! How wonderful!" No, no, no! "Don't say that. Don't celebrate!" says Job at this dark moment of his life. "May that day be dark. Obliterate it! Get rid of it!"

There's another part of this vulnerable testimony that fascinates me. When we get down in the core of his dark perspective, we come to his words, "Let those curse it who curse the day" (v. 8). Job is not very experienced at cursing so he offers those who are familiar with such profane talk to pick up the cursing for him. He adds that they are also those: "Who are prepared to rouse Leviathan."

What in the world is Leviathan? Webster's dictionary offers this definition, "a sea monster represented as an adversary." But it goes further back than that. More specifically, Leviathan was a seven-headed sea monster of ancient Near Eastern mythology. In the ancient Ugaritic literature of Canaan and Phoenicia, eclipses were caused by Leviathan's coming out of the sea, swallowing the sun or the moon, and therefore causing darkness to be cast on this earth. As Leviathan was roused from its sleep in the sea, the myth saw it swallowing up the sun or the moon.

You say, "What?" And I answer: "Poetry." Like I mentioned earlier in this chapter, that's a great way to handle such things as this, isn't it? It's poetry. No, those thoughts are more than poetry, they represent mythology. If you travel to Turkey or Greece these days and you have an individual who is a native of that land now serving as a professional guide on the tour, you will hear a great deal about mythology. I might add, you will hear virtually no theology. Extensive mythology is the basis of the gods of those lands. And in the ancient, patriarchal days it remained a part of their culture and literature.

So, Job picks up the thought and says, in effect, "Oh my, while I'm at it, let Leviathan swallow up the sun of the day, make it dark." Does Job believe in mythology? Not any more than you or I believe in Santa Claus when Christmas comes, even though we may refer to something on earth prompting Santa to do this or that. It's not that we believe in him, it's just that we may refer to him with tongue in cheek.

Last Christmas I got a card from a good friend of mine, a little younger than I. He said, "We go through four stages with Santa. First of all, we *believe* in him. Second, we *don't* believe in him. Third, we *are* him. And fourth, we *look like* him." We joke about Santa and we have fun with all of the myths surrounding that fictional character.

Job, while lamenting that he did not perish at conception and grieving that he lived to see the day of his birth, asks a penetrating question:

> Why did I not die at birth,
> Come forth from the womb and expire?
> Why did the knees receive me,
> And why the breasts, that I should suck?
>
> Job 3:11–12

The latter we understand. Obviously, he is referring to his mother nursing him. But the knees, how curious. Some say that it has reference to the mother as she births the infant. The newborn passes, if you will, through the knees. But this says, "receive." It could be a reference to the mother placing the infant on her knees as she prepares to begin nursing.

It most likely refers to the patriarchal process of a father being given the infant shortly after birth. The child was placed on the knees of the father, and he would there give it the family's blessing. If you ever saw the television documentary, *Roots,* you will remember the African child being held by the father as he lifts the infant up before God and symbolically gives him to the Lord in keeping with their ancient custom. In Job's day, a father would be given the infant and he would bless the child as the infant was placed on the father's knees.

And Job says, "Why was I ever blessed? Why did those knees ever receive me?" In other words, "Why wasn't I simply a lifeless corpse, held in their hands?" And then as he develops the thought of being stillborn, he turns to the blessing of his lifeless body as he describes heaven:

> For now I would have been lain down and been quiet;
> I would have slept then, I would have been at rest.
>
> Job 3:13

> Or like a miscarriage which is discarded, I would not be,
> As infants that never saw light.
> There the wicked cease from raging,
> And there the weary are at rest.
> The prisoners are at ease together;
> They do not hear the voice of the taskmaster.
> The small and the great are there,
> And the slave is free from his master.
> Why is light given to him who suffers,
> And life to the bitter of soul,
> Who long for death, but there is none,
> And dig for it more than for hidden treasures,
> Who rejoice greatly,
> And *exult* when they find the grave?
> Why is light given to a man whose way is hidden,
> And whom God has hedged in?
> For my groaning comes at the sight of my food,
> And my cries pour out like water.
>
> Job 3:16–24

When someone served Job a simple meal, he groaned. The Hebrew term means to shriek. As if he were saying, "Ahhhhhh! *Take that away*, I have no interest in eating anything!" Along with the man's dreadful suffering, he is now starving; his cries pour out like water.

He concludes his lamentation by addressing his fears and his dread. "And my worst fears have transpired, leaving me without hope." Therefore, he sums up his misery:

1. I am not at ease.
2. I am not quiet.
3. I am not at rest.
4. I am full of turmoil.

End of speech!

His friends nearby are staring him down. Analyzing his response from their vantage point of good health, plenty to eat, continued prosperity, and a happy family, they are offended at such raw statements. They will soon rebuke him because he said such things. They are becoming increasingly more convinced, "He's getting what he deserves!"

Did you to see the movie, *The Elephant Man?* What a wonderful film—a film not for the sheltered and naive, but one with an adult theme. It's about a man who struggled with a disease that resulted in deforming and defacing his person. His head becomes enlarged and thick callouslike skin replaces his once-smooth skin, which caused him to appear grotesque. Put bluntly, he ultimately looks like a circus attraction, even though he remains a great man with a good mind and tender emotions. The public is shameless as they treat him like a freak who has escaped from the sideshow.

You'll recall the tragic scene where he's running from the crowd as cameras are flashing and people are yelling and attempting to seize him. He finally finds his way to a railway station and races down the steps to get away from them. He winds up cornered in the public latrine of the station. The mob pours into that place with their flashing cameras as the man struggles to release his words in full volume: *"I am a human being."* You could hear a pin drop in the theater after that line. I can see Job in that setting, screaming: "Oh God, *where are you?"* He's at the end of his rope.

Author John Hartley writes:

> These are the harshest words Job utters against himself in the entire book. They startle us. The friends too are shocked. They fear that his faith in God has melted into distrust . . . Why would one who refused to curse God be so hostile toward his own life? The contrast between the Job of the prologue and the Job of the poem could not be sharper.
>
> Though Job approaches the brink of cursing God, he does not. Instead he vents the venom of his anguish by wishing that he were dead. He survives his darkest hour, since he neither curses God nor takes his fate into his own hands.[5]

Ever felt like that? We've come a long way in church history in the past forty years. My involvement in ministry has unfolded during this four-decade period of time.

Early on (back in the early 1960s) when a Christian suffered from a depression that resulted in this kind of thinking and candid admission, you never said so publicly. You swallowed your sorrow. The first book I read on this subject, covering emotional turmoil and mental illness among Christians was considered heresy by most of my evangelical friends.

The pervasive opinion then was simple: Christians didn't have breakdowns. Furthermore, you certainly didn't stay depressed! You know what term was used to describe those who struggled with deep depression back in the early and midsixties? *Nervous.* "He's got a nervous problem." Or simply, "She's nervous." And if you ever, God help you, if you *ever* had to be hospitalized due to your "nervous" disorder, there just wasn't a Christian word for it. I repeat, you didn't tell a soul. "Shame upon shame that you didn't trust the Lord through your struggle and find Him faithful to help you with your depression."

I remember being told by a seminary prof who talked to us about assisting families with funerals. If you did funerals for those who had committed suicide and the deceased who took his/her own life happened to have been a Christian, we were never to mention that. Frankly, it didn't sound right then, and it doesn't sound right today. Shame-based counsel never sounds right because it isn't right! And I didn't know enough to know that Job 3 was in the Book back then. Had I known, I would have said, "Hey, what about Job?"

WORDS OF COMFORT AND ENCOURAGEMENT

I want to write to you who are reading these lines who may be in the pit, struggling to find your way back. It's possible that things have gotten so dark you need a competent Christian psychologist (or psychiatrist) to help you find your way. The most intelligent thing you can do is locate one and go. In fact, go as long as you need to go. Make sure that counselor really does know the Lord Jesus and is truly competent, able to provide the direction you need so you can work your way through your maze of misery. And I would add, "God bless you for every hour you spend finding your way out of the hole that you have been in. There is hope. Our faithful God will see you through."

I don't know that I would have been mature enough earlier in my life to do this, but today, as I think of hearing Job who is so crushed, with his head in his hands and probably dissolved in tears, I could not restrain myself from walking over to him, putting my arms around him, and telling him how much I love him and respect him. Though admittedly, I'm sure I could never understand how terrible his misery must be.

I want to write these few words to everyone who is engaged in the work of psychology or psychiatry who know our Savior and respects God's Word and trusts in its truths: "Go for it. Stay at it. Help all you can for as long as you can. Many hurting brothers and sisters in God's family need what you can provide. We appreciate you, and our prayers are with you."

THREE STATEMENTS TO PONDER

Having said all that, there are three practical statements I want to give you who can identify with Job's struggle.

First, there are days too dark for the sufferer to see light. That's where Job is as we end this chapter. Unfortunately, his so-called friends will not bring him any relief. Like Job, *you* may not have seen light for a long time either. I'll write more to you in a moment.

Second, there are experiences too extreme for the hurting to have hope. When a person drops so low due to the inner pain, it's as if all hope is lost. That's why Job admits his lack of ease, his absence of peace, and his deep unrest.

Third, there are valleys too deep for the anguished to find relief. It seems, at that point, there is no reason to go on.

We run out of places to look to find relief. It's then our minds play tricks on us, making us think that not even God cares. Wrong! Do you remember the line that Corrie ten Boom used to quote? I often call it to mind: "There is no pit so deep but that He is not deeper still."[6] I know, I know. Those who are deeply depressed don't remember that and can't reason with that. They would deny such a statement because they feel a vast distance between them and God, and it's confusing—it's frightening. But the good news is that God is not only there . . . He cares.

During my student years at Dallas Theological Seminary, Cynthia and I cultivated a friendship with Dennis and Lucy Guernsey. We both lived in the nearby campus apartments (praise God, they have now been torn down!), which meant we were two of only ten couples in that tiny complex, so we got to know everybody around us. Dennis and Lucy became some of our best friends and remained so for years . . . we just loved them.

While at Seminary, they had a little baby boy, whom Dennis absolutely adored. This little boy became Dennis's reason to go on. He and Lucy were such great parents. We had our firstborn, Curt, by then, about the time they had their son.

After Dennis graduated, they moved to Los Angeles where he advanced his education at the University of Southern California, earning his Ph.D. in psychology. He wanted to spend his years helping people who struggled as he had struggled growing up. While Dennis was in the midst of his studies as a Ph.D. student, their little boy stumbled into a swimming pool in a neighbor's backyard and drowned. They lost their precious son, which devastated Dennis.

Years later, Dennis told me how he responded to that loss. "I got in my car, having just lost my boy, and I grabbed that steering wheel and I drove about every freeway in Los Angeles. During those hours I *screamed* out to God expressing all the grief and the anger and the sadness and the confusion from deep within my soul." He added, "I said things to Him in that car that I'd never said before to *anybody.* I screamed it out, and it wasn't very nice. I just vomited everything out to God."

About dawn he finally drove back into his driveway at their little home, his shirt dripping wet with sweat. His hands were still gripping the steering wheel. He turned the key off and dropped his head onto the steering wheel, sobbing with giant heaves. He said, "I was comforted with this thought: God can handle it! He can handle everything I said." Isn't that a great line? "God can handle it!"

The Lord gave the Guernseys two wonderful girls. They grew 'em up right. But, truth be told, there was no one ever to take the place of that little boy they lost. Dennis has since died of brain cancer. Lucy lives on, triumphantly. But I'll never forget his words, "God can handle it!"[7]

I think it is noteworthy that there is no blast against Job at the end of chapter 3. God doesn't say, "Shame on you, Job." God could handle Job's words. He understood why he said what he said. And He understands you. Unfortunately, Job has his words on record for preachers to talk about for centuries. Yours and mine, thankfully, will remain a secret inside our cars, or in the back part of our bedrooms, or along the crashing surf, or perhaps out under tall trees in a forest. God can handle it all, so let it all out. Tell Him all that's in your heart. You never get over grief completely until you express it fully. Job didn't hold back.

I admire him more now than when I first began the book.

CHAPTER SIX

Responding to Bad Counsel

Not all advice is good advice—not even when the one who gives the advice thinks it's the right advice. Sometimes it is given in all sincerity, but it is still faulty. A story I was told recently comes to mind.

A man had finished lunch and was in his car driving toward the next appointment. His mind drifted back to the previous evening. He began to be troubled about the heated argument he'd had with his wife. It was one of those ongoing, unresolved conflicts, so he decided it was time to make up. Feeling guilty over some of the things he'd said, he picked up his cell phone and hurriedly dialed home in the midst of a traffic jam.

When the maid answered the call he said, "I'd like to speak to my wife." She responded, "Well, she told me she didn't want to be disturbed right now." Curious, he asked, "Doesn't want to be disturbed?" The maid said, "That's right—she's upstairs with her boyfriend, and she told me she doesn't want to be interrupted." Infuriated, the husband lost it. "You know where I keep my shotgun? Go get it and put in two shells, then walk upstairs and kill both of them."

She put the phone down, got the double-barrel gun and walked up-stairs. He listened, heard two blasts, then waited. She came back down, calmly picked up the phone, and said, "Okay, it's done, they're dead. What do you want me to do with the bodies?" He said, "Throw 'em in the pool, and I'll take care of the rest when I get there." She said, "We don't have a pool." He paused, then said, "Is this 728-3604?"

Not all advice is good advice. Not even when the person giving the advice thinks that it's the right advice.

GOOD ADVICE . . . BAD ADVICE

Every person reading this chapter has been the recipient of bad advice. You listened as someone gave it to you. You followed the counsel you received and then suffered the consequences. On the other hand, we have all ben-efited from someone's good advice. We were unsure and confused so we reached out to somebody we trusted. We received good counsel, followed the advice, and enjoyed the benefits.

In the Bible there is a book of wise counsel. It's called Proverbs, a thirty-one chapter book, full of wise and helpful advice.

Take for example, Proverbs 12:15: "The way of a fool is right in his own eyes, but a wise man is he who listens to counsel." You and I have experi-enced those very words. We have been foolish, thinking we were right and along came a parent or a teacher, perhaps a friend who talked some sense into our head, thankfully. As a result we benefited from wise counsel.

Another—Proverbs 16:24: "Pleasant words are a honeycomb, sweet to the soul and healing to the bones." I love that! Words given at the right time, Solomon writes elsewhere, are "like apples of gold in settings of silver."

> Like apples of gold in settings of silver
> Is a word spoken in right circumstances.
> Like an earring of gold and an ornament of fine gold
> Is a wise reprover to a listening ear.
>
> Proverbs 25:11–12

Good counsel. Wise reproof. Obedient response. And the benefits come rolling in. The ultimate win-win situation.

This ancient book is chock-full of similar statements:

> Listen to counsel and accept discipline,
> That you may be wise the rest of your days.
>
> Proverbs 19:20

And another:

> Iron sharpens iron,
> So one man sharpens another.
>
> Proverbs 27:17

We all know the benefit of a good friend who sharpens us with wise counsel, even the person's presence "sharpens" our lives. Solomon writes a similar thought in the same chapter.

> As in water face reflects face,
> So the heart of man reflects man.
>
> Proverbs 27:19

I'm sure you have known such occasions. You've had something deep in the well of your heart you've not been able to pull up. Along comes someone who loves you and has the ability to drop a bucket in that deep well of yours, pull it out, then splash the contents around for both of you to see it clearly.

I need to add that wise counsel is not always easy to hear.

> Faithful are the wounds of a friend,
> But deceitful are the kisses of an enemy.
>
> Proverbs 27:6

The Hebrew uses an interesting verb stem in the early part of the verse. It's known as the "causative stem," which allows us to render the statement:

"Trustworthy are the bruises *caused* by the wounding of one who loves you." The bruise that comes after the verbal blow of one who loves you is a trustworthy bruise. In genuine love, your friend confronts you with the truth—you're alone, in private, and you hear the hard thing that needs to be confronted. That bruise stays with you, and you're a better person for it. Such bruising is much more helpful and reliable than a phony embrace, the "kiss" of a flatterer whom Solomon calls our "enemy." Good counsel is a *good* thing, even if it hurts to hear it.

And then, there's *bad* counsel. Some one-liners would sound like this:

- "Look, why don't you go ahead and marry him. He'll change after you're married.
- "You know, since I'm an expert in financial matters, this feels right. I really think it's worth that $10,000 investment in Enron stock."
- "Bright and capable as you are, don't bother about finishing school. Do you have any idea how many millionaires there are today who never graduated from high school?"
- "The weather's pretty bad, but I've flown in worse. Come on, get in. I think we can make it up over the clouds without much difficulty."

Bad counsel.

BACK TO JOB IN THE PITS

We left Job in what we might call "black pessimism." His depression was deep. He despised the day he was born. He hated the thought that he lived after being born. Over and above all that, the silence of God was driving him up a wall. So the man didn't hold back; he said it all. When we left him, the dear man was lower than a whale's belly.

Three friends sitting nearby said nothing as they stared at him. They have completed seven days and seven nights in silence, watching, listening, and forming their opinions. At first, it was hard for them to believe it was really their friend, Job. He looked so different than before. His head is shaved, his face is swollen, he's scabbed over with all these running sores. If you look closely, there are tiny worms in some of them. It's grotesque. He keeps squirming from one position to another. He doesn't feel comfortable sitting on the ground, and he's so miserable lying down, his nights are full of groans and restlessness. Slowly and agonizingly he tries to get into a position that will bring a few minutes' relief—can't do it. As the sun rises, its searing rays burn his skin as he sits in the trash dump of the city. Not even his wife can bring him relief. The man is tormented by his afflictions and broken in spirit. If anyone on earth ever needed the comfort of a friend, Job did. His friends came, but comfort was not to be found.

It was bad enough to have them sit and stare in silence, but when they opened their mouths things only got worse. Talk about bad counsel. Oh, they didn't mean it to be bad—they just lost sight of their purpose. And what was that? Stop and remember. Originally they came *to sympathize* with him and *to comfort* him (Job 2:11). Of the hundreds of business associates and dozens of friends Job knew, only these showed up. In fact, they came for the right reason.

They came to him as we would drive to the hospital to visit a friend who is terminally ill. You and I don't know what to say, so we often stand nearby and say very little. Admittedly, there are times we speak and say the wrong thing. We leave thinking, why did I say that? We wish we had just stayed quiet. Total silence is so much better than inappropriate words. We've all blown it by saying a little more than we should.

But these men go so much further than that. They mix blame and shame, condemnation and judgment, they heap on loads of legalism; to drive their point home they resort to sarcasm and argument. But comfort? Sympathy? Both got lost in the heat of verbal put-downs.

A LITTLE STRUCTURE TO BEGIN WITH

Let me offer a few clarifying comments as we turn the corner in Job's life and begin the dialogue between him and his friends. Four are worth mentioning.

First, the first two chapters of the Book of Job and the final 11 verses of the last chapter, chapter 42, are written in narrative form. As I explained earlier, this style is known as prose. These two sections of prose represent history. Being factual and straightforward, they're easily understood. There isn't a lot of mystery.

You may have questions, of course, with these opening two chapters, but you have no trouble understanding the words and the flow of action. At the end of the book you find yourself thrilled because it all turns out so well. Job gets double everything . . . except children. Since that probably wouldn't have been a blessing to have twice the number of children at his age (!), the Lord is gracious and allows him and his wife to have only ten more children. We like it when people who have suffered wind up living wholesome, fulfilled lives. So much for the prose section.

In between, we find numerous chapters of poetry. Like the Psalms and the book we referred to earlier, Proverbs, Job is mainly poetry. Therefore, as I've mentioned already, it reads like poetry. This means there are repetitious phrases along with colorful word pictures. Some things, as you will soon discover, are beyond our capability to understand fully, which is to be expected. But most of what we read can be grasped. In fact, much of it is beautiful writing. Beautiful, but a bit mysterious, even a little mystical at times. The prose of Job is historical while the poetry is philosophical. That explains why it's sometimes difficult to understand. Philosophical statements can be convoluted.

One of my mentors used to say that a philosopher is a person who talks about things he doesn't understand, but he makes it sound like it's your fault. Philosophy requires that we keep our thinking caps on. And even then, some things don't register clearly. I'll do my best to keep things interesting from one chapter to the next, but you'll need to concentrate with me. As one of our church members noted while I was preaching through Job, "There aren't any car chases to keep the teens on the edge of their seats."

Second, this poetic section, which is the largest part of the book, (Job 3:1–42:6) begins as a mild discussion. It then turns into an intense *debate*. Finally, it ends in a heated *dispute*. Job's first friend, Eliphaz, begins with his hat in his hand as he approaches Job. Initially, he's reluctant and downright civil. But toward the end, there's no hesitation or reservation. By then he's got his index finger jammed against Job's sternum, determined to set him straight. Gentle discussion erodes into an angry debate.

Third, Job's three friends, Eliphaz, Bildad, and Zophar "take turns" as they dialogue with him. Their words appear in cycles—three cycles, to be exact.

In the first cycle, Eliphaz speaks, then Job answers. Next, Bildad talks and Job answers. Finally, it's Zophar's turn. He makes his initial comments, and Job answers. At that point, round one ends.

And then Eliphaz comes back on the scene to start the second cycle of dialogue. He's apparently the oldest of the group. In those days age was given the honor of top priority. So, like before, Eliphaz speaks first and Job answers him. Bildad follows as Job answers him. Zophar again speaks last, then Job answers him.

When we get to the third cycle, for some unrevealed reason Zophar has stepped out of the dialogue. Maybe he got tired of arguing and decided, "I'm outta here. This is going nowhere." Then, you'll remember, by the time we arrive at Job 32, another "friend" comes on the scene, the youngest of the group, named Elihu. Interestingly, Elihu does a monologue, but Job never answers him. Maybe by now Job is thinking, "I have heard all I'm going to listen to." I think the man is simply exhausted. He sees no purpose in providing more answers. I have the feeling he chose to discontinue the argument.

Fourth, one final tip. I should mention that Eliphaz bases his words on experience. He repeats the same phrase: "I have seen . . . I have seen." In light of what he had experienced, Eliphaz said what he did about Job's situation.

Bildad is different. He bases his words on *tradition*. He says to Job, "Inquire of past generations" (Job 8:8). He urges Job to go back into the chronicle of history and check what happened there. In effect, Bildad says, "In light of that, tradition teaches us this."

When we hear from Zophar, (the harshest of the three), we'll find that he throws tact to the wind as he gets in Job's face with both fists clinched. Zophar's impatient and angry words are based on *assumptions*.

Let me add here, *all three are legalistic.* They are judgmental and condemning. To a man, they resort to shame-based counsel. Sometimes you'll shake your head and say, "How in the world could they say that?" Why would they say something like that to somebody they called their friend?" Let's face it—we tend to do that same thing. We get so intent on setting the record straight that we just push ourselves in and bluntly say our piece. At that point, we not only cut to the chase, we do some slaughtering with our tongues. It's like a verbal fistfight. (Which is why it's called a "tongue-lashing.") As the heat of debate intensifies, we will witness that kind of ugliness.

SETTING THE STAGE FOR DIALOGUE

Men, can you remember a major argument you had with your wife? Stop and think back. Maybe it went on for a few hours and it got really intense. So you wound up sleeping on the patio! After about the second night out there you start to feel lonely. So you decide you'd like to come in and kind of get cleaned up. You slowly push the door open and you go, "Hhhhhii, hi. Hi, honey. Hey, nice hair . . . pretty dress!" Something like that. You're sort of breaking into a new conversation. Well, that's the way Eliphaz starts out. He's sat nearby for seven days and nights. He's heard Job unload his truckful of turmoil and torment. He realized—at least here at first—things are awfully tender. Reluctantly, he decides to break the ice and offer a little counsel.

Eliphaz Preaches

Gingerly, he starts, "If one ventures a word with you, will you become impatient? But who can refrain from speaking?" (Job 4:2). We've all been there, maybe with one of our kids. There's been a long period of silence so we try to be sensitive as we ease into a discussion. That's the tone of Eliphaz's opening words. "But who can refrain from speaking?" He adds in so many words: "Silence isn't solving anything."

Our daughter Charissa sent me a funny photograph of a couple of adult lions. One was a big male lion with this thick chunk of mane around his neck. And the other is a weary-looking lioness who has obviously had cubs not too many days ago; she's kind of hanging down to the ground. Big Daddy is dropping by for another little visit. In the photo she's letting out this enormous roar with her fangs fully exposed. She's also got her paw up near his face with long claws extended. Her mouth is wide open as she growls, like she's saying, "Don't even think about it!" The old guy sort of ducks his head and slinks back with his ears flat against his head. Charissa and I had a good laugh over this feisty lioness who is roaring at the old rascal who is suddenly *very* reluctant to come any nearer.

Well, that's Eliphaz. He's hesitant to break the silence . . . so he slides in with a very courteous, "Behold you have admonished many, and you have strengthened weak hands" (Job 4:3). And then he adds, "Your words have helped the tottering to stand, and you have strengthened feeble knees" (Job 4:4). That was true. Job had done all the above.

"But!" With that innocent-sounding "contrastive connective," Eliphaz turns the corner—verbally. He is about to throw his first jab. He does it with heavyweight gloves on, ever so gently. He says, "But now it has come to you, and you are impatient" (Job 4:5).

With that, Eliphaz stops comforting and starts preaching. "You have spent your life giving other people counsel and telling people how to stand firm and how to survive life's storms, and now something difficult has happened to you, and you're irritable!" It's as if he's saying, "As long as you're on the giving end of things, you're good at giving advice . . . but now that you're under it, you're out of control!" Watch how he builds to a climax:

> But now it has come to you, and you are impatient;
> It touches you, and you are dismayed.
> Is not your fear of God your confidence,
> And the integrity of your ways your hope?
>
> Job 4:5–6

"Isn't that about it, Job? I mean, I'm not questioning your integrity . . . but you're impatient with what's happened to you. Seems to me you're not the person everybody thought you were." With that Eliphaz twists in the knife.

> Remember now, who ever perished being innocent?
> Or where were the upright destroyed?
> According to what I have seen, those who plow iniquity
> And those who sow trouble harvest it.
>
> Job 4:7–8

"Look closely, Job, *you're getting what you deserve.*"

The Message puts everything on the bottom shelf.

> Would you mind if I said something to you?
> Under the circumstances it's hard to keep quiet.
> You yourself have done this plenty of times, spoken words
> that clarify, encouraged those who were about to quit.
> Your words have put stumbling people on their feet,
> put fresh hope in people about to collapse.
> But now you're the one in trouble—you're hurting!
> You've been hit hard and you're reeling from the blow.
> But shouldn't your devout life give you confidence now?
> Shouldn't your exemplary life give you hope?
> "Think! Has a truly innocent person ever ended up on the scrap heap?
> Do genuinely upright people ever lose out in the end?
> It's my observation that those who plow evil and sow trouble reap evil
> and trouble.
>
> Job 4:2–8, MSG

That stung! When you analyze those words you see there's shame in them. "Job, if you're that innocent why are you here in this predicament? Frankly, it's my observation that people who suffer like this have got sin in their life." If Eliphaz came to sympathize and comfort, this was a weird way to do it. He didn't lift up his friend, he shoved him down further. Bad counsel does that, and this certainly qualifies as bad counsel. Especially since none of what he's saying is true.

Eliphaz wonders whoever suffered without deserving it. How about every martyr? How about victims of abuse and murder? How about the Son of God, the innocent "Lamb of God who took away the sins of the world?" The One who did no sin, knew no sin, had no sin? Without deserving it, He was nailed to a cross. And He's the One who says, "Father, forgive them, they don't know what they're doing." The classic example of unjust suffering is the Savior's crucifixion.

If I may interrupt for a moment, "Eliphaz, you are *out to lunch.* I don't care how old you are. I don't care how many experiences you've had. You have no right to say this to a man of unquestionable integrity." There, I've said it. And I'd like to say it to every person who twists the truth, ignores the facts, and verbally abuses the undeserving.

Problem is, he's not through. Eliphaz keeps on talking about visions in the night and then about how true it is that mankind is not perfect before God. He went on, telling Job we have a Maker and He's the only perfect One . . . and we're not. Of course, Job knew all of that! As a matter of fact, not everything Eliphaz said was incorrect. He hits the nail on its head when he says to Job, "For man is born for trouble, as sparks fly upward" (Job 5:7). Job certainly knew that too. If only Job's aging friend had stopped there. He goes on to let a little more pride seep in: "But as for me, I would seek God, and I would place my cause before God" (Job 5:8). By Eliphaz saying that, he is implying, "You haven't done that, Job!"

I have a question: How does he know what Job has done? We don't always seek God in stated words. During ultradifficult times we seek God in silence, deep down in our inner soul. Since God is the One "Who does great and unsearchable things, wonders without number" (Job 5:9), seeking Him in silence is altogether appropriate.

Job could have answered, "I know that!" He could have said more: "I'm not sitting here in a carnal state! I'm struggling with my grief and pain, yet I'm fully aware that God does great and wonderful things. I am covered with boils, but I've done nothing to deserve this! And you're pouring forth all this great theology with no understanding. Please, please." He could have said that and so much more, but Job refrained.

Eliphaz doesn't let up. He has the audacity to say at the end of verse 17, "Do not despise the discipline of the Almighty." Again, don't miss the implication: "You're suffering because you're guilty, Job! You're getting just what you deserve. You're not listening to the Lord's reproofs. As a matter of fact, once you repent of your sins, you'll be just fine." How sympathetic and comforting!

He concludes rather bluntly:

> You will know also that your descendants will be many,
> And your offspring as the grass of the earth.
> You will come to the grave in full vigor,

Like the stacking of grain in its season.
Behold this; we have investigated it, and so it is,
Hear it, and know for yourself.

Job 5:25–27

"That's the answer, Job, plain and simple. Take this to heart and you'll be fine. Glad to have been of assistance. This is what you needed to hear. I'm done. No charge."

Somewhere in that bad sermon, accusation overran compassion. And don't think Job missed it. A person in pain doesn't feel well, but that doesn't mean there's a lack of discernment. People who are hurting don't do well when we deliver a mixture of Ghengis Kahn and Mike Tyson rolled into one verbal blast. Furthermore, if you don't have God's clear mind and indisputable facts to prove it, please, just love your hurting friend and keep quiet. If there is insight to be gained, it will be gained through comfort and tender mercy, not rebuke and accusation. On occasion, yes, as we saw earlier in the Proverbs, there are those moments when reproofs are necessary. But while covered with boils? No.

Job Responds

"Oh," says Job at the beginning of his response. Linger over his first statement, "Oh that my vexation were actually weighed" (Job 6:2). Meaning? "Eliphaz, look at me. Consider my circumstances. *I have ten dead children.* Eliphaz, listen to me. *I've lost everything.* Oh that my grief were actually weighed and laid in the balances together with my calamity. If somehow the weight of my grief could be measured with my calamity, the sum of both would be heavier than the sand of the seas." Don't rush on. Eliphaz may not have heard Job, but I want to make sure *we* do. Pause and try to imagine the man's anguish. "Understand, it's with all of that in mind my words were rash." Job is being vulnerable.

When people come to the end of their tether, in the bottomless pit of it all, rash words will come out that they will later regret. But while it's happening we need to cut 'em some slack. Let's go there momentarily. You've got a couple of grown kids going a little nuts . . . cut 'em some slack. They'll finally come around. Later, they will get it together, but realize they have sat through twenty-

84

plus years of your sermons. Allow them to react however they need to for now. Let 'em say whatever they need to say without trying to be an Eliphaz.

To be a good counselor requires enormous timing, great wisdom, a long rope, and great understanding. Job is pleading for all of that as he asks Eliphaz to consider his miserable plight. "I don't think you'd say these things, Eliphaz, if you sat where I sit."

Job also made it clear that he had not "denied the words of the Holy One" (Job 6:10). That's quite a statement. And it was a fact. "I want you to know, Eliphaz, that in all of this—hating the day I was born and in swinging my fist at the fact that I lived and didn't die beyond birth, and the fact that my misery has gotten unbearable, please, Eliphaz, understand I've never once denied the words of the Holy One." Doubt and denial were not in Job's heart. Confusion, yes. And anger? Of course. Again, let's go there. Please give your fellow Christians room to feel confused and express anger in times like this. Job is not defensive, trying to cover some secret sin. His logic unfolds in several questions:

> Have I said, "Give me something,'"
> Or, "Offer a bribe for me from your wealth,"
> Or, "Deliver me from the hand of the adversary,"
> Or, "Redeem me from the hand of the tyrants?"
>
> Job 6:22–23

Have I asked for any of that? No!

> Teach me, and I will be silent;
> And show me how I have erred.
>
> Job 6:24

What a vulnerable, honest offer! "Eliphaz, I haven't asked for something special. I haven't sought for some angle on this that would involve you." He then asks, "What does your argument prove?" His point? "You're missing it."

"Now please look at me, and see if I lie to your face" (Job 6:28). I love that line. "Look, Eliphaz. I don't traffic in lies!" Job knew that lies are absolutely damning to recovery. And so he invites Eliphaz to point out any lie. "Tell me to my face. Look at me. And if you can't, then desist—pull back, turn around. If there is injustice on my tongue, point it out (v. 30)."

In chapter 6, Job speaks to his friend, but in chapter 7 he speaks to his God. In doing so he turns his case over to the Lord. Job says, in effect, "If I could only have my case brought before the living God. He qualifies as the ideal Judge. I would come before Him and I would lay my situation out before Him and I would say, 'Judge rightly, and I will accept whatever You have to say.' But He's so silent. He doesn't speak to me these days."

God's silence is worse than His voice because it's impossible to know what He would say. Job goes on throughout this seventh chapter pouring out his anguish, but God's silence continues. The Lord gives no answer to his grief-stricken soul. He concludes his plea by asking why God had made him His target. "Why am I in Your crosshairs?" Silence.

"Why then do You not pardon my transgression and take away my iniquity?" (Job 7:21). If there's transgression, why haven't you pardoned it? There's nothing I wouldn't confess."

Silence.

Humiliated by the words of Eliphaz and haunted by God's silence, Job speaks like a tormented man, here and later. Physically he's miserable. Emotionally he is at wits' end. Spiritually he is confused. Just remember, in addition to everything he has lost and all the pain he's enduring, he has now been blamed and shamed, rebuked in front of others and soundly judged. It's horrible. There is no other word for it. It's just horrible.

A FEW WORDS OF WISDOM, PLEASE

This is a good place to pause and learn a few hurtful lessons from Eliphaz and after that, some helpful lessons from Job.

HURTFUL LESSONS TO BE LEARNED FROM ELIPHAZ

First, assumptions reduce understanding and insight. I have missed on assumptions so many times in my life. While I'm confessing, I need to add that assumptions have also led me away from the truth several times in my counsel. When your mind is made up and you think you've already figured out what caused this, you can't really understand the truth because you're no longer listening. Your own conclusions have blocked your hearing. You're waiting to get your points across. Because assumptions reduce understanding, insight gets lost. More often than not, as with Eliphaz, words become blunt and condemning.

Second, shame blocks grace and hinders relief. Shame-based counsel leaves us under an extra load of guilt rather than offering the fresh hope of recovery. Shame shoves you further into the tight grip of anguish. In light of that, I hope you will forever remove these three words from your vocabulary: "Shame on you." They do no good.

Third, pride eclipses mercy and compassion. When you come across as though you have the final answer and you imply that you're the model example, you stop the flow of mercy. Pride and compassion cannot coexist.

I read recently of a Christian leader who was traveling with his wife toward Chicago to speak.

As he cruised along, he passed his exit and his wife said, "You missed the exit, honey."

Well, that just made him mad. He said, "I'm driving this car. I know where I'm going. I know if I missed an exit."

She said, "You'd better turn around."

He responded, "There's no need for that."

Silence.

He continued on and the signs ceased to say Chicago. They began telling about Detroit and other cities not so close to Chicago.

She remarked, "Honey, all the signs for Chicago have stopped. You're going the wrong way."

He gritted his teeth and opted for one more exit.

When they reached the exit there was still no sign for Chicago.

His wife piped up again, "Honey, stop being ridiculous and turn around."

At that point, he decided to prove her wrong whatever it took. He began trying to think of a way to get to Chicago without turning around.

There was no way.

Suddenly he realized he was sinning. He confessed his sin, gave up, and turned around.

She said, "See how easy it was."

He smiled. "Now why didn't I do that twenty miles ago?"

"Because you're too proud."[1]

Understand this applies to women just as much as to men. But, guys, we can really be stubborn! I'm sure there are ladies reading this who have learned that we men are willing to drive one hundred miles out of the way to prove we know where we're going.

HELPFUL LESSONS TO BE LEARNED FROM JOB

I find at least two lessons to remember.

First, there are times when others' words only make our troubles worse. That may seem too elementary to mention, so why would I? Well, have you learned it? Are you still listening to everybody? If so, small wonder you're confused.

The counsel of some people only complicates our troubles. Few traps are more disastrous than the trap of believing everything you hear. Let me level with you. Virtually every significant decision I've made in my Christian life, where I've sought the counsel of many people (all of them, very sincere), someone has counseled me incorrectly. They weren't evil people; they just didn't have sufficient understanding, so their advice was skewed. Since bad counsel doesn't stop with Eliphaz, let's make sure we don't give equal weight to everyone's advice. Pick your counselors very carefully. And even then, filter the advice through prayer and common sense.

Second, there are times when God's ways only make us more confused. There I've said it. I've been wanting to say that all through this chapter, and I finally worked up the courage. My point? Don't expect to understand everything that happens when it occurs.

I'm going to close with a simple suggestion that may make you smile. It's something I want you to practice in front of a mirror. I call it, "The Shrug." Stare into the mirror, shake your head and shrug your shoulders, then say out loud, "I don't know." Practice that little maneuver several times a month.

I don't care if you have a Ph.D. you earned at Yale or in Scotland. Just stand in front of the mirror, all alone, nobody around, shrug, and say, "I don't know . . . I really don't know." You can add, "I can't tell you why that happened. I don't know." Repeat the words several times: "I don't know."

The great news is that God never shrugs. He never says that. With acute perception He says, "I know exactly why this happened. I know the way you take. I know why. I know how long you'll be there, and I know what will be the end result." Shrugging and deity are incompatible.

While you're shrugging in genuine humility, saying, "I don't know," He's saying, "Good for you. Rely on Me in the mystery. Trust Me." God never promised He would inform us ahead of time all about His plan, He's just promised He has one. Ultimately, it's for our good and His glory. He knows—we don't. That's why we shrug and admit, "I don't know." So, if you and I meet someday and you ask me a deep, difficult question, don't be surprised if I shrug and say, "I don't know."

But I do know this: The death of His Son was not in vain. And I do know this: Christ died for you. And I do know this: If you believe in Him, He will forgive your sins and you will go to live with Him forever. You'll have heaven and all the blessings of it, I do know that. It's a tough journey, getting there. Full of a lot of confusion, a lot of struggle, a lot of shrugs, followed by a lot of "I don't knows." But when the heavens open and we're there, hey, there will be no more shrugs. "Now I know."

Job finally reaches the place where he can rest his case as he says:

> But He knows the way I take;
> When He has tried me, I shall come forth as gold.
> My foot has held fast to His path:
> I have kept His way and not turned aside.
> I have not departed from the command of His lips;
> I have treasured the words of His mouth more than my necessary food.
>
> Job 23:10–12

What peace this brings! "He knows the way that I take."

CHAPTER SEVEN

Continuing the Verbal Fistfight

J ob and his so-called comforting companions remind me of a folk tale that originated in a forest up in Canada's Northwest Territories. It's about a small pack of porcupines who huddled together to stay warm as the winter winds blew hard. But because their bristles were so sharp, the closer they got the more they pricked each other, which caused them to move away from one another. Before long, they began to shiver as the icy blast of artic winds increased, which forced them to come back together again. This strange dance of the porcupines continued to repeat itself through the long night.

As one wag put it, "They needed each other, but they kept needling each other."

A similar "dance" took place in the ancient land of Uz where Job and his friends verbally slugged it out. What began for all the right reasons got lost in the shuffle of time and tension. It wasn't long before the friends' words became lectures laced with shame and sarcasm. Argument and insult eclipsed comfort and sympathy. Job needed them near as understanding, compassionate friends, but the closer they came the more they bristled with caustic comments and accusations, which pushed them apart.

One author describes their verbal slugfest. Referring to Job, he writes:

> He is wounded by their harshness, stung by their censures, exasperated by their reproaches, and driven into antagonism by their arguments. They are the professed advocates of religious obligation. They represent the cause of God, enforcing his claims on Job and justifying his ways with him, which they do in a spirit that repels him, with assumptions that experience does not sanction, and which his own inner consciousness falsifies. . . .
>
> The insoluble conflict which they assume . . . tends to place before his mind a distorted image of the character of God. God appears to be torturing him for crimes which he has not committed, to be relentlessly pursuing him as an implacable foe, and without justice or reason to be employing his resistless power to crush him to the earth. This is the phantom which his friends·are constantly setting before him, this false notion of God as unjust and pitiless toward him; and this for which he cannot otherwise account, his own intolerable sufferings seem to rivet upon him. This phantom, apparently so real, he is incessantly obliged to fight or it would drive him to absolute despair and force him to give up his confidence and trust in God and thus throw him completely into the tempter's snare. . . .
>
> Here, then, are Job's three friends who . . . are busily engaged in letting fly their poisoned arrows . . . And here is Job himself exposed without shield or buckler to their dangerous attacks.[1]

And so the friends talked. And Job responded. And they kept talking. And he kept responding. And they kept offering their shallow answers and simplistic solutions as Job struggled to survive. The longer they argued, the further they drifted from helping him.

It was H. L. Mencken who said it best: "There is always an easy solution to every human problem—neat, plausible, and wrong."[2] Eliphaz was the first to throw a punch, you will recall. His reasonings came from experience. "I have learned. I have observed. I have seen." He wound up talking a lot, said little, and comforted not at all.

Following Job's vulnerable and honest response, Eliphaz stepped back. Next in the "tag team match" of philosophers is a man named Bildad. If you think Eliphaz was offensive, just wait until you meet Bildad. Talk about a human porcupine. His blunt approach is evidenced in his opening line: "How long will you say these things, and the words of your mouth be a mighty wind?" (Job 8:2). In today's terms, "You windbag!" Now can you imagine sitting there, fevered from the sores that cover your body? The memory of ten children buried on a nearby hillside. Your wife whispering in your ear, "You need to curse God and let Him take you off the earth." Eliphaz coming with his no-help advice. And now, along comes a second friend, a little younger than Eliphaz, with this insulting remark: "You're a bag of wind, Job." Having heard Job's response to Eliphaz, Bildad decided to set Job straight.

Bildad launched into three lines of argument. Here's the way Bildad's "sermon" would look in outline form:

- First, The Character of God—Job 8:3–7
  ("Look Up, Job!")
- Second, The Wisdom of the Past—Job 8:8–10
  ("Look Back, Job!")
- Third, The Evidence of Nature—Job 8:11–19
  ("Look Around, Job!")
- Concluding Comments—Job 8:20–22

Let's follow that outline as we trace Bildad's message—which was more like a lecture on theology.

"LOOK UP, JOB!"

Bildad's opening blow led to further tactless remarks:

> Does God pervert justice?
> Or does the Almighty pervert what is right?
>
> Job 8:3.

And if that's not brutal enough, get this line:

> If your sons sinned against Him,
> Then He delivered them into the power of their transgression.
>
> Job 8:4

Yes, that means exactly what you think it means. I had to read it two or three times to believe a man would say that to a grieving father. As we read in *The Message,* Bildad is saying, "It's plain that your children sinned against him—otherwise, why would God have punished them?" Not only is Job brokenhearted over the loss of his children, he has to listen to this man who has the *audacity* to say that their deaths were due to God's punishing them for their transgressions.

I'm going to be painfully frank—I find it amazing that Job didn't haul off and punch Bildad right in the kisser! But Job, being a man of heroic endurance, restrains himself. (It's a good thing this book is titled *Job* . . . not *Chuck.* Let me just put it to you straight, okay? If that verse were Chuck 8:4, you wouldn't read what you just read). Job's silence is remarkable. He gets hit repeatedly below the belt, but Job allowed the man time to keep swinging. To make matters worse, Bildad says what he says in the name of God. His pious sermon continues . . .

> If you would seek God
> And implore the compassion of the Almighty,
> If you are pure and upright,
> Surely now He would rouse Himself for you
> And restore Your righteous estate.
>
> Job 8:5–6

The implication is obvious. "Since you, too, are sinful, Job, God is not willing to bring you to a state of health and provide you with relief. You're getting what you have coming, man. You're going through this because of divine punishment."

Apparently Bildad thinks Job needed a short course in theology. He didn't; Job's theology was solid and sure. Furthermore, he has already modeled humility by confessing any transgression that may have caused his condition. That wasn't the problem.

"LOOK BACK, JOB!"

Since Bildad got nowhere with his opening volley, he returned to the past. Earlier he said, "Job, look up and consider the character of God. Your sons had this happen to them because of the sinfulness of their lives. You've had this happen to you because of sinfulness in your life. And God, who is holy and just and pure, can do only what He has done." As Job sat silently under that unfair analysis, Bildad said, "I suggest you look back, Job."

> Please inquire of past generations,
> And consider the things searched out by their fathers.
> For we are only of yesterday and know nothing,
> Because our days on earth are as a shadow.
> Will they not teach you and tell you,
> And bring forth words from their minds?
>
> Job 8:8–10

Bildad, being a traditionalist, urges Job to go far back in time and learn from the ancients. He's making two points: First, because we know nothing by comparison, and second, because our lives are so brief ("as a shadow"), we need the wisdom of past ages. All that may be true, theoretically, but is that what Job needs to hear right now? Does that help?

The tactlessness of Bildad really grates on me. I know he had some strong things he wanted to say, but the least he could have done was say them carefully and cushion them with tact. Bildad reminds me of a physician I know who, after giving a particular individual (who is rather portly) a treadmill test, studied the results when the test was over. The patient was sweating and panting and finally stepped off the treadmill as the doc looked at the results and said, "Not bad for a guy as fat as you are." Some people have a great grasp of the obvious, don't they? Bildad qualifies as one of them. He may have been a good theologian and historian, but he made a lousy comforter.

"LOOK AROUND, JOB!"

Now then, with the idea of cause and effect in mind, Bildad turned to the subject of nature.

> Can the papyrus grow up without a marsh?
> Can the rushes grow without water?
> While it is still green and not cut down,
> Yet it withers before any other plant.
> So are the paths of all who forget God;
> And the hope of the godless will perish,
> Whose confidence is fragile,
> And shoes trust a spider's web.
> He trusts in his house, but it does not stand;
> He holds fast to it, but it does not endure.
> He thrives before the sun,
> And his shoots spread out over his garden.
> His roots wrap around a rock pile,
> He grasps a house of stones.
> If he is removed from his place,
> Then it will deny him, saying, "I never saw you."
> Behold, this is the joy of His way;
> And out of the dust others will spring.
>
> Job 8:11–19

He started by urging Job to look up and consider the character of God. He then went to the past and had him look back into the teaching of those who lived before. Now he looks around and philosophically presents his argument in poetic form. He's thinking, just as the cause and effect is true in his life, so it is in the world of nature. Let's see if we can tie this together.

"Can the papyrus grow up without a marsh?" The implication is obviously no. Then in good poetic fashion, he repeats similar words. "Can the rushes grow without water?" The point is this: If these plants do not have water, they will wither and die. And the implication is, "Job, you are withering and dying because you're a hypocrite. It only follows that your hope is perishing because you haven't a pure heart and a right relationship before a holy God."

See how he puts it?

So are the paths of all who forget God.

What's he implying? "Job, you have forgotten God!"

And the hope of the godless will perish.

He's now suggesting Job is godless. Next he mentions a spider's web:

Whose confidence is fragile,
And whose trust is a spider's web.

Can you lean on a spider's web and be sustained? No, of course not. No matter how confident, the web is fragile and will tear. "Job, your confidence is like that. You will soon break and you will fall." And then, having said that, he turns to the plants in a garden. No matter how luxurious the plant, no matter how strong the root system, when it is pulled up, it's finished.

Stretching this analogy, Bildad reasons,

If he is removed from his place,
Then it will deny him saying, "I never saw you."

The implication is, that is what has happened to you, Job! "God has uprooted you. Something has damaged your root system that has led to this deathlike condition in which you find yourself." The man is saying precisely what's on his mind, namely, "You have sinned and God has 'uprooted' you because of it!"

While Bildad is meandering around all these philosophical thoughts, Job must have been sitting there trying to piece them together, thinking *What in the world can I gain from this?* Truth be told . . . nothing. All this verbiage is a waste of time. Talk about a windbag!

BILDAD'S CONCLUSION

Lo, God will not reject a man of *integrity,*
Nor will He support the evildoers.
He will yet fill your mouth with laughter
And your lips with shouting.
Those who hate you will be clothed with shame,
And the tent of the wicked will be no more.

Job 8:20–22, italics mine

After another insulting implication regarding Job's lack of integrity, the man drifts into a set of empty comments about life hereafter, where Job would once again know joy. The bottom line is clear—Bildad missed it by a mile. He had no clue about what Job needed.

Speaking of missing the point . . . a man asked his wife, "If you could have anything in the world for one day, what would you want?" She responded with a smile, "Well, I'd really love to be six again." Early the next morning, the morning of her birthday, he got her up and off they went to a nearby Waffle House for waffles and whipped cream with a tall glass of milk. Next, they headed to a local theme park. What a day! He put her on every ride in the park. The Death Slide, the Cyclone Whip, the Screaming Loop, the Wall of Fear, the Double-Ring ferris wheel—everything they had, she rode. Five hours later, she staggers out of the theme park with her husband . . . her head's reeling, her stomach is still churning. Off to McDonald's next. He ordered her two Big Macs along with extra fries and a thick, chocolate shake. After that they took in an exciting animated movie—the latest Hollywood blockbuster. They had popcorn and Pepsis, a bag of M&Ms . . . topping off the day full of fabulous six-year-old adventures. Exhausted, she stumbles into the house late that evening with her husband and collapses on the bed. That was when he leaned over and softly whispered in her ear, "Well, dear, how'd you like being six again?" One eye opened and she said, "Well, actually, I meant my dress size."[3]

That's how far Bildad missed it with Job. He speaks as if the dear man needed ethereal sermons and theoretical illustrations from the past and philosophical analogies from examples in the world of nature—plants dying without water and spiders' webs and roots around rocks as he came down hard on him. All this time Job must have been thinking, "Look, can you help solve the sores I've got all over my body? Or can't you just say you're here because you care about me . . . and you're praying that I'll survive?" But I don't need to put words in Job's mouth. He can speak for himself.

JOB REPLIES TO BILDAD

Job speaks first to Bildad in Job 9, and then he speaks to God in Job 10.

> So what's new? I know all this.
> The question is, "How can mere mortals get right with God?"
> If we wanted to bring our case before him,
>   what chance would we have? Not one in a thousand!
> God's wisdom is so deep, God's power so immense,
>   who could take him on and come out in one piece?
> He moves mountains before they know what's happened,
>   flips them on their heads on a whim.
> He gives the earth a good shaking up,
>   rocks it down to its very foundations.
> He tells the sun, "Don't shine," and it doesn't;
>   he pulls the blinds on the stars.
> All by himself he stretches out the heavens
>   and strides on the waves of the sea.
> He designed the Big Dipper and Orion,
>   the Pleiades and Alpha Centauri.
> We'll never comprehend all the great things he does;

his miracle-surprises can't be counted.
Somehow, though he moves right in front of me, I don't see him;
quietly but surely he's active, and I miss it.
If he steals you blind, who can stop him?
Who's going to say, "Hey, what are you doing?"
God doesn't hold back on his anger;
even dragon-bred monsters cringe before him.

Job 9:1–13, MSG

Clearly, Job knows how great God is. What he longed for was an audience with Him. "Look at Him! He is the One who does all of this. He is *magnificent in might* and I fear Him. I stand before Him in awe and wonder! All I want is to be able to approach Him and talk this out, and you haven't helped me do that, Bildad."

With that said, there are four lines of questions that follow. Keep in mind, Job has in the back of his mind, his appearing before God in a legal-type setting. He would love to be able to step into a divine courtroom and stand before the Judge, the Lord God. He longs to walk in just as he is, covered with these sores, bankrupt and broken, and argue his case. Not to be a rebel, but simply to be in the same room, face to face, where they could talk all this through. He would come with four questions.

First question: *If I could stand before God, what would I say?*

How then can I answer Him,
And choose my words before Him?
For though I were right, I could not answer;
I would have to implore the mercy of my judge.
If I called and He answered me,
I could not believe that He was listening to my voice,
For He bruises me with a tempest
And multiplies my wounds without cause.
He will not allow me to get my breath,
But saturates me with bitterness.
If it is a matter of power, behold, He is the strong one!

And if it is a matter of justice, who can summon Him?

Job 9:14–19

If it is a matter of power, He wins. So if I could stand before Him what would I say?

That leads to the second question: *If I could declare my own innocence, what good would it do?*

> Though I am righteous, my mouth will condemn me;
> Though I am guiltless, He will declare me guilty.
> I am guiltless;
> I do not take notice of myself;
> I despise my life. It is all one; therefore I say,
> "He destroys the guiltless and the wicked."
> If the scourge kills suddenly,
> He mocks the despair of the innocent.
> The earth is given into the hand of the wicked;
> He covers the faces of its judges.
> If it is not He, then who is it?

Job 9:20–24

Remember, now, this is Hebrew poetry. Some of it requires time to think it through. It would be valuable to turn it over in our minds for another hour as we attempt to plumb the depths of Job's words. His words may seem oblique, but his point is clear: "If I could declare my own innocence, what good would it do?"

Now, his third question: *If I tried to be positive and cheerful, how would that help me?*

> Now my days are swifter than a runner;
> They flee away, they see no good.
> They slip by like reed boats,
> Like an eagle that swoops on its prey.
> Though I say, "I will forget my complaint,

I will leave off my sad countenance and be cheerful,"
I am afraid of all my pains,
I know that You will not acquit me.
I am accounted wicked,
Why then should I toil in vain?
If I should wash myself with snow
And cleanse my hands with lye,
Yet You would plunge me into the pit,
And my own clothes would abhor me.

Job 9:25–31

Those thoughts having been expressed, Job arrives at a major turning point with his fourth question: *Is it possible to have a mediator who could represent my needs before God?*

For He is not a man as I am that I may answer Him,
That we may go to court together.
There is no umpire between us,
Who may lay his hand upon us both.
Let Him remove His rod from me,
And let not dread of Him terrify me.
Then I would speak and not fear Him;
But I am not like that in myself.

Job 9:32–35

Job longs for an arbitrator who could serve as his go-between, communicating with this mighty and holy God. He's wishing for one who could argue his case. Job would love to present his case in God's court, but he doesn't have a mediator. He is saying, in effect, "I would love to come and stand before the holy Judge, this God of mine, but I can't do it. He's not a man to come to me, and I don't have in myself what it takes to come before Him. I need a mediator, a go-between. Is there an arbitrator available?"

Years ago, when I was working my way through school as a machinist, there was the threat of a strike in our shop. The union stood on one side with the laborers while management was on the other side. There was a long list of grievances in between. Interestingly, an arbitrator was hired to come in. He had nothing to gain in the eyes of the union. He had nothing to gain in the eyes of the management. He was neutral, hired to come in and hear both sides. The desire was that some kind of understanding could be reached as the arbitrator could, after hearing both sides, negotiate a settlement and avert a strike. In fact, because he was successful, no strike occurred.

That's what Job wants. But he doesn't have an arbitrator. He doesn't qualify to stand before God on his own because he isn't Deity; and God is not a man that He can come stand before Job—so he's stuck.

Would that Job had lived many centuries later! "There is One Mediator," Paul writes to his younger friend Timothy referring to Him who represents us before God the Father. He is none other than Christ Jesus the Lord.

> This is good and acceptable in the sight of God our Savior, who desires all men to be saved and to come to the knowledge of the truth. For there is one God, and one mediator also between God and men, the man Christ Jesus, who gave Himself as a ransom for all, the testimony given at the proper time.
>
> 1 Timothy 2:3–6

Paul writes of our mediator, our arbitrator, "there is one mediator between God and men," and He is specifically identified as "the man Christ Jesus." When it comes to eternal life, there are not many mediators. There is only one, Christ Jesus. Don't be afraid to be that specific. Jesus wasn't. During His earthly ministry Jesus spoke of Himself as "the Way, the Truth and the Life; no one comes to the Father but through Me" (John 14:6).

People struggle with specificity these days. I hear people say we shouldn't be that narrow or that exact regarding religion. I think, "Do you want people to be specific about the airline flight they take?" You ever call up the ticket agent and hear her say, "Well, it's flight 413 or actually it might be flight 1096, or maybe it's flight 309." You would say, "No no, I want to know specifically, which flight is it?" She pauses, "Well, it takes off from DFW, or that could be Love Field, and the flight departs somewhere around 12:15 . . . or maybe 1:10, or it could be as late as 2:30." How ridiculous! Isn't that amazing? For something as simple as an airplane flight, we want *exact* numbers and precise times and the specific gates. You don't want to walk all over the airport going, "Ahh, let me see. I'm open-minded about departure gates. I'll take whatever flies. Just so the pilot is sincere and the plane looks good, it seems right. Deep down inside I need to feel it deeply when I get on the plane." What a joke!

When it comes to the Person of Christ, He is the *one* and only mediator between God and humanity. He is the one and only Savior! We find ourselves responding, "Oh, Job, there is a mediator. You just haven't met Him, but someday, Job, the world will hear of Him."

The late G. Campbell Morgan writes:

> The cry of Job was born of a double consciousness which at the moment was mastering him; first, that of the appalling greatness and majesty of God; and secondly, that of his own comparative littleness. This was not the question of a man who had dismissed God from his life and from the universe, and was living merely upon the earth level. It was rather the cry of a man who knew God, and was overwhelmed by the sense of His greatness. . . .
>
> Over against that was the sense of his own comparative smallness. He felt he could not get to this God. He was altogether too small. . . .
>
> It is as though Job had said: There is no umpire, there is no arbiter, there is no one who can stand between us, interpreting each to the other; me to God, and God to me. There is no one to lay his hand upon us. . . .
>
> Here then was Job crying out for some one who could stand authoritatively between God and himself, and so create a way of meeting, a possibility of contact.
>
> We now turn from the elemental cry of Job, and from the Old

Testament, to consider the apostolic word concerning Jesus. "There is one Mediator between God and man." That is the Gospel in brief. That is Christianity fundamentally.[4]

JOB RESPONDS TO GOD

Having replied to Bildad, Job now turns to God Himself. He writes with a heavy sigh:

> I loathe my own life;
> I will give full vent to my complaint;
> I will speak in the bitterness of my soul.
> I will say to God, "Do not condemn me;
> Let me know why you contend with me."
>
> Job 10:1–2

Job is still struggling. Eliphaz left him cold. He has received neither comfort nor insight from Bildad. He has no mediator to represent his case; therefore, he is very candid. Matter of fact, he's returning to questions he asked earlier. He has every right to ask them. He's confused. He still doesn't get it. So, understandably, he asks:

> Why then have You brought me out of the womb?
> Would that I had died and no eye had seen me!
> I should have been as though I had not been,
> Carried from womb to tomb.
> Would he not let my few days alone?
> Withdraw from me that I may have a little cheer.
>
> Job 10:18–20

"Why didn't He just take me from the womb and carry me to the tomb?" Oh, Job, you're back where you started. In fact, as he ends his response, he is back in the doldrums. He writes of his own "gloom" and "deep shadow" and "darkness." Out of respect for Job's private struggle, I suggest we draw all this to a close. This ends sadly, but so it is with Job as Bildad frowns, then walks away. And God stays silent.

TWO LINGERING LESSONS

We end sadly, but not without lessons to remember.

First, when misery breaks our spirit, philosophical words don't help us cope. All Job's so-called comforting companions had to offer were hollow words in the form of philosophical meanderings and theoretical concepts. That brought him no relief, no break in his misery. Philosophical words fall flat when they're mouthed before those in misery.

Second, when a mediator can't be found, futile searches won't give us hope. We're surrounded by people today on a search for hope to go on . . . to make it through the maze of their misery. Many of them long for a mediator, someone who can represent their cause and plead their case. You may be that person. If so, you can know what Job didn't know. The mediator he longed for is not only alive, He is available and ready to hear your story. Unlike Job's friends, He's no philosopher. He's the Redeemer. His name is Jesus. Anyone who comes to Him for comfort will find it. He has more mercy than you have misery.

CHAPTER EIGHT

When Rebuke and Resistance Collide

As time passes, conflicts have a way of getting more complicated instead of simplified. They're like roaches; you simply cannot ignore them. If you don't deal with them—by that I mean kill everyone you see—they will take over. Folks who have never lived in the South just don't understand.

When I moved back to Texas, I had a friend tell me when he saw me in cowboy boots one day, "You know why we wear cowboy boots here in Texas?" I said, "Well, I thought I did, but I think I'm about to learn a new reason right now." He said, "Yeah, it's so you can kill roaches in a corner." Funny comment.

When we were at Dallas Theological Seminary, as I mentioned earlier, Cynthia and I lived in the old Campus Apartments. But back in our day, we lived in Campus Apartment number nine (almost sounds like a prison cell, doesn't it?). I'm telling you, we had roaches. I said to Cynthia one evening, "We don't have a single roach in our place." She stared at me like I was absolutely nuts. I said, "Actually, they're all married and have large families." Problems are like that. And when they get worse, almost without exception, they lead to conflicts. Often when you try to solve them, they only intensify.

I have a feeling there is not a person reading this who has not attempted to make things right with another individual only to have it blow up in your face. It sure is easy to forget the original agenda.

When one person is bankrupt, has lost everything and everyone, then he's gotten sick and his friends show up to bring encouragement, the agenda is really very simple: express sympathy and demonstrate genuine compassion. That's precisely what Job's friends set out to do. Great agenda.

But somewhere between their leaving with the right agenda and the passing of a few days, the original agenda got lost. Amazingly, you cannot find a sentence of sympathy or one act designed to bring comfort. In the entire central section of Job—chapters 4 through 31—there is nothing but anger and accusation. There is lots of blame and lots of shame. There are insults, sarcastic remarks, finger pointing, sermon preaching, and judgmental condemnation.

Not surprisingly, Job winds up, as we're soon going to see, saying, "It had been better if you had just stayed silent." He's right. What is it our mothers taught us? If you can't say something nice, don't say anything at all. If you cannot bring sympathy and comfort, bring nothing at all. Just let your presence do the talking.

NOW IT'S ZOPHAR'S TURN

Job's third friend is your classic legalist. His tone and his words are saturated with abrasive legalism.

- "You are guilty, Job" (Job 11:1-4).
- "You are ignorant, Job" (Job 11:5-12).
- "You are sinful, Job (Job 11:13-20).

Check out the man's opening comment. It is heartless.

> Shall a multitude of words go unanswered,
> And a talkative man be acquitted?

> Job 11:2

How's that for openers? He heard the word *windbag* earlier and decides to use it again. He's saying, in effect, "We have listened to you about as long as we plan to listen, Job. How many more things do you think you have to say to convince us you're full of words? The fact is your life is devoid of righteousness."

> Shall your boasts silence men?
> And shall you scoff and none rebuke?
> For you have said, "My teaching is pure,
> And I am innocent in your eyes."
>
> Job 11:3–4

Let's stop right here in the middle of Zophar's put-down. Job never said that. It was hard enough for Job to be dealt with rudely and tactlessly, but to be misquoted is a terribly painful thing to take sitting down.

Earlier, Job was vulnerable enough to say:

> Teach me, and I will be silent;
> And show me how I have erred.
>
> Job 6:24

He then added . . .

> Now please look at me,
> And see if I lie to your face.
>
> Job 6:28

How open is that? He sincerely meant what he said. But these critics are given to generalization, placing blame. So they pound on Job with both fists. Having misquoted him, Zophar then tells him that he's guilty. If that isn't enough, he now implies, "You are one ignorant man!"

Can you recall when Job was identified as the greatest man of the East? The biblical account also says that he feared God and turned away from evil. In light of all that, I'd say he was neither guilty nor ignorant of God.

But you need to understand when legalists make their statements, they don't work with facts, all they need is volume and the opportunity to put you down, (they're good at both), in hopes that you'll be intimidated by their presence.

Listen to Zophar:

> But would that God might speak
> And open His lips against you.
> (He is calling down judgment from heaven.)
> And show you the secrets of wisdom.
> For sound wisdom has two sides.
>
> Job 11:5–6 (Parentheses mine)

He probably means the side we can understand and the side we can't— the side we can see and the side we can't see. He's talking about the invisible wisdom of God: "Know then that God forgets a part of your iniquity" (Job 11:6).

Zophar is delivering a lecture in Theology 101—as if Job needs another lecture.

I should warn you that Zophars are still on the loose. If you haven't met one, just wait. He'll come along—with zero capacity to connect the dots. They have no ability even to color by numbers. Though they don't get it, they have a severe message for you. That message is a put-down, because you are not doing what they believe you ought to be doing. Or you are doing what they believe you should not be doing.

In this case, since Zophar sees Job as ignorant of God, he decides he needs to teach him about God. And he tells him of God's length and breadth and depth and width and height and reminds Job that this God cannot be restrained. And then, as if that isn't enough, he adds the insulting implication:

> For He knows false men,
> And He sees iniquity without investigating.
>
> Job 11:11

Before landing the ultimate blow:

An idiot will become intelligent
When the foal of a wild donkey is born a man.

Job 11:12

Pause here for a few moments. The word *idiot* comes from a Hebrew term that means, "to be hollow, empty." When used of a person, it's referring to one who is empty-headed, like our colloquialism, *airhead*. He's calling Job, by implication an "empty-headed man," suggesting there is no more possibility a person like that could ever become wise, than a donkey could give birth to a human.

For the next few moments, try to imagine yourself there, sitting at the city dump. You've lost it all including your health. You haven't been able to sleep; you can't eat; you're running a fever and everything being said is demoralizing and condescending. You're in the ring with your critics for the third round of this first cycle of dialogues, and things are getting worse by the minute. Now, of all things, you're called a hollow-brained idiot from this clown who, himself, can't connect the dots.

Warren Wiersbe writes insightfully,

> How sad it is when people who should share ministry end up creating misery. . . .
>
> How tragic that these three friends focused on Job's words instead of the feelings behind those words.
>
> A Chinese proverb says, "Though conversing face to face, their hearts have a thousand miles between them." How true that was at the ash heap! After all, information is not the same as communication. Sidney J. Harris reminds us, "Information is giving out; communication is getting through."[1]

Ever worked for a person like that? You may be married to one. It is a dreadful existence. You may talk together and live your lives face to face, but your hearts have a thousand miles between them. Nothing really "gets through." How true that was at the ash heap. Harris is correct: Giving out information is not to be confused with in-depth communication.

My desire in writing all this is to urge you to take the side of the person who has no friend in his corner. Job is unusual—even without such support he hangs in there. That's why I've chosen the word *heroic* to describe his endurance.

Suddenly he receives another jab from Zophar:

> If you would direct your heart right
> And spread out your hand to Him,
> If iniquity is in your hand, put it far away,
> And do not let wickedness dwell in your tents;
> Then, indeed, you could lift up your face without moral defect,
> And you would be steadfast and not fear.
>
> Job 11:13–15

Now the man is accused of having a "moral defect." In addition to that inaccurate denouncement, he is condemned for lacking stability and faith. Remarkably, Job allowed Zophar to finish with a flair without interrupting him:

> For you would forget your trouble,
> As waters that have passed by, you would remember it.
> Your life would be brighter than noonday;
> Darkness would be like the morning.
> Then you would trust, because there is hope;
> And you would look around and rest securely.
> You would lie down and none would disturb you,
> And many would entreat your favor.
> But the eyes of the wicked will fail,
> And there will be no escape for them;
> And their hope is to breathe their last.
>
> Job 11:16–20

With that serving as a wrap-up, Zophar's through. Well, not really, he's coming back. But thankfully it will not be for a while. The sheer arrogance of a man as legalistic and condemning as Zophar is shocking.

Before we turn to Job's reply, I need to point out that Zophar makes an error in judgment that commonly occurs among legalists. While he correctly acknowledges the infinitude and greatness of God and urges Job to understand such truths and realize their implications, he then exhorts Job to fall in line. Arrogantly, he assumes he knows something that Job isn't willing to admit. He's keeping his sins a secret, and Zophar is bound and determined to expose them.

We Christians can be terribly judgmental, assuming we know why others are going through hard times. Furthermore, we can paint with too broad a brush as we criticize folks because it seems like they're implicated by the sins of another. We need to stay with the facts, not allowing ourselves to yield to suspicions and jump to false conclusions. It is unfair to see someone as guilty because others around them have failed.

A gentleman who was a partner with Arthur Anderson stopped me after a worship service to say a few words to me about what he was learning from our study of the life of Job. Graciously, he said it had been very helpful. He mentioned that his division of Arthur Anderson was guilty of nothing; their group was as clean as a whistle, but the smear campaign from the media had left everyone thinking that all Arthur Anderson people lack integrity. That's a bad call.

When the Jim and Tammy Bakker scandal hit the news back in the 1980s, our *Insight for Living* broadcast ministry suffered from the fallout for quite a long period of time. Though I had never met either one of them and did not agree with or participate in that style of religious work, many assumed guilt by association. How unfair . . . even insulting to suggest that because of one extreme example, all are equally tainted. The overarching message in this? Guard against judgmental generalizations. Zophar would have been wise to get his facts straight before he took on a man as faithful as Job. How much better it would have been for him to disagree with his two frowning colleagues and speak in defense of Job's integrity. Legalists, unfortunately, rarely break ranks.

JOB RESPONDS TO ZOPHAR

Frankly, I admire Job's guts. I'm pleased he doesn't cave in and say, "Well, maybe you're right, Zophar. You sound like those other two men, so I'm not going to disagree and fight you on this." No way! The strong rebuke of

Zophar is met by an even stronger resistance from Job. This, by the way, is the only way to deal with a legalist. They, too, are like roaches! You leave them alone and let them have their way, they proliferate. They attract others. And before you know it, the legalists take over. Bullying their way into leadership is their favorite approach. And if they can't bully, they take their ball and bat and go elsewhere (thank the Lord). They leave.

There was a time in my life when I allowed legalists to take more control of me than they should have been allowed. I'm making up for lost time now. Age has its benefits. I've learned the hard way, you need to fight fire with fire when bullies are determined to take charge. Job would have nothing to do with that! He put the stop to Zophar like Paul resisted the legalistic Judaizers and "did not yield in subjection to them for even an hour" (Galatians 2:5).

When Job finally does speak, he says, in effect, "Okay. That's enough." He stood up to them. I, for one, greatly admire Job for not sitting there any longer taking it on the chin.

When our older son, Curt, was in high school, he played the flute in the school band. In their particular seating arrangement, flute players sat in front of the trombone section. At that time, Curt was a sophomore and there was a trombone player who sat behind him who was not only an upperclassman, he was a bigger kid than our Curt. He was also a bully. Now, you may not know that a trombone has a "spit valve" at the bottom end of the slide. And, of course, courteous trombonists are careful when they open that valve and blow their saliva out of their slide. But to this crude kid in high school, courtesy wasn't high on his list of virtues. He found a cruel sense of satisfaction in opening the spit valve and blowing his spit all over Curt's shoulder. That went on for a few days until our son decided he'd had enough. So he quietly turned around and said to the bully, "Don't do that anymore. Stop blowing your spit on me." Well that kid couldn't wait to work up more spit. I mean he was just looking for another opportunity, and it wasn't long before he did it again. Curt said to him, "You know, you're gonna wish you hadn't done that if you do it one more time." It wasn't ten minutes later before the fella blew out another load. Instantly, Curt threw his elbow back against the bell of the kid's trombone—whomp—which drove the mouthpiece through the kid's lips, loosening a couple of his front teeth. Suddenly ol' hot lips looked like the opposite of Bugs Bunny. Blood squirts down his chin as Curt quietly returns to playing his flute. The kid couldn't play trombone for weeks . . . and, amazingly, that was the last time he blew his spit on Curt. When Curt told me that story, I was so proud of him I raised his allowance.

Job's response is like an elbow hitting the bell of Zophar's trombone. It's his way of saying, "I've had enough of you!"

Job has learned a little sarcasm from his friends by now. He starts with an exaggerated statement, "Truly then you are the people." By the way, it's plural. (We'd say, "y'all" here in Texas.) "Truly then y'all are the people. And with all y'all's wisdom it will die when y'all die. Ah! What a shame! All y'all experts are going to die, and there won't be any more wisdom left on the planet!" Isn't that a great line? "Truly y'all are unbelievable."

Job goes on:

> Truly then you are the people,
> And with you wisdom will die!
> But I have intelligence as well as you;
> I am not inferior to you.
> And who does not know such things as these?
>
> Job 12:2–3

I love that! Like my son, he's saying, in effect, "You're not going to keep blowing your spit on me. Who does not know the things you've told me about the living God? Gentlemen, I didn't just fall off the turnip truck. I've been there and back. And in your eyes, I'm a joke" (v. 4). He called it what it was. They didn't have the gall to call him what they thought of him, and he knew it.

> I am a joke to my friends,
> The one who called on God and He answered him;
> The just and blameless man is a joke.
>
> Job 12:4

Would there be a greater insult in life than being seen in the eyes of another as "a joke?" Probably not. Especially since Job was really the one who has talked with the Living God. The one who understands who He is and what He is about. Yet he was viewed as a joke in their eyes.

THE GREATNESS OF GOD

Job demonstrates his knowledge by addressing God. He asks his arrogant friends to visit the beast of the field and the birds of the air, the fish of the sea . . . and learn some things from that field trip.

> Who among all these does not know
> That the hand of the LORD has done this,
> In whose hand is the life of every living thing,
> And the breath of all mankind?
>
> Job 12:9–10

"It is of God, Zophar. It's all of God, Bildad and Eliphaz. Listen to me! It is of God! You can't explain it. But the beasts of the field acknowledge it. Built within them are all of these God-given instincts. They would be able, if they could speak our language, to tell you their story."

Job then "gets on a roll," we might say, as he begins his list of God's mighty acts. Take the time to track his thoughts:

> With Him are wisdom and might;
> To Him belong counsel and understanding.
> Behold, He tears down and it cannot be rebuilt;
> He imprisons a man and there can be no release.
> Behold, He restrains the waters, and they dry up;
> And He sends them out, and they inundate the earth.
> With Him are strength and sound wisdom.
> The misled and the misleader belong to Him.
> He makes counselors walk barefoot
> And makes fools of judges.
> He loosens the bond of kings
> And binds their loins with a girdle.
> He makes priests walk barefoot
> And overthrows the secure ones.

He deprives the trusted ones of speech
And takes away the discernment of the elders.
He pours contempt on nobles
And loosens the belt of the strong.
He reveals mysteries from the darkness
And brings the deep darkness into light.
He makes the nations great, then destroys them;
He enlarges the nations, then leads them away.
He deprives of intelligence the chiefs of the earth's people
And makes them wander in a pathless waste.
They grope in darkness with no light,
And He makes them stagger like a drunken man.
Behold, my eye has seen all this,
My ear has heard and understood it.

Job 12:13–13:1

Job declares, "It is all about our God! It is the inscrutable, Almighty God who is in charge of all things. Don't you think I know that?" And what a creative way to say it! "The God I serve takes delight in undoing human activities and in dismantling human enterprises, and in the process, executing His miraculous undertakings. He alone is in full control."

Job is making it clear that God alone is the One before whom he bows, and in doing so he implies, "I'm not sure you've ever met Him. Don't bully me. While I cannot answer why I'm suffering like this, I can tell you somehow and in some way the God of heaven, the silent God, the One who seems to be absent from my perspective, is still in control."

And to think they considered Job an airheaded idiot!

THE INTEGRITY OF JOB

Job then returns to and repeats his earlier comment:

What you know I also know:
I am not inferior to you.

Job 13:2

With that said, he drives home another verbal blow:

> But I would speak to the Almighty,
> And I desire to argue with God.
> But you smear with lies;
> You are all worthless physicians.
> O that you would be completely silent,
> And that it would become your wisdom!
>
> Job 13:3–5

In Proverbs 17:27–28 we find support for Job's strong advice:

> He who restrains his words has knowledge,
> And he who has a cool spirit is a man of understanding.
> Even a fool, when he keeps silent is considered wise;
> When he closes his lips, he is considered prudent.

Here's some helpful advice we need to remember. If you open your mouth everyone will know that you're a fool. If you don't, they'll think you're wise. There you have it. That's precisely what Job is getting at. Their silence would have been so much more encouraging and comforting than their speech.

Because they failed to implement verbal restraint, Job calls it like it is: "You're worthless physicians." Look at the indictment of what follows: "Will it be well when He examines you?" Great question. One wonders if Zophar even heard it.

> O that you would be completely silent,
> And that it would become your wisdom!
> Please hear my argument
> And listen to the contentions of my lips.
> Will you speak what is unjust for God,
> And speak what is deceitful for Him?
> Will you show partiality for Him?
> Will you contend for God?

Will it be well when He examines you?
Or will you deceive Him as one deceives a man?
He will surely reprove you
If you secretly show partiality.
Will not His majesty terrify you,
And the dread of Him fall on you?
Your memorable sayings are proverbs of ashes,
Your defenses are defenses of clay.

Job 13:5–12

DECLARATION OF JOB'S FAITH

Read Eugene Peterson's paraphrase of this section of Job's response in *The Message* (13:13–17):

So hold your tongue while I have my say,
then I'll take whatever I have coming to me.
Why do I go out on a limb like this
and take my life in my hands?
Because even if he killed me, I'd keep on hoping,
I'd defend my innocence to the very end.
Just wait, this is going to work out for the best—my salvation!
If I were guilt-stricken do you think I'd be doing this—laying myself
on the line before God?
You'd better pay attention to what I'm telling you,
listen carefully with both ears.
Now that I've laid out my defense,
I'm sure that I'll be acquitted.
Can anyone prove charges against me?
I've said my piece. I rest my case.

Job 13:13–19, MSG

With that, he temporarily closes his comments to the men, and he turns to the God he loves. The One with Whom he longs to have an audience.

JOB'S RESPONSE TO GOD

Job concludes his response by opening his heart before his God. He hides nothing as he declares his own pain as well as his confusion.

> Only two things do not do to me,
> Then I will not hide from Your face:
> Remove Your hand from me,
> And let not the dread of You terrify me.
> Then call, and I will answer;
> Or let me speak, then reply to me.
> How many are my iniquities and sins?
> Make known to me my rebellion and my sin.
> Why do You hide Your face
> And consider me Your enemy?
> Will You cause a driven leaf to tremble?
> Or will You pursue the dry chaff?
> For You write bitter things against me
> And make me to inherit the iniquities of my youth.
> You put my feet in the stocks
> And watch all my paths;
> You set a limit for the soles of my feet,
> While I am decaying like a rotten thing,
> Like a garment that is moth-eaten.
> Man who is born of woman,
> Is short-lived and full of turmoil.
>
> Job 13:20–14:1

The Living Bible renders that last line, "How frail is man, how few his years, how full of trouble!" I would call that an accurate commentary on life.

Job then uses three word pictures to describe himself: "a flower, a shadow, a hired man." All humans are frail like a flower. All are fleeting like a shadow. All are full of trouble like a hired man. This is raw, unguarded vulnerability. Humanity on display. Job doesn't see himself ever getting better, so he now leaps to the life beyond.

> For there is hope for a tree,
> When it is cut down, that it will sprout again,
> And its shoots will not fail.
> Though its roots grow old in the ground
> And its stump dies in the dry soil,
> At the scent of water it will flourish
> And put forth sprigs like a plant.
>
> Job 14:7–9

When you clear a field, the old, seasoned woodsman always advises you to dig up the stump. Don't leave it in the ground. You leave a stump, soon as the rain falls, the stump sprouts. The tree will come back; even the once-large shrub will return green. That's the way it is with a plant, with a tree. But man?

Again, Job's depression shines through. He states what he believes, based on what he knows.

> But man dies and lies prostrate.
> Man expires, and where is he?
> As water evaporates from the sea,
> And a river becomes parched and dried up,
> So man lies down and does not rise.
> Until the heavens are no more,
> He will not awake nor be aroused out of his sleep.
> Oh that You would hide me in Sheol,
> That You would conceal me until Your wrath returns to You,
> That You would set a limit for me and remember me!
> If a man dies, will he live again?
>
> Job 14:10–14

This is an ancient book written during the patriarchal era, when the progress of revelation had hardly begun to run its course. Job knows very little about the doctrine of resurrection. Understand, what Job writes is not meant to suggest that's all there is to know about resurrection. Hardly. We have a whole Bible full of further truth. The progress of revelation provides increasingly more light on any subject, so that today we can pretty well describe what happens at death as well as beyond death. Thanks to further revelation, we now know much more about the ultimate destinies of heaven and hell. But back then? There were more questions than answers. Therefore Job sincerely asks,

> If a man dies, will he live again?
> All the days of my struggle I will wait.
> Until my change comes.
>
> Job 14:14

The chapter ends in something like a depressed whimper. *The Message* renders it this way:

> Meanwhile, mountains wear down
> and boulders break up,
> Stones wear smooth
> and soil erodes,
> as you relentlessly grind down our hope.
> You're too much for us.
> As always, you get the last word.
> We don't like it and our faces show it,
> but you send us off anyway.
> If our children do well for themselves, we never know it;
> if they do badly, we're spared the hurt.
> Body and soul, that's it for us—
> a lifetime of pain, a lifetime of sorrow.
>
> Job 14:18–22, MSG

Suddenly we're at the end of Job's response. We now know that when we die, we live on. Jesus himself taught, "I am the resurrection and the life; he who believes in Me will live even if he dies, and everyone who lives and believes in Me will never die" (John 11:25–26).

In fact, we all have life everlasting, but our destinies are different. Some will spend eternity with God in heaven, some will spend eternity without God in hell. Those represent the two alternatives. Sobering. Yes, Job, when we die we live again. In fact, we live on. But up to this point, Job has only questions.

THREE QUESTIONS YOU MUST ANSWER

Let's stay with questions as we bring this chapter to a close. Three come to mind—three questions I'd urge you to consider. Turn them over in your head. Each one deserves your attention. One has to do with depth; one has to do with discovery; one has to do with destiny.

First, are you seeking to know the depths of God, or are you just skimming the surface?

> Can you discover the depths of God?
> Can you discover the limits of the Almighty?
> They are high as the heavens, what can you do?
> Deeper than Sheol, what can you know?
>
> Job 11:7–8

Let me repeat the question: Are you seeking to know the depths of God, or are you just skimming the surface? Only you know the answer. Our current culture is so busy we can become proficient at faking it. We can look like we're going to the depths when in fact we're just skating. So you must answer for yourself. Are you seeking to know the depths of God? Or do you find that you're just attending a lot of religious meetings, reading a few religious books, and learning all the religious-sounding language?

One of Larry Crabb's latest books is titled *The Pressure's Off*. In it he writes,

> As a culture, present-day Christianity has redefined spiritual maturity. The reformers knew we were saved to glorify God. We moderns live to be blessed. The mature among us are now thought to be the successful, the happy, the effective people on top of things and doing

well. . . . We're more attracted to sermons, books, and conferences that reveal the secrets to fulfillment . . . than to spiritual direction that leads us through affliction into the presence of the Father. . . .

We seem more interested in managing life into a comfortable existence than in letting God spiritually transform us through life's hardships.[2]

That cuts to the quick, doesn't it? Don't run from the hardship. Don't seek a friend who'll help you get out from under it quickly. Stay there. Stay in it. The Lord God will get you through it. As a result you'll stop skating. This question is for you to answer. Are you seeking to know the depths of God, or are you just skimming the surface?

Next, please look again at Job 13:9:

Will it be well when He examines you?
Or will you deceive Him as one deceives a man?

Now the question: *Will it be well when God examines your life, or will it be a disappointing discovery?* I repeat, I can't speak for you because I have no idea. But I do know "we must all appear before the judgment seat of Christ, so that each one may be recompensed for his deeds in the body, according to what he has done, whether good or bad" (2 Corinthians 5:10). Is that going to be a disappointing discovery, or will it be well with you? Probing thought, which is why I've urged you to give these questions such serious consideration.

Now, the third question. Look at Job 14:14 one more time:

If a man dies, will he live again?
All the days of my struggle I will wait
Until my change comes.

Here's what I'd like you to think about: *When you die, where will you live again?* Will it be with the Lord or away from His presence forever? The choices are as I stated earlier in this chapter: heaven or hell. Will it be eternal bliss filled with joy and relief and the rewards awaiting God's people?

Or eternal judgment, away from God and all those things you hold dear? Only you can determine which.

C. S. Lewis wrote this:

> There's no doctrine which I would more willingly remove from Christianity than the doctrine of hell, if it lay in my power. But it has the full support of Scripture and especially of our Lord's own words; it has always been held by Christendom and it has the support of reason.[3]

C. S. Lewis was no intellectual pushover. His words deserve serious consideration. I started this chapter by describing how problems have a way of multiplying. The good news is—that's true only in this life—"How frail . . . how few our years . . . how full of trouble." But once we're in our Lord's presence, all that changes.

On the other hand, should you choose to ignore this opportunity to secure such hope, the alternative results will be dreadful beyond imagination. Come to think of it, that kind of future would make Job's trials seem like a piece of cake. Who wants a destiny like that?

Don't go there!

CHAPTER NINE

Graceless Words for a Grieving Man

I f you're like me, there are mornings you get a song on your mind and it keeps returning through the day. It happened to me last Thursday. It went into the afternoon, and on into Friday morning. While sitting in my study I kept going over the same old spiritual that used to be sung by choirs in the Deep South:

> Heav'n, Heav'n
> Ev'rybody talkin' 'bout Heav'n ain't goin' there
> Heav'n, Heav'n
> Goin' to shout all over God's Heaven.[1]

Well, the more I ran those words through my head, the more unusual they seemed to be. As I remembered the smiling faces of former choir members singing about *not* going to heaven, I wondered why they were smiling. And, frankly, it reminded me of how we talk about grace. Everybody's talkin' about grace, *ain't goin' there either!* Funny, isn't it? Everywhere we turn we hear about grace, but most folks wouldn't know grace if they met it face to face. Most people aren't ready to accept it even when it's presented to them.

Not long ago a student from a college in Missouri wrote this in an e-mail:

I left work early so I could have some uninterrupted study time right before the final in my class. When I got to class, everybody was doing their last minute studying. The teacher came in and said he would review with us for just a little bit before the test. We went through the review, most of it right on the study guide, but there were some things he was reviewing that I had never heard of. When questioned about it, he said that they were in the book and we were responsible for everything in the book. We couldn't really argue with that.

Finally, it was time to take the test.

"Leave them face down on the desk until everyone has one and I'll tell you to start," our prof instructed.

When we turned them over, every answer on the test was filled in! The bottom of the last page said the following:

"This is the end of the Final Exam. All the answers on your test are correct. You will receive an 'A' on the final exam. The reason you passed the test is because the creator of the test took it for you. All the work you did in preparation for this test did not help you get the 'A'. *You have just experienced . . . grace.*"

He then went around the room and asked each student individually, "What is your grade? Do you deserve the grade you are receiving? How much did all your studying for this exam help you achieve your final grade?"

Now I am not a crier by any stretch of the imagination, but I had to fight back tears when answering those questions and thinking about how the Creator had passed the test for me.

Discussion afterward went like this: "I have tried to teach you all semester that you are a *recipient* of *grace*. I've tried to communicate to you that you need to demonstrate this gift as you work with young people. Don't hammer them; they are not the enemy. Help them, for they will carry on your ministry if it is full of *grace!*"

Talking about how some of us had probably studied hours and some just a few minutes but had all received the same grade, he pointed to a story Jesus told in Matthew 20. The owner of a vineyard hired people to work in his field and agreed to pay them a certain amount. Several different times during the day, he hired more workers. When it was time to pay them, they all received the same amount. When the ones who had been hired first thing in the morning began complaining, the boss said, "Should you be angry because I am kind?" (Matthew 20:15).

The teacher said he had never done this kind of final before and probably would never do it again, but because of the content of many of our class discussions, he felt like we needed to experience grace.[2]

After reading of that true event, I thought: "Why didn't I have a teacher like than when I was taking all of my final exams?"

These days, seems like everybody's talking about grace, but we ain't goin' there. Not on your life! We love it coming from God, but just don't expect it from fallen folks like us. And even when it does, we're shocked. Too bad!

Of all the things Job had to endure, the ultimate test was enduring the graceless words and responses from his alleged friends.

We have just completed the first cycle of insults which came from Eliphaz, then Bildad, and finally, Zophar. As we saw, Job answered each man, no doubt hoping that would put a stop to all their heartless accusations. Not a chance.

ONE CRUEL STATEMENT FOLLOWS ANOTHER

In the second cycle, which starts in chapter 15 of the Book of Job, Eliphaz takes off the gloves and starts swinging barefisted, thinking it's time to really get down to business. Hard as it is to imagine, there is not a hint of grace. It's now "same song, fourth verse . . . could be better . . . but it's going to be worse." Much worse.

A Litany of Rebukes

Eliphaz throws more verbal punches in the first round of this second cycle. They are nothing more than graceless words for a grieving man. In case you wonder what those kind of words sound like, they begin with *pride*.

> Should a wise man answer with windy knowledge
> And fill himself with the east wind?
>
> Job 15:2

The word *himself* is really "belly" in the Hebrew. Should a wise man (Eliphaz, of course) fill his belly with a lot of wind? Eliphaz's pride is followed by *insult*. Still referring to himself, he says,

> Should he argue with useless talk,
> Or with words which are not profitable?
> Indeed, you do away with reverence
> And hinder meditation before God.
>
> Job 15:3–4

Then there's *guilt*,

> For your guilt teaches your mouth,
> And you choose the language of the crafty.
>
> Job 15:5

(You deceiver, you.)

> Your own mouth condemns you, and not I;
> And your own lips testify against you.
>
> Job 15:6

So, there's *condemnation* as well.

In the words that follow we find *exaggeration* and *sarcasm*, where one humiliating question follows another.

> Were you the first man to be born,
> Or were you brought forth before the hills?
> Do you hear the secret counsel of God,
> And limit wisdom to yourself?
> What do you know that we do not know?
> What do you understand that we do not?
>
> Job 15:7–9

Can you imagine the unmitigated gall it took to stand before a man shaking and shattered by pain and unloading such a diatribe on him? This is verbal abuse at its lowest level, intensified by the pride in this man's heart who is delivering the blows so relentlessly.

The sarcastic interrogation continues:

> Are the consolations of God too small for you?
> Even the word spoken gently with you?
> Why does your heart carry you away?
> And why do your eyes flash,
> That you should turn your spirit against God.
> And allow such words to go out of your mouth?
> What is man, that he should be pure,
> Or he who is born of a woman, that he should be righteous?
> Behold, He puts no trust in His holy ones,
> And the heavens are not pure in His sight;
> How much less one who is detestable and corrupt,
> Man, who drinks iniquity like water!
>
> Job 15:11–16

He tears Job apart with his sharp teeth, never even pausing to give the grieving man a chance to answer.

Reminders of Wrong

Having rebuked him, he follows up with reminders of the fate of the wicked as he ends his speech. He says, in effect, "Job, because you're wicked, you writhe in pain. Plain and simple, that's why you're in pain. You're only getting what you deserve."

> Sounds of terror are in his ears;
> While at peace the destroyer comes upon him.
> He does not believe that he will return from darkness,
> And he is destined for the sword.
>
> Job 15:21–22

"So, my friends and I are not surprised you're going through such terror, loss, and torment."

> He wanders about for food, saying, 'Where is it?'
> He knows that a day of darkness is at hand.
> Distress and anguish terrify him,
> They overpower him like a king ready for the attack.
>
> Job 15:23–24

"Small wonder you're experiencing this overpowering distress and anguish."

> Because he has stretched out his hand against God
> And conducts himself arrogantly against the Almighty.
>
> Job 15:25

"That's it, Job! It's your arrogance!" Eliphaz backs away and stares at him with that glare, saying, again, "You are getting exactly what you deserve!"

The style of communication Eliphaz employs is not that unusual to those who lack grace. It may not always be this brutal, but haven't you noticed this tone when you're around people who evidence no grace? When you're down, they kick you. When you're drowning, they pull you under.

When you're confused, they complicate your life. And, when you're almost finished, they write you off. Other than that, they're pretty good folks.

It is easy to forget the grief Job was trying to get past—the shocking loss of his adult children. Releasing the vise grip of grief that comes from a sudden death takes an enormous toll.

Dr. Lucy Mabry-Foster, a longtime friend to Cynthia and me, died suddenly back in the spring of 2002. Lucy and her family were not strangers to tragedy. Lucy's first husband, Dr. Trevor Mabry, was killed in an airplane crash while returning from a Focus on the Family retreat in Montana. Trevor was a splendid ear, nose, and throat surgeon, trained at the Mayo Clinic, and practicing in the Dallas area. All four of the fine men of God on that plane died in the crash.

The Mabrys' older son, Dan, was on his honeymoon at the time. Hearing that the plane had not returned as scheduled, Dan immediately returned home and joined in the search, hoping for a sign of survival. Ultimately the family members had to face the tragic reality that their husband and father had perished in that fatal crash.

The city of Dallas mourned as the news of their multiple deaths made the headlines. All of us who knew and loved those men reeled in disbelief, sorrow, and grief.

Lucy determined that she would not give up. The Christian community and her family surrounded her with love and support. All the children put their arms around their mother as they worked their way through the loss. During the next ten years Lucy finished her education, earned her Ph.D., and became the first woman teacher at Dallas Theological Seminary. It's a wonderful story of her strong determination through years of grief.

Ultimately, the Lord brought to her side a fine Christian gentleman, C. L. Foster from South Texas. Over the passing of many months, C. L. and Lucy fell in love. And along with many others, Cynthia and I were in the church the day C. L. and Lucy were joined in marriage. It was absolutely charming. All of us were thinking how great of God to do this. Their wedding was a joy to everyone.

Five years later—almost to the day—on a Monday morning, Lucy breathed her last in the arms of her beloved husband. They were in an emergency vehicle racing to the hospital in hopes of saving her life. We buried her the following Thursday. Lucy's sudden demise was almost too surprising to believe.

It was my privilege to sit for more than two hours and talk with the family who had already been through the shocking loss of their dad, and now these same three were having to deal with the sudden loss of their mother. And C. L., who had lost his first wife in a car crash, was quietly sitting beside them. You could see the wheels turning as the tears ran from his eyes. The grief mixed with the shock left them stunned.

C. L. Foster and those adult children didn't need any rebuke or condemnation. They didn't need to be blamed for anything or to be asked any insulting, humiliating questions. They needed reassuring comfort and genuine sympathy. In a word, they needed grace.[3]

I can't help but think of that when I see Job, as he sits there enduring this, awash in his grief, trying his best to believe his ears—that this man who was once a friend is saying such graceless words. I'm left with one thought: "Lord, if you are teaching us anything through Job's endurance, teach us the value of *grace*. Teach us about demonstrating *grace*. Show us again that grace is *always* appropriate. *Always* needed. Not just by a student in Missouri taking a final exam. Not only by a grieving family in Dallas. *All* of us need it! The person sitting near you in church next Sunday, the lady pushing that cart in the grocery store, the one who's putting gas in his car at the next pump, the man behind you at the movies, waiting to buy his ticket, the student across from you at school. You have no idea what that person is going through. If you did, chances are you'd be prompted to show grace or to say a few encouraging words even quicker. Remember this please: Grace is *always* appropriate, *always* needed!

JOB'S STRONG RESPONSE

I'm starting to sit back and silently admire Job. Like right now. He has listened and now he responds. He says, in effect, "You want to fight with bare fists? Fine with me. My hands may be covered with sores, but I'll do as you have done and take the gloves off."

I find four responses from Job that are both admirable and realistic. Personally, I do not find them shocking, though you may.

He Is Disgusted

First off, Job is downright disgusted with Eliphaz, and rightly so! He chooses not to sit there and take another punch in the face by this insulting, proud man. Job's self-respect steps up in spades. "Sorry comforters are you all" (Job 16:2). How's that for an opening line of disgust? Choice description: *Sorry comforters.* Talk about an *oxymoron!* You may not be familiar with that term. Webster defines an oxymoron as "a combination of contradictory words," like government intelligence. Another comes to mind: teenage submission. Sorry comforters! "You think *this* is comfort? What a sorry group of comforters you are, Eliphaz, Bildad, and Zophar!"

One man describes the scene like this:

> Job complains that often he has *heard many such things* as the comforters speak. But in his present plight such pious platitudes serve only to increase his sorrow. Therefore, he accuses his friends of being *miserable comforters.* . . . The byword *miserable comforters* is a pungent oxymoron; i.e., the more words they speak to comfort, the more pain they inflict. This interchange boldly marks the difference between Job's perspective and Eliphaz's. Whereas Eliphaz believes that the speeches of the friends are the very consolations of God (15:11), Job considers them to be harbingers of misery. And whereas Eliphaz concludes his speech with the aphorism "conceiving mischief . . . bearing iniquity" (15:35a), Job retorts that it is their theologizing that conceives mischief to produce misery in him.
>
> With a biting rhetorical question Job charges Eliphaz with uttering *windy words* . . . i.e., eloquent speech devoid of content. He is directly countering Eliphaz's reproach that his knowledge is empty wind (15:2) and Bildad's retort that his words are a mighty wind (8:2). Next Job asks Eliphaz *what irritates* . . . him so much that he feels compelled to *keep answering.* Job cannot fathom why Eliphaz is so upset with him. [4]

No extra charge for this reminder. People who are graceless and insulting don't get a clue unless you are equally strong in return. So, sometimes, like Job, you have to plant a firm verbal blow in their brain. To be sure you are getting through, there are times you must fight fire with fire. You have to be just as blunt or they'll walk all over you and stomp you into the dirt. Which explains why Job calls them "sorry comforters." He doesn't smile and act pious—he responds truthfully. His integrity is revealed in his honesty.

Speaking the truth cuts through the fuzzy, vague, feel-good verbiage that often characterizes a lot of religious clichés. That's why I urge with such passion that we all learn how to speak truth, ideally in love. Let me add here, if I've got to make an either/or choice, I'll take truth. It's better with love, of course, but truth is absolutely essential. "Truth hurts" is a familiar saying. But, I repeat, there are times its unvarnished, direct blows are needed. Sometimes *we* are the ones in need of hearing them. A good example would be when you lose your job—and you're the reason. The one in authority has the unhappy task of facing you with reality. If there's truth in the communication, the person who is letting you go at that moment is telling you things you should never forget. He or she is cutting through all the nice-sounding veneer and addressing the specific reason you have lost the job. Be sure you are hearing the truth, hard as it may be to take it. It will help you if you accept it and make the necessary changes.

In this case, Job is saying to Eliphaz, "Your words are wrongly stated. You've misjudged me and your reasoning is incorrect. Furthermore, the words you've used are harsh, and therefore I'm telling you, you are a sorry comforter."

He's Distressed

Job is not only disgusted with Eliphaz, he is distressed over God's apparent absence and very obvious silence. That may sound shocking to some who read those words, but it happens, especially among those who are hurting. Keep that in mind as you read Job's distressing words.

> I feel worn down.
> God, you have wasted me totally—me and my family!

You've shriveled me like a dried prune,
showing the world that you're against me.
My gaunt face stares back at me from the mirror,
a mute witness to your treatment of me.
Your anger tears at me,
your teeth rip me to shreds,
your eyes burn holes in me—God my enemy!
People take one look at me and gasp.
Contemptuous, they slap me around and gang up against me.
And God just stands there and lets them do it,
lets wicked people do what they want with me.
I was contentedly minding my business when God beat me up.
He grabbed me by the neck and threw me around.
He set me up as his target,
then rounded up archers to shoot at me.
Merciless, they shot me full of arrows;
bitter bile poured from my gut to the ground.
He burst in on me, onslaught after onslaught,
charging me like a mad bull.
I sewed myself a shroud and wore it like a shirt:
I lay face down in the dirt.
Now my face is blotched red from weeping;
look at the dark shadows under my eyes,
Even though I've never hurt a soul
and my prayers are sincere!
 O Earth, don't cover up the wrong done to me!
Don't muffle my cry!
There must be someone in heaven who knows the truth about me,
in highest heaven, some Attorney who can clear my name—
My Champion, my Friend,
while I'm weeping my eyes out before God.
I appeal to the One who represents mortals before God
as a neighbor stands up for a neighbor.
Only a few years are left

before I set out on the road of no return.
My spirit is broken,
my days used up,
my grave dug and waiting.

Job 16:7–17:1, MSG

Strong, deeply emotional words from a distressed man.

If you'd find fault with Job, it's because you've never been there. There's not a counselor who has been in that kind of work very long before she or he meets up with someone who is distressed over the way God has treated them. Their words are strong, full of anguish, because they don't understand how a loving, gracious, good God could allow such devastating events to happen to one of His own.

Remember, Job still doesn't know the arrangement between Satan and God. We were introduced to it very carefully and clearly before it occurred. But Job was never in on that flow of information. He still doesn't know why one day, completely out of the blue, the bottom drops out, bringing tornadoes and fires, destruction and multiple deaths . . . finally ill health with such force. Not once does God give him a word of explanation. Remember, all of his adult life Job has walked intimately with God. He has been obedient and submissive—now this! No wonder he's distressed.

I'll confess to you, I've known that kind of confusion—but certainly not like Job. During such times, I have said in unguarded moments, "God what in the world are You up to? What is this about? To the best of my knowledge, I am not doing anything wrong. And I'm not doing it with the wrong motive. I haven't gone into this to please myself or to impress somebody else. I'm trying to walk in obedience. But everything has backfired! What's going on, Lord?"

It's like driving home from work after a terrible day at the office. In bumper-to-bumper traffic, the guy behind you smashes into you. You then hit the car in front of you, and it happens to be a new Porsche. Porsche drivers tend not to like that when you hit them from the rear. You get everything documented by the police. And the Porsche owner is so angry he threatens to sue you. And when you finally do get home, you don't have any milk. Your dog's hungry and he's been gnawing on the cabinet. Your kids are mean, so they're gnawing on each other. And the mail is full of overdue bills, and you're out of money. And your wife tells you she got the results of the biopsy . . . and the doc wants both of you to come see him first thing in the morning. That does it! You think, "What is this all about, God? And while I'm at it, where are You?"

And no answer comes . . . and tomorrow is worse than today. And next week is intensifying all of it, making last week look like a downhill slide. On top of all of that, you are about to lose your job. And the guy in the Porsche *does* sue you. And. And. And. And.

In unguarded moments when the lights are out and the doors are closed, and your pastor isn't around to listen, and nobody's going to tell on you, you do slump and start wondering. If you don't you're weird. Don't tell me you're too spiritual to think like that. Like Job, your spirit is broken, your days leave you exhausted and confused, and it's like your grave is dug and awaiting your arrival. The result? *Again, he is depressed.* And how could anyone be surprised?

What, specifically, brought Job to this point of depression? I believe it's best expressed in the Latin words, *Deus absconditus.* I came across those words this week. . . . *Deus* is the Latin word for God. *Absconditus* gives us our English word *abscond.* Webster says it means "to conceal, to depart secretly and hide oneself." God has secretly split the scene. That's it, exactly!

"He's gone. I can't figure Him out. When I pray I don't get answers. When I devote myself even more deeply to doing His will for all the right reasons, I continue to lose. When I pray, zip happens. God has *absconded* with the blessings."

C. S. Lewis describes the frustration perfectly in *A Grief Observed.*

> Meanwhile, where is God? This is one of the most disquieting symptoms. When you are happy, so happy that you have no sense of needing Him . . . you will be—or so it feels—welcomed with open arms. But go to Him when your need is desperate, when all other help is vain, and what do you find? A door slammed in your face, and a sound of bolting and double bolting on the inside. After that, silence.

You may as well turn away. The longer you wait, the more emphatic the silence will become.[5]

Deus absconditus. That expresses the problem without any literary ruffles or lace. He's hit bottom. Disgusted, distressed, depressed, Job finds himself ready to die. So . . .

He's Despondent

We could call the following words, Job's Requiem.

> My life's about over. All my plans are smashed,
> all my hopes are snuffed out—
> My hope that night would turn into day,
> my hope that dawn was about to break.
> If all I have to look forward to is a home in the graveyard,
> if my only hope for comfort is a well-built coffin,
> If a family reunion means going six feet under,
> and the only family that shows up is worms,
> Do you call that hope?
> Who on earth could find any hope in that?
> No. If hope and I are to be buried together,
> I suppose you'll all come to the double funeral!
>
> Job 17:11–16, MSG

Disgusted
    Distressed
        Depressed
            Despondent

The man has reached absolute rock bottom. Death seems his only recourse, the one refuge of relief. Right now, the grave seems mighty inviting.

You know what he's thinking?

> Ev'rybody talkin' 'bout Heav'n ain't goin' there
> Heav'n, Heav'n
> Goin' to shout all over God's Heaven.[6]

You know what he's missing? He is missing what only grace can bring him. Hope. He has no grace from anybody around him, so he's left with no hope. Nobody there to reassure him. He is totally confused. He can't find his way.

Phillip Yancey in his outstanding book, *Disappointment with God*, tells this true story.

> Once a friend of mine went swimming in a large lake at dusk. As he was paddling at a leisurely pace about a hundred yards offshore, a freak evening fog rolled in across the water. Suddenly he could see nothing: no horizon, no landmarks, no objects or lights on shore. Because the fog diffused all light, he could not even make out the direction of the setting sun.
>
> For thirty minutes he splashed around in panic. He would start off in one direction, lose confidence, and turn ninety degrees to the right. Or left—it made no difference which way he turned. He could feel his heart racing uncontrollably. He would stop and float, trying to conserve energy, and force himself to breathe slower. Then he would blindly strike out again. At last he heard a faint voice calling from shore. He pointed his body toward the sounds and followed them to safety.
>
> Something like that sensation of utter lostness must have settled in on Job as he sat in the rubble and tried to comprehend what had happened. He too had lost all landmarks, all points of orientation. Where should he turn? God, the One who could guide him through the fog, stayed silent.
>
> The whole point of The Wager was to keep Job in the dark. If God had delivered an inspiring pep talk—"Do this for me, Job, as a Knight of Faith, as a martyr"—then Job, ennobled, would have suffered gladly. But Satan had challenged whether Job's faith could survive with no outside help or explanation. When God accepted those terms, the fog rolled in around Job.
>
> God ultimately "won" The Wager, of course. Though Job lashed out with a stream of bitter complaints, and though he despaired of life and longed for death, still he defiantly refused to give up on God:

"Though he slay me, yet will I hope in him." Job believed when there was no reason to believe. He believed in the midst of the fog.

You could read Job's story, puzzle over The Wager, then breathe a deep sigh of relief: *Phew! God settled that problem. After proving his point so decisively, surely he will return to his preferred style of communicating clearly with his followers.* You could think so—unless, that is, you read the rest of the Bible. I hesitate to say this, because it is a hard truth and one I do not want to acknowledge, but Job stands as merely the most extreme example of what appears to be a universal law of faith. The kind of faith God values seems to develop best when everything fuzzes over, when God stays silent, when the fog rolls in.[7]

NEEDED: A LOT OF GRACE

You know why I love the Bible? Because it's *so* real. There's a lot of fog rolling into Job's life just like in our lives. On this earth nobody "lives happily ever after." That line is a huge fairy tale. You're living in a dream world if you're waiting for things to get "happy ever after." That's why we need grace. Marriage doesn't get easier, it gets harder. So we need grace to keep it together. Work doesn't get easier, it gets more complicated, so we need grace to stay on the job. Childrearing doesn't get easier. You who have babies one, two, three years old—you think you've got it tough. Wait until they're fourteen. Or eighteen. Talk about needing grace!

Everything gets harder. You thought you were fat when you got married. Take a glance in the mirror this evening. That's why I often tell brides and grooms, "Enjoy the wedding pictures; you'll never be *thinner*." That's tough to face, but it's the truth. So? We need *grace* as we gain weight! We need *grace* to go on! Grace and more grace—*God's grace*. We need *grace* to relate to each other. We need *grace* to drive. We need *grace* to stay positive. We need *grace* to keep a church in unity. We need *grace* to be good neighbors. We really need *grace* as we get older. Let's never forget what Job's treatment teaches: When folks are out of hope, don't kick 'em, don't hold 'em under. *Administer grace! Lots of grace.*

I'll be painfully honest here. If I called the shots, I would have relieved

Job five minutes after he lost everything. I'd have brought all his kids back to life the very next day. I would have immediately re-created everything he lost, and I would really deal with those sorry comforters! I'd have cut the lips off of Eliphaz after about three sentences. And if that didn't shut him up, I'd take the neck. I mean . . . who needs that clod? But you know what? You would never mature under my kind of treatment. You'd just enjoy the comfort. We'd all go to picnics then on a motorcycle ride and have tons of fun. That's my style. Which explains why Cynthia says to me, "Honey, if everybody handled things like you wanted, all we'd bring to the party is *balloons*. Nobody would think to bring the food." As usual, she's right.

So, the fog's rolled in. As all hell breaks loose, grace takes a hike. Welcome to the human race, Job.

I started this chapter with an old song. I'll end it with an even older one.

> Thru many dangers, toils and snares,
> I have already come;
> 'Tis grace hath brought me safe thus far,
> And grace will lead me home.[8]

That's the ticket. Even in the fog, grace will lead us home. Our dear, beat-up friend, Job, thinks he's going to miss heaven. He's so miserable he's not even thinking beyond the grave. We understand. We know there is a tomorrow and by God's grace there is a home beyond. Job can't see it right now. The fog's too thick. Everything has fuzzed over. If you listen closely, you can almost hear him humming that tune. He can't get it off his mind:

> Ev'rybody talkin' 'bout Heav'n ain't goin' there
> Heav'n, Heav'n . . .

Chapter Ten

Reassuring Hope for the Assaulted and Abused

What did you talk about at breakfast on the morning of September 11, 2001? You don't remember, do you? There is a small group of people who will never forget what they talked about at breakfast that morning.

They had gathered at the Pentagon in Washington D.C. with the secretary of defense, Donald Rumsfeld. They listened as he spoke of what seemed to most of them little more than a theoretical concern. A few might have gone so far as to say it sounded like a studied prediction. He said something to the effect, "At some time in the next several months there will be an event in the world that will remind people how important it is that our nation have a strong, healthy defense department."[1] Little did Rumsfeld or any of those who sat at the breakfast at 8:00 a.m. that morning have any idea that Flight 77 was on its way from Dulles International to crash into the Pentagon. Little did any of them realize how prophetically the secretary of defense had spoken.

Jeffrey Krames, author of *The Rumsfeld Way*, describes Rumsfeld's immediate reaction when only minutes after those words had fallen from his lips, the plane crashed into the other side of the Pentagon, taking the lives of 180 of Rumsfeld's colleagues, friends, and other high-ranking officers in the military.

Krames writes, "Instinctively, Rumsfeld dashed out of the room, asked if anyone knew what had happened, then ran toward the smoke. Surrounded by chaos and rubble and rescue workers, he helped get some of the wounded onto stretchers."[2]

The Economist, released shortly after that horrific event, reported, "He (Rumsfeld) had done what soldiers have to do: stand fast when the world explodes around you. He had led by example."[3]

During that emergency and in the hours that followed, what some were calling an "out-of-touch secretary of defense" was transformed into a courageous "secretary of war" with a vital mandate that he has not forgotten to this day. The same man who had spoken theoretically of the possibility of "an event" found himself engaged in it that very morning, less than an hour later.

Reminds me of Job. Remember how his story began? "Now there was a day." Those words seem so innocuous. Like the dawning of the day on the eleventh of September . . . just another clear and sunny morning. The smell of early autumn was in the air. Children were being hustled off to school. Moms and dads were busy about their work. Buses and subways were full of commuters as the whirl of commerce was just getting started.

And with Job? I can imagine his standing at the kitchen window as his wife is finishing breakfast. He says to her, "You know sweetheart, let's stop for a few minutes and give thanks. Our fields are full and green. The camel caravans are loaded and about to leave. Look over there—another group of them coming through the gate. And look over there at our son's place . . . look at that." She walks over and looks with him as she smiles and puts her arms around his waist. He says, "You know honey, we are wonderfully blessed, but we need to remember it may not always be like this. Who knows? Before we know it, this could all change."

While Satan is meeting with the Lord God, light years removed, offering a sinister strategy, Job and his sweet wife finish the conversation with a quiet prayer of gratitude, a soft kiss before they sit down for breakfast to talk of home and family, God's blessings, and the future. In only a matter of minutes everything for that couple will change. Everything! Like Secretary Rumsfeld on that fateful September morning, Job would soon be running toward the smoke, surrounded by chaos and rubble. He would find his buildings scattered like pieces of firewood thrown in the air. And there would be one servant after another shouting horrible news, followed by worse news, until the ultimate: *All ten children* have perished! In only minutes they lose it all. Possessions and staff, livestock and camels, the ability to make a living and all their children, everything. And, literally, before the smoke clears, there dawns a new day. "There was a day . . ." Another one of those familiar sunrises.

Satan returns for a second session with the eternal God, saying with something of a sneer, "You are protecting Job . . . no wonder he still believes in You. But if You let pain touch his body, he will curse You to Your face." Satan had been forced to witness that Job "did not sin nor did he blame God" (Job 1:22). But he isn't about to quit. "Who wouldn't serve You in good health?"

But in all this, we are told, "Job does not sin with his lips." I wonder if he thought, when sitting there after his wife came close to suggest that he simply curse God and die, if he said something like, "I remember honey, when you and I were standing at the kitchen window and I casually mentioned that things could change. . . ."

Secretary of Defense Rumsfeld must have replayed his breakfast speech a hundred times in his mind during the weeks that followed. Remember when I said, "At some time in the next several months. . ."

Job, many centuries earlier, led by example. And as a result, he has become a model of remarkable patience. To this day we have the saying, "the patience of Job." Who knows how many have been strengthened by his example? I can tell you when Cynthia and I have been stunned by sudden and shocking events that have hit us completely out of the blue, we have reminded each other that it takes the endurance of Job to stay at it, to press on in spite of the pain.

In Job's case, as if the grief and the pain and the loss of health were not bad enough, along come these so-called friends. We are told in the biblical account, "They made an appointment together to come to sympathize with him and comfort him" (Job 2:11). As we've already noted, that was their original objective. They communicated with one another, each living in a different place, and they agreed on the same purpose for visiting Job. They would go and they would put their arms around their hurting friend, and they would do their best to thank him for his life and sympathize with him in his pain, in hopes of encouraging him.

But, as we have discovered, something got lost in the process. Their agenda got blurred. They sat for a week and stared at him, "No one speaking a word to him, for they saw his pain was very great" (Job 2:13). It was not their silence that troubled him. That was not a problem. The problem came when they decided to speak! From that point on, a worse pain than Job had ever known emerged and stayed with him interminably.

You and I know people who have lost their home for whatever reason. We also know people who have gone belly-up in business. We even know people who have buried not one, but several children. I know of one couple who buried four of their children in one day. But I doubt that we know anyone who was verbally assaulted and abused after all of that by people who came afterward and criticized and blamed and condemned them. But that is exactly what these men did. In fact, they took turns!

Satan must have danced with glee. He hadn't planned on having a tag team of cynical partners. That was a wonderful bonus! Without knowing it, those men became Satan's spokesmen. The Adversary might have thought, *This is going to work. Job will cave under this abuse, and God will hear the man curse Him to His face. No one can hold up under that kind of barrage.* The first full cycle of assault runs it course from chapter 3 through chapter 14 of Job as Eliphaz, followed by Bildad, and then Zophar take their turns venting their spleen on the suffering soul. And then round two begins immediately (chapter 15). Eliphaz, probably the oldest, unloads his invective and then steps aside as Bildad walks up for his next turn.

BILDAD'S SECOND ASSAULT

This would be a good time to pause and compare. Go back and consider the first time Bildad spoke. He began, "How long will you say these things, and the words of your mouth be a mighty wind?" (Job 8:2). Now look at his opening line as he speaks again to Job. Talk about "same song, second verse." Bildad is obviously getting agitated.

How long will you hunt for words?
Show understanding and then we can talk.
Why are we regarded as beasts, as stupid in your eyes?
O you who tear yourself in your anger—
For your sake is the earth to be abandoned,
Or the rock to be moved from its place?

Job 18:2–4

Is God going to hold His breath while you get your life straightened out? That seems to be the implication of these sarcastic remarks. I'd call that an insulting beginning.

George Bernard Shaw once compared the average conversation to a phonograph with only half a dozen albums. You soon weary of hearing them over and over again.

How long, Job, *how long?* Bildad sees this whole thing as a wearisome repetitious group of monotonous words. Clearly, the man is no longer interested in Job's pain. He's only interested in Job's shutting up and admitting that he's sinful. Period.

Here's the way Bildad thinks. God is just and fair. God not only punishes the wicked, He blesses the righteous. If you repent, God will bless you and relieve you of your affliction. If you don't repent, He'll keep judging you and your pain will continue. *Repent!* Here's the snag: Job isn't in need of repenting because he hasn't done anything wrong. But, like some folks to this day, Bildad's theology doesn't have room for mystery. Everything is black or white. If you obey, you will be blessed. Those in God's will enjoy great prosperity and good health. But if you suffer, you're *out* of God's will. He wants *everybody* well. What flawed theology! Since God is sovereign and all powerful, if He wanted everybody well, we'd all be well. After all, He's God . . . but it's not like that.

He's running the show, if you will. He deliberately allows sickness. For mysterious reasons beyond our comprehension, He permits pain. And then there are other times for reasons that are clearly revealed, He tests us. The point is, He is in charge. That means we're not. (I'm sounding like Yogi Berra.) If we pray for the healing of an individual, and healing doesn't occur, we are not to conclude it's his or her fault. Because *God doesn't want everyone well*. Please read that sentence again.

Paul prayed three separate times that his thorn in the flesh would be taken from him. And the Lord answered "No, no, no." Paul not only stopped praying for relief, he accepted God's firm no as final. Then he responded with an acceptance speech that cannot be improved on:

> He has said to me, "My grace is sufficient for you, for power is perfected in weakness." Most gladly, therefore, I will rather boast about my weaknesses, so that the power of Christ may dwell in me. Therefore I am well content with weaknesses, with insults, with distresses, with persecutions, with difficulties, for Christ's sake; for when I am weak, then I am strong.
>
> 2 Corinthians 12:9–10

What a magnificent, mature response! Paul was willing to accept the mystery of God's will in leaving him with the affliction after he had urgently prayed for relief three times!

But Bildad left no room for mystery. What was in Bildad's mind? Something like this: "It's clear to us that there is secret sin somewhere in your life. If we press the issue long enough you will finally admit it." I think the only sin that Job wrestled with about now is: "How do I silence these guys?" (No extra charge for that. Frankly, that's a thought I would have had, had I been sitting there in the city dump, covered in boils, and having to endure their shame-based condemnation.)

Death Is Near

A closer look reveals that Bildad visits Job with one reminder after another of death. How's that for a caring counselor? He pulls out all the stops as he underscores the presence of the "king of terrors" (Job 18:14). This is poetry, remember. He uses poetic language, allegory, and word pictures in his presentation. Bildad portrays Job's dying in four different word pictures.

First, a light going out:

Indeed, the light of the wicked goes out
And the flame of his fire gives no light.
The light in his tent is darkened
And his lamp goes out above him.

Job 18:5–6

Second, a person who is trapped, heading for death. There's an implication that Job has a scheme he is not willing to admit. He's not confessing it. Notice the word pictures for this trapped person.

His vigorous stride is shortened,
And his own scheme brings him down.
For he is thrown into the net by his own feet,
And he steps on the webbing.
A snare seizes him by the heel,
And a trap snaps shut on him.
A noose for him is hidden in the ground,
And a trap for him on the path.

Job 18:7–10

Third, Job is portrayed as a fugitive who is being pursued. It's here Bildad introduces the "king of terrors."

All around terrors frighten him
And harry him at every step.
His strength is famished,
And calamity is ready at his side.
His skin is devoured by disease,
The firstborn of death devours his limbs.
He is torn from the security of his tent
And they march him before the *king of terrors*.
There dwells in his tent nothing of his;
Brimstone is scattered on his habitation.

Job 18:11–15 (italics mine)

Glance back at that last vivid statement: "Brimstone is scattered on his habitation." "Can you believe it?" Bildad says. "Fire and brimstone, that's what's coming Job. You're on your way to hell!"

Fourth, he portrays Job as an uprooted tree.

> His roots are dried below,
> And his branch is cut off above.
> Memory of him perishes from the earth,
> And he has no name abroad.
> He is driven from light into darkness,
> And chased from the inhabited world.
> He has no offspring or posterity among his people,
> Nor any survivor where he sojourned.
> Those in the west are appalled at his fate,
> And those in the east are seized with horror.
>
> Job 18:16–20

He ends with the ultimate insult: "You do not even know God!" He fires both barrels at point-blank range.

Here sits Job itching madly, fever intensifying, his head is shaved, he's dirty and hot and enduring pain at its most excruciating level. Standing over him is this man with the audacity to dress him down and conclude he doesn't even know God.

Now why? Why would the Lord our God include this scene in His Word? At the risk of repeating myself too often, because the spirit of Bildad still lives. There are times it surfaces in the form of a harsh, judgmental, marital partner who, no matter what, cannot offer a word of encouragement or affirmation. Other times it emerges in the form of a boss who criticizes incessantly. And let me add, sometimes it is displayed by a preacher who uses the pulpit as a hammer to beat and abuse the sheep. I've seen it in the response of a harsh and impatient nurse who will be glad when you're gone so she can get the hospital room cleaned out and get somebody else in there. Count on it, the spirit of Bildad still lives.

Two Major Mistakes

As I analyze the man's approach, two glaring mistakes come to the surface. First, he is talking to the wrong person. And second, he's speaking with the wrong motive. Bildad says things about death, about being haunted by "the king of terrors," and being driven to this dreadful state of mind—all of which are true if a person doesn't know the Lord. As long as he's thinking of one who is an unbeliever, Bildad is right. "There is a way which seems right to a man, but its end is the way of death" (Proverbs 14:12). You and I know people who do not know the Lord and so we try every gracious way we can to present Him to them . . . explaining the hope He offers, the assurance of life hereafter, promising forgiveness. There are times we weave into the conversation a reminder that death is sure, it's coming. They blink and look at us with something like, "No, we'll make it on our own." Well, what Bildad has described is precisely what you get when you try to make it on your own. This is what the person who does not know God has to face. But in this case, Bildad has no right to say this to a fellow believer. For sure, Job knew the Lord. Bildad had the wrong audience. And as we've seen, he spoke with a wrong motive.

JOB'S STRONG RESPONSE

Pause here and read Job's first words of reply, slowly and thoughtfully. Don't miss how he uses Bildad's words to begin his own, "How long?"

Then Job responded,

> How long will you torment me
> And crush me with words?
> These ten times you have insulted me:
> You are not ashamed to wrong me.
>
> Job 19:1–3

I have those four passionate verbs underlined in my Bible: *torment, crush, insult, wrong*. What brutal blows Job took! What a blast of hot air from the furnace of Bildad's mouth. How devastating!

Let me step in here before we probe deeper into Job's response and clarify that reproof is a good thing when communicated correctly. We all need accountability. No question about it. Some don't like and don't want to be held accountable. So any kind of reproof is resisted.

Some pastors and evangelists, even a few missionaries love to be free of reproof so they quote the verse (out of context), "Do not touch my anointed ones" (1 Chronicles 16:22). They think, "I am a man of God who proclaims His truths, so you have no right to correct me. I'm above all that. I am the one who corrects you." No, the fact is we all need reproof. Such "wounds are trustworthy," says Solomon. "Faithful are the wounds of a friend" (Proverbs 27:6), remember? If the reproof comes from the right person in the right way and is done with the right motive, we're wise to accept it and be grateful for it. It's truly trustworthy.

That's why growing up in the right kind of home can be so beneficial. Good moms and trustworthy dads reprove. Some of the best and most helpful reproofs many of us ever got came from faithful moms and dads who corrected us when they saw we needed to be corrected. Occasionally, they spanked us. They didn't let us get away with being sassy or impudent, deceptive or cruel in our behavior. The tongue of the wise can bring great benefit to those who are willing and humble enough to accept it. The tongue, on the other hand, can be a deadly thing. It can torment and crush, insult and wrong others. When David wrote Psalm 57, he was fleeing from Saul. In fact, he was a fugitive for about twelve years. It is in that context he records some descriptive expressions regarding the destructive power of the tongue:

> My soul is among lions;
> I must lie among those who breathe forth fire,
> Even the sons of men, whose teeth are spears and arrows
> And their tongue a sharp sword.
>
> Psalm 57:4

David pictures fire-breathing hotheads whose words are like sword thrusts, shoved in, twisted—shoved in again so brutally. He is describing abusive speech—assaulting people with our tongues. David had been the target of that.

Again, read from Psalm 64:

Hear my voice, O God, in my complaint;
Preserve my life from dread of the enemy.
Hide me from the secret counsel of evildoers,
From the tumult of those who do iniquity,
Who have sharpened their tongue like a sword.
They aimed bitter speech as their arrow,
To shoot from concealment at the blameless;
Suddenly they shoot at him, and do not fear.

Psalm 64:1–4

What a potent weapon is the tongue! And this is especially true when we are attacked in secret, behind the scenes. Things are said against us, and we neither know it nor realize the impact that it's having on people who once believed in us. And those sword thrusts keep going on. The contrasting role the tongue can play is set forth eloquently in Proverbs 12:18.

There is one who speaks rashly like the thrusts of a sword,
But the tongue of the wise brings healing.

Proverbs 15:4 provides a similar thought:

A soothing tongue is a tree of life,
But perversion in it crushes the spirit.

Bildad blamed Job because he considered him a sinful man. Therefore, he erroneously concluded, what he was going through was the appropriate consequence prompted by wrong. Job realized there was no sin he hadn't confessed, so he saw what he was going through as a mystery. When you add mystery to the silence of God and a feeling of distance from the presence of God, life becomes borderline unbearable. Which explains Job's periodic loss of control. But those men refused to cut him any slack.

There is a fine piece I've carried with me for years, entitled *The Builder*. It asks penetrating questions toward the end:

I saw them tearing a building down,
A group of men in a busy town,
With a hefty blow and a lusty yell,
They swung with zest,
And a side wall fell.
Asked of the Foreman,
"Are these men skilled? The kind you would hire if you had to build?"
He looked at me, and laughed, "No, indeed! Unskilled labor is all I
   need.
Why, they can wreck in a day or two,
What it has taken builders years to do."
I asked myself, as I went my way,
Which of these roles have I tried to play?
Am I a builder with rule and square,
Measuring and constructing with skill and care?
Or am I the wrecker who walks the town,
Content with the business of tearing down?[4]

Anonymous

Job's friends qualified as *wreckers*. The longer they spent with him, the more Job realized they didn't represent the truth. They continued to condemn.

Some who are reading this book are no longer married because you were abused by a partner. You were verbally assaulted; you never knew what it was to be affirmed and encouraged. Receiving nothing but put-downs and never an understanding hug, you couldn't continue and survive. And, tragically, some of you are abusive in your marriage. The amazing thing is that you don't know it. Chances are good you're thinking, "Oh, I've never laid a hand on—" No, it's not that. I'm talking about verbal abuse: ugly comments, insults, words that stab and lacerate like sword thrusts, sarcasm, and snide remarks.

To be fair, I don't think Bildad sat on the edge of his bed that morning thinking, "Let's see, how can I possibly insult Job today?" Verbal abuse is committed most often by those with huge blind spots. Like Bildad, it got worse the longer they talked.

God's Silence and Distance

Job calls such abuse tormenting, crushing, insulting, and wrong. But that isn't all that was troubling him. There was also the distance he felt from God.

> Behold, I cry, "Violence!" but I get no answer;
> I shout for help, but there is no justice.
>
> Job 19:7

The heavens were tarnished brass. God was mute. Referring to that maddening silence, Job says:

> He has walled up my way so that I cannot pass,
> And He has put darkness on my paths.
>
> Job 19:8

Our heart goes out to the man as he further describes his anguish:

> He has stripped my honor from me
> And removed the crown from my head.
> He breaks me down on every side, and I am gone;
> And he has uprooted my hope like a tree.
>
> Job 19:9–10

Others' Absence and Resistance

Not only is God silent, others who were once close to Job are now estranged from him. And when he hears from them, they are turned off by him.

> He has removed my brothers far from me,
> And my acquaintances are completely estranged from me.
> My relatives have failed,
> And my intimate friends have forgotten me.
> Those who live in my house and my maids consider me a stranger.

I am a foreigner in their sight.
I call to my servant, but he does not answer;
I have to implore him with my mouth.
My breath is offensive to my wife,
And I am loathsome to my own brothers.
Even young children despise me;
I rise up and they speak against me.
All my associates abhor me,
And those I love have turned against me.

Job 19:13–19

"You, Bildad. You, Zophar. You, Elipahz. You've all turned against me!" What a tragic, pitiable existence was his. As far as earthly companionships were concerned, he had no one. Perhaps bent over and through tears he sobs:

Pity me, pity me, O you my friends,
For the hand of God has struck me.
Why do you persecute me as God does,
And are not satisfied with my flesh?

Job 19:21–22

The one wish he had was that there might be some way to preserve his words so that other generations might read them and learn from them.

Oh that my words were written!
O that they were inscribed in a book!
That with an iron stylus and lead
They were engraved in the rock forever!

Job 19:23–24

Job's Longing

Job longed for his words of woe to be etched into granite so that people through time could enter into all the things he was enduring. He thought his words would be forgotten.

When I first read that, I was reminded of our sixteenth president, Abraham Lincoln, on the nineteenth of November 1863. He stood at Gettysburg surrounded by the horrendous aftermath of that bloody battle, with bloated bodies still lying in the fields under the sun. He stood with this simple little speech written by his own hand. For sure, he believed his words would soon be forgotten.

> The world will little note, nor long remember what we say here, but it can never forget what they did here.[5]

Realizing how permanently his words have been etched in everyone's memory, each time I read his speech I think, "Mr. President, our nation will *never* forget what you said in that address!" Most of us are unable to remember all that those soldiers did there, but we'll never forget the immortal words Lincoln spoke there.

Job had no idea that his words would survive him. Yet—think of it—God chose to include them in His eternal Word! Along with scriptures like Genesis 1, Psalm 23, Romans 8, 1 Corinthians 13, and Revelation 22, we call to mind Job 19:25–27 to this day!

> As for me, I know that my redeemer lives,
> And at the last He will take His stand on the earth.
> Even after my skin is destroyed,
> Yet from my flesh I shall see God;
> Whom I myself shall behold,
> And whom my eyes shall see and not another.
> My heart faints within me!

Thanks to Handel's *Magnum Opus*, every Christmas season we hear that message over and over again. Little did Job realize in his dreadful anguish that his Lord would honor his name by preserving his words for all the world to hear *and sing!*

Your Own Hope

I need to pause right here and write to you whose God is distant and silent. And, perhaps (like Job), your friends have begun to turn against you. There is a future that is brighter beyond your wildest dreams! As Job will one day experience, justice will win out, God will replace evil, and right will eclipse wrong.

In the end, God wins. And so will we.

Job will be vindicated and remembered and respected. And all the Zophars and the Bildads and the Eliphazes will be judged, silenced, and forgotten.

> Then be afraid of the sword for yourselves,
> For wrath brings the punishment of the sword,
> So that you may know there is judgment.
>
> Job 19:29

In all his misery, Job had not lost sight of who was right and who was wrong. He reminded all three men that "judgment and punishment are not coming my way, they're coming *yours*."

LESSONS LEARNED FROM A CONTEXT OF PAIN

Two lasting lessons live on as I complete this tenth chapter. The first one is about hope, and the second one is about assurance.

First, there is nothing like hope in the truth to clarify perspective and keep you going. Enduring a painful journey can be done a lot more easily if you embrace truth as your traveling companion. Not only will it give you hope, it will clarify your perspective. Truth reminds us that God is alive and just and good. I say again— wrong will ultimately be judged. Today may seem dark and terribly long, but there will be a bright tomorrow.

Second, there is nothing like a lack of assurance to haunt your steps and make you afraid. Let me put it to you straight: If you are without the Lord Jesus Christ in your life, your steps are marked by uncertainty. And deep into the night when the lights are out and your head is sunk into the pillow, thoughts of your ultimate future will haunt you. Few thoughts are more frightening than not knowing where you will be when you die. If you die without Christ, you're facing a fearful judgment. "It is appointed for men to die once and after this comes judgment" (Hebrews 9:27). To have inner peace you need to know without a doubt where you're going.

My wife and I have a commitment regarding giving our money while we're alive. I like the old saying, "Do your givin' while you're livin', then you're knowin', where it's goin'." With that in mind, be sure you're believing right while you're living, then you'll be knowing where you're going. It's scary not knowing where you're going.

Evangelist Billy Graham was invited several years ago to speak at the old-but-still-elegant Waldorf Astoria Hotel in New York City. I have a friend who was there and heard him speak. Dr. Graham apparently had some trouble getting there—in fact, he was a little late arriving. When he stood up to speak, he told a story about the world-renowned physicist, Albert Einstein, who was taking a train to a big city many years ago. The conductor came by to gather the tickets. When he got to the Great Thinker, he waited to collect his ticket. The old gentleman began to search through all his pockets, but he couldn't find it. By now the conductor noticed who he was, so he said to him, "Oh, Dr. Einstein, don't worry. I know who you are . . . I trust you. You don't have to show me your ticket," and he continued his rounds.

A few minutes later the conductor was returning with his pouch full of tickets, and he noticed that Einstein was down on his hands and knees, looking under the seats for his lost ticket. He leaned over and whispered, "No, please get up. It's no problem. We trust you. You don't need to show me your ticket." At that point, Einstein paused, looked up, and said, "Young man, this isn't a matter of trust, but direction. I'm searching for my ticket because I don't know where I'm going."[6]

Do you really know where you're going? Is your eternal destination guaranteed? Amazingly, Bildad talked to the wrong man with the wrong motive. He had a strong message, but it was for some other person. Could that person be you? If so, there is reason to be concerned.

CHAPTER ELEVEN

Responding Wisely When Falsely Accused

Threatment the most treacherous enemy in the church is the tongue. The human tongue has done more damage and caused more heartaches than any other source of trouble. What we say cuts far deeper than any knife or sword. The Bible occasionally presents the tongue as a sword that thrusts its way into others' lives causing deep, lingering hurt. We're not surprised, therefore, to read of lying in the list of the Ten Commandments, "You shall not bear false witness against your neighbor" (Exodus 20:16).

When Solomon wrote the Proverbs, he included the seven things the Lord hates. Among them, "A false witness who utters lies" (Proverbs 6:19). Nevertheless, liars are still on the loose. If you have been the brunt of someone's lying tongue, more specifically, if you have been falsely accused, you don't need me to describe real pain. You've not only been there. You've discovered how difficult it can be to defend yourself. You try, but folks are hard to convince once they've heard convincing lies. The venom from a poisoned tongue has already taken its toll. Tragically, churches can be a feeding ground for loose lips and lying tongues. It takes courage to stand up to liars.

While I was ministering with Ravi Zacharias at a Bible conference several years ago, he told a terrific story that I'll never forget. There was a young pastor who went to a church that had gone through a devastating split. As a result, the little church had been reduced to bare survival. When the strong-hearted young man arrived, he was determined to open his Bible and boldly preach the truth from God's Word week after week. He had the courage to call a spade a spade, which God honored.

Not surprisingly, the church got back on its feet and began to grow. Before long the congregation was bulging at the seams. This resulted in multiple services on Sunday; it was obvious that they needed to build a larger place of worship. Only one major problem: The new worship center would cost a million dollars. Though they didn't have that kind of money, no one could deny reality—they needed the building.

In this growing church were two brothers living carnal lives. They were sorry rascals, and they were very wealthy. Rich reprobates living notoriously godless lives. One of them suddenly died. The surviving brother soon came to the pastor and said, "Here, I have something for you." He handed the pastor an envelope. "It's a check for one million dollars. I want you to use it to pay for the new sanctuary. All I ask in return is, when you preach my brother's funeral, tell everybody attending the funeral service that *he was a saint.* That's all I'm asking you to do."

The pastor thought for a moment and said, "Okay, it's a deal." He took the check, deposited it that same afternoon, and began to prepare his funeral message. The service was held several days later, and the church was packed. The coffin rested in front of the pulpit as the pastor stood to deliver his message. The people sat in silence, wondering what in the world could be said since they knew the kind of life he'd lived. They were stunned by the pastor's opening words. "This man was a reprobate. He was unfaithful to his family. He lived a life of hypocrisy and immorality. He was dishonest in his business. He was a liar . . . not a man that you could trust. He was a major cause of this church's troubles and struggles before and after I arrived as pastor . . . a real heartache to many of you. But compared to his brother, *he was a saint.*"[1] There are several ways to speak the truth, but that young preacher refused to be blackmailed. Pastors that gutsy are rare.

BIBLICAL CHARACTERS FALSELY ACCUSED

You may be surprised to find how often false accusations were leveled against innocent people in the Scriptures. Let's think of several examples—all of them the victims of unfair, damaging words.

Let's start with a man named Joseph, who learned a new language, became familiar with a completely different culture, and earned his way to a place of great responsibility as the manager of Potiphar's belongings. He was a model of integrity, but at the height of his career Joseph was falsely accused of rape by Potiphar's wife. He wound up in jail. How unfair.

Moses was faithful even at eighty years of age to obey God's voice and accept God's commission from the burning bush to go back to Egypt and deliver his people from bondage. Following the Exodus, while still wandering across the wilderness, the very people he had delivered turned on him and falsely accused him of bringing them into that wilderness to watch them die. Nothing was further from the truth.

David, after killing the giant and demonstrating a life of courage and integrity, was falsely accused of trying to dethrone King Saul by the jealous and insecure king himself. David became a fugitive for a dozen or more years, falsely accused of something that was not at all true. How undeserving.

Nehemiah rebuilt the wall around ancient Jerusalem having motivated the people to accomplish that difficult task. Just before the project reached completion, several of his enemies spread the word that Nehemiah had an ulterior motive. "He's building the wall so that he can ultimately become the new king. Nehemiah is in it for himself," was their lie. How unfair for that to be said of godly and diligent Nehemiah.

Peter and John were accused of preaching a false Christ, clearly a false accusation. Unfairly, they were beaten for it.

Paul was accused of being a phony convert shortly after his conversion. The apostles wouldn't even allow him in their circle since they were suspicious about his not being born again. He was later accused of causing a dissension among all the Jews. How exaggerated can stories get? The same man was later accused by Governor Festus of being insane because of his "great learning." How unfair was that?

And who could ever overlook Jesus himself, "a man of sorrows and acquainted with grief." Much of His sorrow and grief was spawned by false accusations. From His earliest months in public ministry He was accused of being of illegitimate birth. During His incredible ministry, He was accused of being a drunkard because He sat and ate with sinners. The Pharisees also accused Him of being demon-possessed, an instrument of Satan, as He healed people. Ultimately, He went to the cross due to false accusations of blasphemy and tyranny. Talk about unfair!

We're not surprised when Jesus began to deliver His immortal Sermon on the Mount that He included these words:

> Blessed are you when people insult you and persecute you, and falsely
> say all kinds of evil against you because of Me. Rejoice and be glad,
> for your reward in heaven is great; for in the same way they perse-
> cuted the prophets who were before you.
>
> Matthew 5:11–12

If you are being falsely accused these days, I'd suggest you read those words again, this time a little more deliberately. Don't miss the promise: Your heavenly reward will be great. Today your misery may be enormous. You may have found that you're unable to defend yourself. A mind made up is almost impossible to persuade otherwise.

ENTER ZOPHAR . . . ACCUSING FOR THE SECOND TIME

> Then Zophar, the Naamathite answered,
> Therefore my disquieting thoughts make me respond,
> Even because of my inward agitation.
>
> I listened to the reproof which insults me,
> And the spirit of my understanding makes me answer.
>
> Job 20:1–3

Zophar has "disquieting thoughts." He then admits to "inward agitation." He also feels "insulted." I'll be honest with you: I don't find anything that's disquieting, agitating, or insulting from what Job has said. He has simply voiced his disagreements with Zophar. Those who wish to set others straight and gain control over them are often disquieted, agitated, and insulted because they don't agree. They don't want to listen; they want to talk. They don't want to learn; they want to instruct, preferably lecture. And they certainly don't want to be disagreed with!

Zophar's acrid tongue has not softened as he's waited his turn to speak again. He has three messages to say to Job. Not surprisingly, he says each one in an exaggerated manner. First, he wants Job to understand *the wicked do not live long* (Job 20:4–11). Second, *the pleasures of the wicked are temporal* (Job 20:12–19). Finally, he affirms *God's judgment falls hard on the wicked* (Job 20:20–29). There's one major problem with those messages—they are wrong when you interpret them as Zophar intends.

Zophar is delivering his lecture not unlike a novice coloring by the numbers—*his* numbers. To this man, everything is crystal clear and overly simple. Everything can be reduced to simplistic axioms, which explains why Zophar stands so firm in his comments about the brevity of life, the temporary pleasures of wickedness, and the judgment of God. Job will soon point out the error of Zophar's analysis, but first, let's be sure we track the man's thinking.

> Do you know this from of old,
> From the establishment of man on earth,
> That the triumphing of the wicked is short,
> And the joy of the godless momentary?
>
> Job 20:4–5

Zophar sees Job as wicked, therefore, he believes it's his responsibility to tell him that he is not long for this world.

> Though his loftiness reaches the heavens,
> And his head touches the clouds,
> He perishes forever like his refuse;

Those who have seen him will say, "Where is he?"
He flies away like a dream, and they cannot find him;
Even like a vision of the night he is chased away.
The eye which saw him sees him no more,
And his place no longer beholds him,
His sons favor the poor,
And his hands give back his wealth.
His bones are full of his youthful vigor,
But it lies down with him in the dust.

Job 20:6–11

In all this verbosity, Zophar is implying that Job's life is convoluted, twisted, and strange; it's weird and then all of a sudden, (poof!) you're gone. People won't be able to find you because the wicked don't stick around; God removes them.

When Zophar refers to his youthful bones lying down with him in the dust, he's not talking about natural causes, he's saying it's due to God's judgment. He says, in effect, "Because you've lived like you've lived, because you've kept your secret sins from us while all of us thought you were righteous, judgment will soon come." What Zophar lacked in tact he made up for in cruelty! Can you imagine Job's enduring such a blast? Trying to handle his misery and grief, he now hears, "You will die sooner than you think."

That's not all. Zophar bears down even further. As you read his words, put yourself in Job's place.

Though evil is sweet in his mouth
And he hides it under his tongue,
Though he desires it and will not let it go,
But holds it in his mouth,
Yet his food in his stomach is changed
To the venom of cobras within him.
He swallows riches,
But will vomit them up;
God will expel them from his belly.

He sucks the poison of cobras;
The viper's tongue slays him.
He does not look at the streams,
The rivers flowing with honey and curds.
He returns what he has attained
And cannot swallow it;
As to the riches of his trading,
He cannot even enjoy them.
For he has oppressed and forsaken the poor;
He has seized a house which he has not built.

Job 20:12–19

Those closing blows must have hurt. In addition to his insulting and condemning words, he accuses Job of taking unfair advantage of others because of his wealth. He implies that Job used his riches to exploit and oppress the poor by pushing them out of their houses, then seizing their property. All this to say, "Your pleasures are over, Job. The jig's up. Your wickedness has finally caught up with you." Is it any surprise why the Lord comes down so hard on "a false witness who utters lies?"

Unfortunately, Zophar isn't through. His final words can better be understood in the way Eugene Peterson paraphrases them in *The Message*.

Such God-denying people are never content with what they have or
who they are; their greed drives them relentlessly.
They plunder everything
but they can't hold on to any of it.
Just when they think they have it all, disaster strikes;
they're served up a plate full of misery.
When they've filled their bellies with that,
God gives them a taste of his anger,
and they get to chew on that for a while.
As they run for their lives from one disaster,
they run smack into another.
They're knocked around from pillar to post,

beaten to within an inch of their lives.
They're trapped in a house of horrors,
   and see their loot disappear down a black hole.
Their lives are a total loss—
   not a penny to their name, not so much as a bean.
God will strip them of their sin-soaked clothes
   and hang their dirty laundry out for all to see.
Life is a complete wipeout for them,
   nothing surviving God's wrath,
There! That's God's blueprint for the wicked—
   what they have to look forward to.

Job 20:20–29, MSG

One of the sources I've been using in my study of Job makes this insightful comment: "This is the last time we hear from Zophar and we will not miss him."[2] In life, tragically, some people are so harmful and demoralizing, the best thing they do is ride off into the sunset and never return, since they've made everyone so miserable. As they walk out you think, "Good riddance." That's the way we feel about the Zophars in our lives. Job may have lived many centuries ago, but some of his encounters have a relevant ring to them. This kind of stuff still goes on.

ZOPHAR'S APPROACH APPLIED

Let's fast-forward momentarily and face the music. Some of you who are reading these words have awfully sharp tongues. You say things that cut, but you couch your words in phrases that sound pious and even eloquent. They can sound superreligious at times, but they're hurtful and damaging. They imply much more than is actually said. It is here that self-control plays such a vital role. How valuable it is to think before we speak and then, even after giving our words careful thought, to measure their tone, their possible impact, their truthfulness. Zophar did none of the above. With reckless abandon he dropped his harsh words like depth charges. Though Job was a seasoned and mature man of God, they must have hurt as they exploded in his mind. Even for the strong, false accusations hurt.

Forming habits of self-restraint is an essential discipline. When receiving information about another, it's best to ask the source: "How do you know that? Who told you? Is this information credible?" Those questions have a way of silencing people who tend to pass along damaging and exaggerated information. They assist in getting to the bottom of rumors. Furthermore, truth is given the opportunity to flourish, replacing lies. But you need to know that that kind of truth-talking comes with a price.

I recently read a true story about a minister . . .

> whose congregation persistently refused to accept his message. He wanted to lead God's flock into the green pastures and beside the still waters, but they were unwilling to be led. His choir, with their ungodly practices, brought things to a head.
>
> The position became so untenable that he invited the choir to resign. The choir not only resigned, but persuaded the congregation to desist from taking any part in the singing on the following Sunday. The result was that whatever singing was done, had to be done alone by this minister, while the choir and congregation enjoyed his discomfiture. This state of things continued for some time and the minister was greatly dejected and perplexed at the turn events had taken.
>
> He was at his wits' end when God spoke to him. One day he was sitting on a seat in a park when he saw part of a torn newspaper before him on the ground. The torn piece bore a message for him which exactly suited his need. It was this:
>
> No man is ever fully accepted until
> he has, first of all, been utterly rejected.
>
> He needed nothing more. He had been utterly rejected for Christ's sake, and his recognition of that fact was the beginning of a most fruitful ministry. Though utterly rejected by man, he had been fully accepted by God.[3]

Throughout Zophar's lecture Job has been listening to what my mother used to call "a lot of palaver." Just a lot of lip flapping—he's been talking nonsense. What he's saying against Job isn't true, even though Zophar delivers his words poetically and eloquently. Job has patiently endured, but he refuses to let those words slide by.

I've heard it said that no matter what, when false accusations are made, you just sit quietly and say nothing; God will defend you. There are some occasions when that may be appropriate. Not always. I often call to mind a motto from the American Revolution: "Trust in God but keep your powder dry."[4] Wise counsel! If your reputation is being ruined by lies, if your company is going down the tubes because of false accusations, if your church is being destroyed and demoralized because of wrong information from lying lips, there are times it is necessary to step up and set the record straight. Truth has a way of silencing lies.

JOB'S STRONG RESPONSE TO ZOPHAR

I'm impressed that Job refuses to take it on the chin. He doesn't shrug his shoulders and whisper, "Oh well, whatever." This was no time for passivity. Zophar's words were insulting, exaggerated, and inappropriate. His lies needed to be confronted, and his accusations denied. In fact, Job's opening lines reveal strong determination.

Then Job answered,

> Listen carefully to my speech,
> And let this be your way of consolation.
> Bear with me that I may speak;
> Then after I have spoken, you may "mock."
>
> Job 21:1–3

He starts by telling Zophar to "listen (for a change) to my speech." It's an imperative, like we would say, "*You listen to me!*" Not unlike a line often used by authority figures in military uniform, "Okay, listen up!"

Secondly, he tells Zophar, "Bear with me." That was another needed imperative because people who are guilty of making false accusations are usually poor listeners. They're not known for patiently gleaning truthful information. Knowing that, Job says, in effect, "I want you to do two things: I want you to *listen,* and I want you to *be patient* as you reason your way through what I have to say." He throws in, "After I have spoken, you may mock." A well-timed counterpunch, which one of my references referred to as a "sarcastic imperative" in the Hebrew. Isn't that good? "After you've heard me out, go ahead and mock me, but at least give me my day in court. After listening and patiently sifting your way through this, then feel free to mock on." Perhaps his accusers have been reacting to Job's answers with hisses and disruptive gestures. He wants that to stop. He urges them to listen for a change.

> Look at me, and be astonished,
> And put your hand over your mouth.
>
> Job 21:5

There's Job's third command: First, listen to me! Second, bear with me! Third, look at me! How can they do all three? "Put your hand over your mouth." By now those three critics must have been lecturing into space. They're no longer looking at him. So, Job says, "You look at me," as if to say, "Say what you have to say, but say it to my face." False accusers don't do that either. They go around us. They go behind our backs. They go to people who are weak and gullible and willing to listen to lies, and they infect them with their verbal germs. So, Job gets the attention of his accusers with these staccato-like commands.

If you take the time to analyze Job's answer, you'll see that he follows Zophar's outline, addressing all three of his points. Put in the form of questions:

1. Who says the wicked always die young? (Job 21:7–16)
2. Where's the proof that the godless always suffer calamity? (Job 21:17–22)
3. How can you say that death always falls hard on the wicked? (Job 21:23–26).

Let's take them in that order.

First, who says the wicked always die young? Job begins his defense by asking

Zophar an excellent question amplified—"If the wicked always die young, why do so many continue on, becoming more powerful?" (Job 21:7).

> Their descendants are established with them in their sight,
> And their offspring before their eyes,
> Their houses are safe from fear,
> Neither is the rod of God on them.
> His ox mates without fail;
> His cow calves and does not abort.
> They send forth their little ones like the flock,
> And their children skip about.
> They sing to the timbrel and harp
> And rejoice at the sound of the flute.
> They spend their days in prosperity.
>
> Job 21:8–13

The realistic analysis doesn't look very grim. And yet there's no question—they really don't know God.

> They say to God, "Depart from us!
> We do not even desire the knowledge of Your ways.
> Who is the Almighty, that we should serve Him,
> And what would we gain if we entreat Him?"
>
> Job 21:14–15

The truth of the matter is, Zophar, "the counsel of the wicked is far from me" (Job 21:16). In other words, "I'm not wicked—I'm sick. Nobody (including you!) knows why I'm sick, but nevertheless I'm sick. It's a huge mystery, but get this straight, I'm definitely not in the category of the wicked."

Second, where's the proof that the godless always suffer calamity? Just because they don't have the Lord God in their lives doesn't mean that all in that camp go to an early grave. Furthermore, they don't always suffer calamity. Follow Job's logic here. Read his words thoughtfully.

How often is the lamp of the wicked put out,
Or does their calamity fall on them?
Does God apportion destruction in His anger?
Are they as straw before the wind,
And like the chaff which the storm carries away?
You say, "God stores away a man's iniquity for his sons."
Let God repay him so that he may know *it*.
Let his own eyes see his decay,
And let him drink of the wrath of the Almighty.
For what does he care for his household after him,
When the number of his months is cut off?
Can anyone teach God knowledge,
In that He judges those on high?

Job 21:17–22

Job is saying, in effect, "Your argument doesn't hold water, Zophar. There are numerous opposing examples of what you're suggesting."

Let me show you a verse you may have never considered before. I learned it years ago, and it comes to mind when I refer to subjects like this. These are among Solomon's ancient words of wisdom:

Because the sentence against an evil deed is not executed quickly, therefore the hearts of the sons of men among them are given fully to do evil.

Ecclesiastes 8:11

Do you follow his thinking? He's saying this: Because every time a person does wrong he's not immediately judged or doesn't suddenly become a victim of calamity, he keeps on doing wrong. He determines he can do evil over and over again since he keeps on getting away with it. The lack of quick consequences prompts the wrongdoer to do more of it. You steal ten bucks and get away with it, you seriously consider stealing another ten. After stealing twenty and not getting caught and punished, you're tempted to be a professional thief, doing more of the same. Job had that idea in mind as he tells Zophar that calamity doesn't always follow close on the heels of the unbeliever.

We need to get stereotyped images of lost people out of our minds. Far too many Christians have the idea that because a person is an unbeliever, he's stupid. Not true! Many of the lost are brilliant. In fact, some are more brilliant than many of us will ever dream of being. Furthermore, many of the lost live easier lives than many of us. And they aren't instantly judged or taken from this earth before turning forty. Many of them live well and live long, even though they live alienated from the Almighty. It's easy to let that reality confuse us.

Not long ago I read of a pastor and a deacon who made plans to do some visiting of the lost in their neighborhood. One particularly notorious unbeliever, who was well known in the community, had visited their church the previous Sunday. He had signed a visitor's card, including his address. So they decided to drop by and talk with him about the Good News. They rode together in the same car, and when they arrived in this exclusive residential section they wound their way around the long driveway which circled in front of his large, gorgeous home. The lawn was thick and manicured, and the landscaping was elegant. Kids were playing hopscotch out in the driveway. They could see past the inner motorcourt into the backyard where there was a beautiful pool with a large, splashing fountain. There were three luxurious cars sitting beyond the brick arches, all of them new and spotless. Tucked away in the fourth garage was a classic, bright red Ferrari. Parking their car out front, both men could see the man of the house through the window of the study. He was sitting in his large soft leather chair, laughing with his friends and having the greatest time, munching on a handful of popcorn with a tall, icy beverage in the other hand. At that moment the young deacon turned to his pastor and said, "Now, tell me again, what kind of good news do we have for this guy?"[5]

Never forget, our Good News is about the life beyond. Believing that Good News does not mean you will suddenly become affluent. Nor does it mean if you don't believe it you're doomed to poverty or a life in prison. Our theology needs to be clearly understood and articulated apart from economic lifestyles or personal preferences or narrow-minded prejudices— as if the wealthy can never be godly or the poor can never be wicked. That's where Zophar missed it, "Look at you, Job. Look at the condition you're in. Sick as you are and destitute as you've become, you obviously have sin in your life. You just haven't told us because only the wicked suffer like this." Job is setting the record straight: "No, that's not true. It isn't uncommon for the wicked to live very prosperously or for those who know God to suffer." But remember this: In death, all distinctions disappear.

Third, how can you say that death always falls hard on the wicked?

> One dies in his full strength,
> Being wholly at ease and satisfied;
> His sides are filled out with fat,
> And the marrow of his bones is moist,
> While another dies with a bitter soul,
> Never even tasting anything good.
> Together they lie down in the dust,
> And worms cover them.
>
> Job 21:23–26

"Zophar, you've missed it in my case; I'm not in that category." And look at Job's final response to Zophar's erroneous counsel:

> How then will you vainly comfort me,
> For your answers remain full of falsehood.
>
> Job 21:34

You've got to admire Job's honesty. Like the pastor who refused to be bribed by the surviving, rich brother, Job says it straight. That kind of truth-talking needs to be practiced in public. Falsehood has no redeeming value and must be confronted head-on. The word *falsehood*, in the Hebrew, means, "treachery or fraud." In other words, "Zophar, your answers remain full of treachery. They can't be counted on. I am not as you have falsely accused me. You need to hear the truth, since you're neither saying it nor hearing it." I cannot help but wonder if this strong rebuke explains Zophar's sudden exit from any further dialogue.

FOUR RESPONSES TO FALSE ACCUSERS

I began this chapter by addressing the power of the tongue. As we've worked our way through the last of the three accusers in this second cycle, we've seen repeatedly how devastating false accusations can be. Chances are good that many of you who are reading these lines are currently the target of someone's lying accusations. That can be an anguishing cross to bear. I've been there so I speak from painful experience. Since this is an ongoing issue for many of us, it should be helpful to draw a few guidelines to follow based on the way Job handled his accuser. I find from Job's example at least four responses worth mentioning. Each is followed by a strong two-word suggestion.

First, listen to what is being said, considering the character of the critic. STAY CALM! You will be tempted to jump in and rashly react in the flesh, saying things you will later regret. Do your best to listen to what is being said. While doing so, keep in mind the character of the person who is the source of the accusation. Calmly take it all in. Job did that, which prepared him for his further response.

Second, respond with true facts and accurate information knowing the nature of your accuser. SPEAK TRUTH! Stay on the side of accuracy, regardless. The other person may be a former husband or former wife. He or she could be your previous or current boss, an employee, a neighbor, a pastor, or a friend. It doesn't matter who the individual is. If you are being accused you need to focus only on true facts. Don't *react* or ponder ways to *retaliate*. If you yield to either temptation, you'll come off sounding like the accuser. God honors integrity. Maybe not immediately, but ultimately you'll be vindicated. Remember David's prayer: "Vindicate me, O LORD, for I have walked in my integrity" (Psalm 26:1). Truth will prevail among people who traffic in it and make their decisions based on it.

Abraham Lincoln was told that he needed to fire his postmaster general. All kinds of accusations were being leveled against the man. Lincoln weighed rumor against hard evidence, and on July 18, 1864, he wrote Secretary Stanton a letter saying he was not going to do that because the information was based on hearsay, not accurate facts. In that letter he correctly concluded, "Truth is generally the best vindication against slander."[6] Wise response.

Stay with the truth. Don't exaggerate it, don't deny it, and don't hesitate to say it.

Third, use examples that represent reality and balance, trusting your defense to the Lord. LEAN HARD! Stop and think. Job did precisely that. While speaking the truth he left the defense of his own character in the Lord's hands. He was firm and deliberate, but he remained in control. I repeat, I understand what it's like to be unjustly maligned. I have been accused of things, and that rumor has kept me awake. It has made my stomach churn. It has taken away my appetite. I have determined not to pay any attention to it, yet found that I was unable to turn it off in my mind. Not until I decided to leave things in the Lord's hands and rest in His sovereign control, did I find inner peace. Without exception (please hear this!) *without exception*, not until I deliberately stepped back and leaned hard on my God, did my mind begin to relax, my emotions settle down, and my inner peace return. I say again, the truth will win out. And God *will* be glorified.

Fourth, refuse to let the accusations discourage and derail you, remembering they are nonsense and lies. GET TOUGH! Returning to that one-liner from the Revolutionary War, "Trust in God but keep your powder dry," is essential to keeping your balance. You may be trusting the Lord for safety, but you still lock your doors every night, hopefully, and turn on your alarm. When you get in your car, you lock your doors, don't you? You roll up your windows, don't you? If you don't, you are playing with fire. Trusting God is not naive presumption. Wisdom must be applied to a life of faith. Going through hard times requires a get-tough mind-set. Go there. That may seem harsh, but it's realistic. Realism is a powerful message.

I recall the true story of a physician-father who lived in Paraguay. Several years ago he stood against the unscrupulous military regime there, especially exposing its human-rights abuses. The law enforcement officials were corrupt. As a result of being exposed, they took out their revenge on the outspoken medical doctor by arresting his teenage son and torturing him to death. The townsfolk were outraged. They wanted to turn the boy's funeral into a huge protest march. The doctor chose a better means of protest. At the funeral, the father displayed the son's body as he had found it in the jail—naked, scarred from the electric shocks, cigarette burns, beatings, and stabbings. All the villagers filed past the corpse, which lay not in a soft, clean casket but on a dirty blood-soaked mattress from the prison, exactly where he found his boy. It proved to be the strongest protest imaginable. It put injustice on grotesque display.[7]

That's what God did with Christ at His crucifixion. He didn't wrap Him in a clean, white bedsheet, saying to the world, "No, no, it's too hard for you to look at that." Jesus wasn't crucified in a dark, private basement so people wouldn't see. He was on a hill, at a place of public humiliation, *hanging there*. Exposed. Finally limp, gray, *dead*. The method, representing a bold message, was *impacting*, and that cross is still impacting all who will look and live. Look at it yet again. Let your mind picture it. Bearing the sins of the world called for an agonizing, ugly scene.

Let me write these closing words to you who are going through a time of false accusation. May God strengthen you in it. May He hold you close through it. May He give you wisdom and grace in responding to it. May He become real and personal to you, even giving you songs in the night and quiet rest with the assurance that He is defending your integrity. And I would add, may He toughen your hide so you don't cave in while awaiting vindication.

And let me say to you who are spreading rumors, lies, and slander against another: There is nothing more treacherous you could be doing than that. Nothing. If you claim to be a follower of Christ, that must stop. Now. You hurt the body. You disease the church. You ruin the testimony of Christ. There is nothing the lost world loves to hear and see more than the family of God fighting each other.

To all of us I would add a final comment. Before we cluck our tongues at Zophar and Bildad and Eliphaz, let's do some soul-searching. Let's follow the psalmist's example and pray: "Search me, O God, and know my heart; try me, know my anxious thoughts; and see if there be any hurtful way in me, and lead me in the everlasting way" (Psalm 139:23–24).

Let the soul-searching run its course before turning to the next chapter.

CHAPTER TWELVE

How to Handle Criticism with Class

E rnest Hemingway reduced his definition of courage to three words, "Grace under pressure."[1] Those words aptly describe courageous people down through the centuries who pressed on against the relentless blast of opposition and criticism. Each one could have sat for a portrait titled *Grace under Pressure*. There was a day when the devil approached Martin Luther and tried to accuse him of his many sins. He presented the Reformer with a long list and started reading from the top. When Satan had finished, Luther said, "Think a little harder. You must have forgotten some. This the devil did and added more to the list. For several more exchanges they went on until the devil could come up with nothing more. Then Luther simply said, "That's fine. Now write across that long list in red ink, 'The blood of Jesus Christ, his Son, cleanses me from all sin.' And the devil had to slink away."[2]

Our nation's sixteenth president was another magnificent model of handling personal assaults on his character. Public criticism against him intensified during the last seven years of his life. One of his biographers writes:

Abraham Lincoln was slandered, libeled, and hated perhaps more intensely than any man ever to run for the nation's highest office. . . .

He was publicly called just about every name imaginable by the press of the day, including a grotesque baboon, a third-rate country lawyer who once split rails and now splits the Union, a coarse vulgar joker, a dictator, an ape, a buffoon, and others. The *Illinois State Register* labeled him "the craftiest and most dishonest politician that ever disgraced an office in America. . . ." Severe and unjust criticism did not subside after Lincoln took the oath of office, nor did it come only from Southern sympathizers. It came from within the Union itself, from Congress, from some factions within the Republican Party, and, initially, from within his own cabinet. As president, Lincoln learned that, no matter what he did, there were going to be people who would not be pleased. . . . As his enemies increased, so did the criticism against him. But Lincoln handled it all with a patience, forbearance, and determination uncommon of most men.[3]

Lincoln had four ways of responding to all that criticism. First, and most often, he simply ignored it, calling it "petty." Second, he answered back only when it was important and would make a difference. Third, he formed the habit of sitting down and writing lengthy letters in defense of his integrity and reputation, venting his anger and emotions . . . then tearing them up and never mailing them. Fourth, he always looked on the brighter side of life and kept a good sense of humor. Grace under pressure.

One of my favorite historical characters is the colorful and brilliant leader, Sir Winston Churchill. He not only handled criticism with class, he invited it. Biographer, Steven Hayward, verifies this:

He was thought to be stubborn, though it should be recognized that stubbornness is the twin of determination, and therefore requires to be kept in proportion. In fact, an important part of Churchill's method and success was his independent judgment and self-criticism. "Every night," he remarked to one of his aides during the war, "I try myself by Court Martial to see if I have done anything effective during the day. I don't mean just pawing the ground, anyone can go through the motions, but something really effective."

Despite Churchill's tendency to dominate meetings with his volubility, he always encouraged a complete discussion of issues, and never penalized or fired anyone from openly or vigorously disagreeing with him. "Opportunity was always given for full discussion," one of his wartime aides wrote. Lord Bridges wrote after the war, "I cannot recollect a single Minister, serving officer or civil servant who was removed from office because he stood up to Churchill and told Churchill that he thought his policy or proposals were wrong." Moreover, Churchill never overruled the service chiefs of staff, even when he strenuously disagreed with their decisions.[4]

One of the most eloquent examples in all of time would be King David when Absalom led a rebellion that overthrew his father. David was forced to abdicate the throne after Absalom stole the hearts of the people through deception and flattery. David, not wanting to bring harm to his own son, simply left without a fight, escaping for his life with his mighty men. While en route through a distant region, an irritating enemy named Shimei suddenly appeared at a safe distance shouting curses at the dethroned king.

Second Samuel 16 records the event, where we read, "He came out cursing continually as he came" (v. 5). Then we're told, "He threw stones at David and at all the servants of King David" (v. 6). As Shimei threw the stones he screamed, "Get out, get out, you man of bloodshed, and worthless fellow!" (v. 7). Classic example of kicking a guy when he's down. But that's the kind of man Shimei was, a real loser.

The pertinent question is: How did David respond to this nut on the loose throwing stones at him and screaming these put-downs and curses? Well, before we hear David's response, let me mention Abishai's (one of David's bodyguards) response, "May I go over there and cut off his head?" (I love that line! Had I been David, I would've nodded, and Shimei wouldn't have known his throat was cut until he sneezed.) But David graciously responded:

> Behold, my son who came out from me seeks my life; how much more now this Benjamite? Let him alone and let him curse, for the Lord has told him. Perhaps the Lord will look on my affliction and return good to me instead of his cursing this day.
>
> 2 Samuel 16:11–12

Again, grace under pressure.

One of my longtime friends and a fellow author, David Roper, has captured the essence of such grace and its lasting benefits:

> Our Lord was nailed to the cross; you can count on being nailed to the wall. It's helpful to see each ordeal that way—as being crucified with Christ. . . .
>
> God gives us over to such bruisings because they are part of the process to make us what he intends us to be. The hurting makes us sweeter, more mellow. We lose the fear of losing out; we learn to let go of what we want. We're not so easily provoked to wrath by harm or reproof. We learn to absorb abuse without retaliation, to accept reproof without defensiveness, to return a soft answer to wrath. It makes us calm and strong.[5]

BACK TO JOB . . . STILL ENDURING

There is no finer example of grace under pressure than the man we're examining. Job has suffered the destruction of all possessions, the heartbreaking deaths of all his children, and finally, the loss of health and happiness. On top of all this came the frowning presence of his friends, who are determined to wrench a confession of guilt from him, since no one would undergo such suffering if he were innocent—or so they thought.

From chapters 3 through 37 the merciless, monotonous assault continues. Two complete cycles have run their course, and Eliphaz is back for round three. You'd think by now, he would cut Job some slack. Not a chance. Matter of fact, his criticism intensifies.

ROUND THREE WITH ELIPHAZ . . . STILL CRITICIZING

According to the biblical record, Eliphaz makes three critical statements. He is neither tactful nor subtle.

- You are suffering because you have sinned. (Job 22:1–11)
- You're a hypocrite because you've hidden your sins. (Job 22:12–20)
- You need to repent because your sins are obvious to us. (Job 22:21–30)

You would think by now Job's critics would back off, but they refuse to let up. With a whole new round of verbal ammunition, Eliphaz returns to the same, third verse. He is determined to press the issue until Job comes clean.

"You are a sinner!" With sarcasm Eliphaz indicts Job:

> Is it because of your reverence that He reproves you,
> That He enters into judgment against you?
> Is not your wickedness great,
> And your iniquities without end?
>
> Job 22:4–5

Why would he say that? Remember his reasoning. Nobody suffers like this unless he is guilty. Nobody loses everything including business and family, home and health without being guilty of sin! Eliphaz makes a correct observation: Job has lost everything. But he's come to an incorrect conclusion: It wasn't because he was sinful. Job demonstrates grace under pressure by not uttering a word.

Eliphaz presses the issue:

> For you have taken pledges of your brothers without cause,
> And stripped men naked.
>
> Job 22:6

He's got a vivid imagination. Job never did that, but he's being accused of it. It's another wrong assumption.

To the weary you have given no water to drink,
And from the hungry you have withheld bread.

Job 22:7

Job never did those things either, but he sits in silence and allows it to be said.

You have sent widows away empty,
And the strength of the orphans has been crushed.

Job 22:9

Wrong again. Never did that. Harsh statement, but Job restrains his lips.

Therefore snares surround you,
And sudden dread terrifies you,
Or darkness, so that you cannot see,
And an abundance of water covers you.

Job 22:10–11

Remember, this is poetry. "Job, you have received the full reaction of the living God who can't abide sinfulness, the kind you have been hiding. Because you are sinful, you are going through all these treacherous calamities."

Can we go back to the original facts? Job's character was so pure before all his trouble started that Satan picked him out as the one he wanted to bring down and expose as a hypocrite. The Lord allowed it, knowing that Job's solid integrity and stable maturity would be able to withstand it. It was Job's unquestioned life of consistency that characterized the man— the opposite of what he's being accused. The critic Eliphaz didn't know his facts. How could he have known them? He hasn't been on the scene prior to the series of calamities. He showed up after the sickness occurred. Eliphaz didn't know what he was talking about. He's slicing and dicing Job on the basis of imaginary surmisings.

Habitual critics never get their facts straight. To make matters worse, they have lurid imaginations. They only need a little bit to go on in order to build a sandcastle full of lies. Some even feel it's their "calling" to make you squirm as they put together a twisted mass of information that cannot be proven. But, oh, the damage it can do! Even though it's hard to sit there and take it, especially when you realize that other people are listening and some believing, Job shows a lot of class as he restrains himself from responding.

"*Job, you are a hypocrite!*" The critic turns the heat up as he steps into that next realm. He now sees Job as a hypocrite, guilty of hiding his sins. He invites Job to look back.

> Is not God in the height of heaven?
> Look also at the distant stars, how high they are!
> You say, "What does God know?
> Can He judge through the thick darkness?
> Clouds are a hiding place for Him, so that He cannot see;
> And he walks on the vault of heaven."
> Will you keep to the ancient path
> Which wicked men have trod,
> Who were snatched away before their time,
> Whose foundations were washed away by a river?
> They said to God, "Depart from us!"
> And "What can the Almighty do to them?"
>
> Job 22:12–17

In our words, Eliphaz is "telling him off." It's hard enough to be told you're a sinner, but to be charged with hypocrisy adds an even lower blow. Demonstrating grace under pressure at a time like that is especially challenging for someone like Job who was the antithesis of a hypocrite.

I appreciate how Warren Wiersbe defines hypocrisy:

> A hypocrite is not a person who fails to reach his desired spiritual goals, because all of us fail in one way or another. A hypocrite is a person who doesn't even try to reach any goals, but he makes people think he has. His profession and his practice never meet.[6]

The old, Puritan preacher, Stephen Charnock, said it straight, "It is a sad thing to be Christians at a supper, heathens in our shops, and devils in our closets."[7] No question about it, hypocrisy is an awful reality. Jesus was death on it. In His earthly ministry He exposed hypocrisy more vehemently than any other vice. A major reason He delivered His Sermon on the Mount was the unashamed hypocrisy of the Pharisees.

Our God despises hypocrisy. All the more reason that Job "the servant of God" was not guilty of it. He's hiding nothing. We can be sure that, by now, Job has confessed everything. Have you ever hurt so badly that you mentally rehearsed the history of your life, revisiting all the dark corners? We can be certain that Job has been there, done that! In fact, he has admitted more than once that he's brought his life before the Lord. This is a wonderful man, whom Eliphaz is treating like a piece of trash.

"Job, you need to repent!" Eliphaz goes further. He decides to preach an evangelistic sermon to Job and maybe the man will get saved. And so he launches into an excellent evangelistic sermon. The problem is, Job's already in God's family.

Eliphaz delivers it nevertheless.

> Yield now and be at peace with Him;
> Thereby good will come to you.
> Please receive instruction from His mouth
> And establish His words in your heart.
> If you return to the Almighty, you will be restored;
> If you remove unrighteousness far from your tent,
> And place your gold in the dust,
> And the gold of Ophir among the stones of the brooks,
> Then the Almighty will be your gold
> And choice silver to you.
> For then you will delight in the Almighty
> And lift up your face to God.
> You will pray to Him and He will hear you;
> And you will pay your vows.
> You will also decree a thing, and it will be established for you;

And your light will shine on your ways,
When you are cast down, you will speak with confidence,
And the humble person He will save.

Job 22:21–29

He's going on and on with this salvation message as Job patiently sits and listens.

Showing maximum class, not once does Job interrupt Eliphaz's long-winded speech. He doesn't even attempt to set the record straight or lift his hand to ask a question. In fact, when Job does respond, he doesn't bother to defend himself. He talks to the Lord and about the Lord, but he ignores all the criticism and innuendo. Once again he models grace under pressure.

JOB RESPONDING . . . DEMONSTRATING CLASS

As we get to chapters 23 and 24 of Job we observe three calm, vulnerable responses from him. Take the time to read through these two chapters—they're magnificent! Job's first theme seems to be *"I am unable to locate the presence of God, but I trust You, Lord."* I find that coming through loud and clear in the first twelve verses of chapter 23—where our hero openly admits,

Oh that I knew where I might find Him,
That I might come to His seat!

Job 23:3

It seems that Job has a courtroom in mind. "I wish I knew the bench on which Almighty God sits. I wish I knew where I could locate Him. Some place—anyplace—on this earth that I could get to Him."

He continues:

I would present my case before Him
And fill my mouth with arguments.
I would learn the words which He would answer,
And perceive what He would say to me.

189

> Would He contend with me by the greatness of His power?
> No, surely He would pay attention to me.
>
> Job 23:4–6

Hidden within these passionate words is found one of the great things about our God. When we come to Him as we are, we never hear Him shout, "Shame on you!" God hears our pleading, our feelings of need, and He is quick to respond, "I forgive you. I love you. I understand you. I'm here; I commend you for facing the truth."

Did you notice how Job refers to the Lord's response?

> Would He contend with me by the greatness of His power?
> No, surely He would pay attention to me.
> There the upright would reason with Him;
> And I would be delivered forever from my Judge.
>
> Job 23:6–7

All of God's people find here a valuable truth we can learn from our God. When people come, open and vulnerable with their confession, there is one appropriate three-word response: *I forgive you.* They don't need to be put on the spot or shamed because they failed. They need the assurance of forgiveness. He asks, "Would He contend with me?" Then answers, "He would not contend with me, even though He's much more powerful. He would pay attention to me. I could reason with Him, and I would be delivered forever from my Judge." How wonderful is that?

But Job struggles, finally admitting his frustration: he cannot find Him.

> Behold, I go forward but He is not there,
> And backward, but I cannot perceive Him;
> When He acts on the left, I cannot behold Him;
> He turns on the right, I cannot see Him.
>
> Job 23:8–9

Ever been there? Of course, all of us have! There are days we search in vain for some visible evidence of the living God. I'm thinking, wouldn't it be great to wake up in the middle of a full-moon sky tonight, peek out my bedroom window, and see some skywriting, "Dear Chuck, I hear you. I'm right here. I'm in charge. Love, God." I would love for that to happen! I'd love to get into my pickup after a tough day at the church, turn the radio on, and have God interrupt, saying, "Before you listen to this station, Chuck, I want to talk to you for a few minutes." Let's face it, all of us would love to hear an audible voice or read a visible message from God. But that's not the way it works. Our walk with Him is a walk of faith.

I'll never forget hearing about the tragedy that struck a family of one child. The mother died abruptly and early in the child's life. The father and the daughter were suddenly left with only the memory of this wonderful wife and mother. Their grief and sorrow went deep. The night following the funeral, as the father tucked his daughter in bed, his heart went out to her, seeing that she was fighting back the tears. And he decided that he would move a cot in there. He pulled it up close beside his daughter's bed, and they soon fell asleep. In the middle of the night, he heard her crying. And he called her name. Through her tears she said, "Daddy, it's so hard. I just miss her so much." Fighting back his own tears, he reached over and took her hand. She said, "Oh, that's so much better." And she put her hand over on his shoulder and on his chest. Wanting to comfort her he said, "You know, sweetheart, we have the Lord to lean on." She said, "I know that, Daddy . . . but tonight I just need someone with skin on."[8]

If you live alone, you sometimes feel that. If you have been left alone because of a broken relationship, and where you once had close companionship, now it's only you, you must awaken sometime in the night and think, I wish I could see God right here. Right now. I wish I could reach out and touch Him or I could at least hear His words. How reassuring that would be.

Job is a great and godly man. He is a mature saint, no doubt about it. Nevertheless, he longs to witness God's presence. "Oh, that I could know where He is. But I cannot see Him, behold Him, or perceive Him."

With that, Job pauses and ponders. His perspective changes from regret to a reassurance. In the words that follow, we have some of the greatest verses found in all the Bible. I'm referring to Job 23:10–12. Many years ago I committed these three verses to memory. I must have repeated them hundreds of times to others and also to myself during the dark days I've struggled through trials. To be honest, I think I may have quoted these verses more than any other passage of Scripture. I have framed them in a box marked in bold print in my Bible; I suggest you do the same. Talk about having grace under pressure! These words will point you there. Read them slowly and carefully.

> But He knows the way I take;
> When He has tried me, I shall come forth as gold.
> My foot has held fast to His path;
> I have kept His way and not turned aside.
> I have not departed from the command of His lips;
> I have treasured the words of His mouth more than my necessary
>   food.
>
> Job 23:8–10

Though unable to locate the presence of God, Job states his trust in Him. "Eliphaz, Bildad, and Zophar, you can say whatever you wish against me. God knows the way that I take. He knows the truth. He is my Justifier. He and I are on speaking terms. I trust Him. I believe in Him. Furthermore, after the trial is over, and He has accomplished His purpose within me, 'I shall come forth as gold.'"

You can count on that, my friend. When the trial has passed, you will be deeper and richer for it. Gold will replace alloy. I want you to allow those words to burn their way into your brain so deeply that they become like a divine filter for everything that happens in your life from this day forward. God knows the way that you're taking.

One of the heretical ideas floating around these days is the "openness of God." "Open Theism" is its theoretical name as I mentioned in an earlier chapter. It says that God is still learning as He watches us respond to situations. In other words, omniscience is not really omniscience. God is engaged in a kind of progressive knowledge. Nonsense! The God of our lives is fully aware and completely in charge of the way we take. Your need and mine is to "hold fast to His path, to keep His way and not turn aside . . . nor depart from the command of His lips."

Stop and think. To what does "the command of His lips" refer? His Word. It's as if God is speaking through His lips when we open His Book. His Word teaches us, instructs us, counsels us, comforts us, reproves us, and directs our steps.

> But He knows the way I take;
> When He has tried me, I shall come forth as gold.
>
> Job 23:10

Job is embracing God's Word—it's more important than bread and water. Job states that he esteemed God's words more than anything that kept him alive. That explains the man's endurance. It helps us understand how he continued to demonstrate grace under pressure.

And so can you!

Job now makes a second declaration, which further reveals his vulnerability: "I'm unable to understand the plan of God, but I trust Him." Remember his first statement? "I'm unable to locate the presence of God, but I trust Him." Putting the two together will keep us balanced. And in each situation, we still trust Him. Job admits that God's plan is unfolding, yet he's not able to understand it. In fact, he refers to God as "unique."

> But He is unique and who can turn Him?
> And what His soul desires, that He does.
>
> Job 23:13

That's a very important statement. "What His soul desires, that He does." God doesn't ask our permission. He doesn't tell us His plan ahead of time. He doesn't give us a preview of coming attractions and then add, "Is that okay with you?" And He doesn't explain why it's so hard. He doesn't let you know how it's going to end. He doesn't tell you how long this particular episode is going to last. And so? You and I trust Him. We trust *Him*. We wait. We serve Him. We keep our feet on His paths. We treasure His Word, and whatever God desires that is what He does. We keep leaning on Him, even though we can't understand what He's up to. (And don't bother to call me. I can't explain it either!)

To make matters even more interesting, read on: "He performs what is appointed for me" (v. 14). There's a uniqueness there. Nobody else was Job, and Job had what was appointed for Job, which became his life, his lifestyle, his destiny. Just as He is performing what is appointed for you (don't get your hopes up), "many such decrees are with Him." He has a whole bunch of 'em waiting to implement once you get through this one. Isn't this exciting!

> Therefore, I would be dismayed at His presence;
> When I consider, I am terrified of Him.
>
> Job 23:15

That's great vulnerability. Go ahead and admit it—"terrified." Job finally says it. It's okay. I think the Lord loves to hear us say that on occasion. "Lord, You frighten me!"

I heard about one of the great preachers of the past who was so exasperated the Lord was taking such a long time, he went into his study, closed the door, and he said out loud, "God, hurry up! You're so slow." Job says out loud: "You frighten, You terrify me!" If you say that to Him, God will fully understand.

Saint John of the Cross, one of the fathers, wrote, "God perceives the imperfections within us." (I'll repeat that; this is deep.) God perceives the imperfections within us, and because of His love for us urges us to grow up. His love is not content to leave us in our weaknesses, and for this reason:

> He takes us into a dark night.
>
> He weans us from all the pleasures by giving us dry times and inward darkness. In doing so He is able to take away all these vices and create virtues within us. Through the dark night pride becomes

humility, greed becomes simplicity, wrath becomes contentment, luxury becomes peace, gluttony becomes moderation, envy becomes joy, and sloth becomes strength.

No soul will ever grow deep in the spiritual life unless God works passively in that soul by means of the Dark Night.[9]

Job's final response is recorded in chapter 24 of his divinely inspired journal. Since he was unable to locate the presence of God, he backed off and admitted, "I trust Him." Unable to explain the plan of God, he quietly stated, "I trust Him." (Paschal once wrote, "The eternal silence of those infinite spaces frightens me.")[10]

Job's third declaration, woven through this chapter, is equally profound: "I'm unable to justify the permissions of God, but I trust Him." What does Job mean? He starts in the country (vv. 1–11) where he sets forth several situations God permits. He then goes to the city (vv. 12–17), and he does the same. Finally at the end (vv. 18–24), he levels curses against the wicked, and leaves it at that.

For example:

> Some remove the landmarks;
> They seize and devour flocks.
>
> Job 24:2

God doesn't step in and stop them.

> They drive away the donkeys of the orphans;
> They take the widow's ox for a pledge.
>
> Job: 24:3

God doesn't stop them either; he permits it.

> They push the needy aside from the road;
> The poor of the land are made to hide themselves altogether.
>
> Job 24:4

This is not only great poetry, it's true.

> Behold, as wild donkeys in the wilderness
> They go forth seeking food in their activity,
> As bread for their children in the desert.
> They harvest their fodder in the field
> And glean the vineyard of the wicked.
> They spend the night naked, without clothing
> And have no covering against the cold.
>
> Job 24:5–7

God doesn't stop any of that.

> They are wet with the mountain rains
> And hug the rock for want of a shelter.
>
> Job 24:8

And God doesn't step in and stop it. He permits the hardship.

> Others snatch the orphan from the breast,
> And against the poor they take a pledge.
>
> Job 24:9

And on and on and on it goes down through verse 11. Job is saying these things occur by God's permissive will. Why does He permit that? We can't explain it, we only know He does.

Job then addresses many of the wrongs in the city.

> From the city men groan,
> And the souls of the wounded cry out;
> Yet God does not pay attention to folly.
> Others have been with those who rebel against the light;
> They do not want to know its ways
> Nor abide in its paths.
>
> Job 24:12–13

And God lets it happen.

> The murderer arises at dawn;
> He kills the poor and the needy,
> And at night he is as a thief.

Job 24:14

And God doesn't stop it.

> The eye of the adulterer waits for the twilight,
> Saying, "No eye will see me."
> And he disguises his face.
> In the dark they dig into houses,
> They shut themselves up by day;
> They do not know the light.
> For the morning is the same to him as thick darkness,
> For he is familiar with the terrors of thick darkness.

Job 24:15–17

We could go all the way down through this list, all the way to the end. There are wrongs, there are failures, and there are injustices. There were robberies and sexual sins and hidden wrongs done in the dark, and where is God? He is permitting it. Why? "I don't know," says Job. "I think His point here is that these things are allowed for purposes unknown to us, exactly like what's happened to me. God has permitted it all!" Those who do wrong get away with it. Those who take advantage of others get away with that. Unexplainable suffering falls into the same category.

You and I could mention events in our lifetime that the Lord could have stopped, but He didn't. This isn't just about the Jewish Holocaust. This isn't simply about the wrongs of the Crusade Era. This isn't only about the priests in the Roman Catholic Church who have molested young boys. This is also about all kinds of things that we could name, and God could have stopped each one—but He didn't. *It's a mystery!* That's the point. "I can't justify the permissions of God, but I trust Him." That's a major step, especially if one of the molested boys is your son. Or if one of the children kidnapped is your child. Or if the test on trust is aimed specifically at a trial that you and your family must endure. And so Job finishes his response by leveling curses against all the wicked.

> While Job awaits God's answer, his mind turns to the topsy-turvy affairs in the world that allow the wicked, given to self-serving, brutal deeds of violence, to oppress the weak and powerless. His own sufferings have made him more sensitive to widespread human suffering. He longs for God to rectify matters on earth. While he grieves at social evil, he remains so confident that God does eventually execute justice that he pronounces a series of curses against the wicked. Job's concern for injustice leads him to challenge the theology of his day, but at the same time, because of his profound faith in God, his lamenting drives him to God for an answer. He is anxious that God curse the wicked, holding them accountable for their evil deeds.[11]

Job is saying in effect, "You think I'm wicked? I'm telling you, if I had my way with God He would curse every one of them doing wrong. I'd stand against everything that I've named here." And verse 25 is pretty assuring, isn't it? "Now if it is not so, who can prove me a liar, and make my speech worthless?"

Can any stand up and say, "This is nonsense"? No one could say that, not even Eliphaz. Job's passionate response leaves his critics sitting in silence.

LESSONS THAT LINGER . . . EVEN TO THIS DAY

The major message Job leaves us is fairly obvious by now: Even though God is elusive and mysterious, strange and silent, invisible and seemingly passive, *He is trustworthy.* In light of that, I want to suggest these three lessons that linger.

First, resist the temptation to explain everything; God knows.

Second, focus on the future benefits, not the present pain; God leads.

Third, embrace the sovereignty of the Almighty; God controls.

Refuse to believe that life is based on blind fate or random chance.

Everything that happens, including the things you cannot explain or justify, is being woven together like an enormous, beautiful piece of tapestry. From this earthly side it seems blurred and knotted, strange and twisted. But from heaven's perspective it has an incredible pattern. Best of all, it is for His greater glory. Right now, it seems so confusing, but someday the details will come together and make good sense.

Early in this chapter I quoted from Dave Roper's book, *Elijah, a Man Like Us*. I return to it for a story he tells that vividly illustrates my point.

Recently Carolyn and I were on the first leg of a flight from Frankfurt, Germany, to our home in Boise, Idaho. Our first stop was Boston.

It had been an exhausting week and I dropped off to sleep as soon as I found my seat, but I was soon awakened by a disturbance in the aisle.

The steward and a passenger who had been seated on Carolyn's left were arguing about the man's seat assignment. Somehow, he had been separated from his fiancée who was seated several rows behind us.

The man grew increasingly angry and argumentative until another passenger, seated by the man's fiancée offered to trade places. The swap was made and Carolyn's new seat-mate settled into his place, drew out a legal pad, and began to work on some project.

Unfortunately, there was a garrulous little French boy seated on his left—a charming child—who wanted to talk. The man, who seemed to be the soul of patience, gave up his project after a few minutes and began to chat amiably with the boy. Carolyn was soon drawn into the conversation.

I heard the man say he was from Los Gatos, California, a town close to Los Altos, California, where Carolyn and I had lived for eighteen years. He was on the Frankfurt-to-Boston leg of a flight to San Francisco. I heard Carolyn remark on the fact that we had many friends in the Bay Area and then I went back to sleep.

When I awakened an hour or so later, I found Carolyn sharing her faith with her new-found friend, scribbling on his pad of paper, drawing diagrams, and animating her story. He was listening intently and asking questions. I sat there quietly and prayed for her and the man.

At one point he said, "You believe as my wife does."

"Oh?" Carolyn replied. "And how did she become a follower of Christ?"

"Through Bible Study Fellowship," he responded.

"How did she find out about Bible Study Fellowship?" Carolyn asked.

"A friend of hers, Nel King, invited her to attend."

"That's remarkable!" Carolyn exclaimed. "Nel King is one of my best friends!"

And then the coin dropped: A few months before we moved to Boise, Nel had asked Carolyn to pray for a friend who had just become a Christian through Bible Study Fellowship and for her husband who was not yet a believer—the man now seated on Carolyn's left—there "by that power which erring men call chance."[12]

There it is—part of God's perfect plan unfolding. You can't explain it. You couldn't piece it all together if you tried. You aren't able to understand it and there will be times you won't like it. But, as we're learning from Job, He's not going to ask your permission. And so? We trust God. I'll write it once more: Those who do that discover without trying to make it happen that they have begun to demonstrate grace under pressure. To settle for less is a miserable existence.

CHAPTER THIRTEEN

The Futility of Unscrewing the Inscrutable

The study of Job is essentially the study of God Himself. Think about it.

- It was God who first met with Satan and struck the deal regarding Job.
- It was God who released the Adversary to go after Job.
- It was God who set the boundaries, placing limitations on each attack.
- It was God who permitted all of it to happen, start to finish.
- It was God (as we shall see in chapter 17) who broke the silence and spoke to Job.

And it was God who finally set the record straight, rebuking the "sorry counselors" and rewarding His faithful servant.

All the way through the story, it is God who captures our attention and makes us wonder. Better stated, He confuses us.

We who were reared in the church learned from our earliest years that God is good, loving, merciful, compassionate, just, fair, holy, full of mercy and grace. He "sympathizes with our weaknesses" (Hebrews 4:15), "knows what you need before you ask Him" (Matthew 6:8), and "satisfies your years with good things" (Psalm 103:5). Remember the memorized mealtime prayer? "God is great, God is good, let us thank Him for this food. Amen."

Then we encounter Job. And we see God stepping back into the shadows, permitting Satan to afflict His godly servant, as He stays silent, keeps a distance, and refuses to answer when Job pleads for an explanation. I'll go ahead and say it—all that seems downright cruel. If not cruel, it is certainly in conflict with the God we met as kids in Sunday school.

And so we're left with one of two conclusions. Either we weren't given a complete and correct understanding of our God, or we do not really understand the story of Job. I suggest it's the former. The picture we were given in Sunday school was incomplete.

Paul wrote a brief yet profound statement regarding the Lord our God in Romans 11:33. I ask you to pause and let its words sink in. Read it slowly, preferably aloud, and read it more than once before going on.

> Oh, the depth of the riches both of the wisdom and knowledge of God!
> How unsearchable are His judgments and unfathomable His ways!

Please take the time to ponder two words in that second sentence. Unsearchable. Unfathomable. Allow them to land with full weight on your mind.

As far back as the first century, when Paul penned his letter, he informed his readers in Rome (ultimately us), that God is *unfathomable* and *unsearchable*. Now, don't misunderstand. That doesn't mean He stops being good, and it doesn't mean He is no longer loving and merciful. He is still all of that but so much more. He is also incomprehensible. He is deep. His ways are beyond our understanding, seeming mysterious and inexplicable to us. The longer we think on this the more we realize there is a lot about God we were never taught. In the midst of our study of Job, we are forced to dig much deeper into His character and discover new depths. In a word, God is *inscrutable*.

One of the first times I remember that word making a dent in my brain occurred when I was graduating from seminary in the spring of 1963. The president of Dallas Seminary was the late Dr. John F. Walvoord, a man I always admired for his clear-thinking, theological mind. He told our graduating class that he would hope all of us would continue to remember that our God is inscrutable. He then quoted Romans 11:33. Looking around the campus chapel audience, he added with a wry smile, "There will be times you will try to unscrew the inscrutable. You cannot do so!"[1] As usual, Dr. Walvoord was right. But we so want to do that. Everything within us longs to explain everything about God and interpret all His ways and come to a full understanding of all the workings of God.

After all, God made us intelligent beings. Furthermore, He instructs us to know Him. Longing to do that, we continue to pursue this divine understanding, but the deeper we dig, the more unfathomable He becomes. Why, of course! That shouldn't surprise us, but we're frustrated not knowing. We prefer things fathomable, or, if you will, "scrutable." We want to be able to explain and correctly analyze *whatever*, so that we understand the whole story. But that is impossible when it comes to the living and reigning God.

It is especially important that we realize He is not like us, neither are His methods like ours. Not even a little bit. As the prophet Isaiah reminds us of God:

> For My thoughts are not your thoughts,
> Neither are your ways My ways," declares the LORD
> "For as the heavens are higher than the earth,
> So are My ways higher than your ways
> And My thoughts than your thoughts."
>
> Isaiah 55:8–9

We are finite; He is infinite. Our ways are limited; His unlimited. We are small; He is vast. An imaginary journey into outer space assists in realizing the enormity of God.

> If it were possible to travel the speed of light, you could arrive at the moon in 1 1/3 seconds. But continuing at that same speed, do you know how long it would take you to reach the closest star? Four years.

New York City's Hayden Planetarium has a miniature replica of our solar system showing the speeds and sizes of our planets. What is interesting is that the three outer planets are not even included. There wasn't room for Uranus, Neptune, and Pluto. Uranus would be in the planetarium's outer corridor. Neptune would be around Eighth Avenue. And Pluto? Another three long avenues away at Fifth Avenue. By the way, no stars are included, for obvious reasons. Can you imagine (on the same scale) where the nearest star would be located? Cleveland, Ohio. Vast! And, remember, that's just our own local galaxy.

A scientist once suggested another interesting analogy. To grasp the scene, imagine a perfectly smooth glass pavement on which the finest speck can be seen. Then shrink our sun from 865,000 miles in diameter to only two feet . . . and place a ball on the pavement to represent the sun.

Step off 82 paces (about two feet per pace), and to represent proportionately the first planet, Mercury, put down a tiny mustard seed. Take 60 steps more and for Venus put down an ordinary BB. Mark 78 more steps . . . put down a green pea representing earth. Step off 108 paces from there, and for Mars, put down a pinhead. Sprinkle around some fine dust for the asteroids, then take 788 steps more and place an orange on the glass for Jupiter. After 934 more steps, put down a golf ball for Saturn.

Now it gets really involved. Mark 2,086 steps more, and for Uranus . . . a marble. Another 2,322 steps from there you arrive at Neptune. Let a cherry represent Neptune. This will take 2 1/2 miles, and we haven't even discussed Pluto.

We have a smooth glass surface 5 miles in diameter, yet just a tiny fraction of the heavens, excluding Pluto. Now, guess how far we'd have to go on the same scale before we could put down another two-foot ball to represent the nearest star. We'd have to go 6,720 miles before we could arrive at that star. Miles, not feet! And that's just the first star among millions. In one galaxy among hundreds, maybe thousands. And all of it in perpetual motion . . . perfectly synchronized . . . the most accurate timepiece known to man.[2]

David, in Psalm 139, makes the appropriate comment, "*Such* knowledge is too wonderful for me; it is too high, I cannot attain to it" (v. 6). If David lived today, he would write, "This blows my mind." The vastness of God's inscrutability has a way of doing that to us—and so it should.

Addressing the subject of God's inscrutability, A. W. Tozer writes,

> Left to ourselves we tend immediately to reduce God to manageable terms. We want to get Him where we can use Him, or at least know where He is when we need Him. We want a God we can in some measure control. We need the feeling of security that comes from knowing what God is like, and what He is like is of course a composite of all the religious pictures we have seen, all the best people we have known or heard about, and all the sublime ideas we have entertained.
>
> If all this sounds strange to modern ears, it is only because we have for a full half century taken God for granted. The glory of God has not been revealed to this generation of men. The God of contemporary Christianity is only slightly superior to the gods of Greece and Rome, if indeed He is not actually inferior to them in that He is weak and helpless while they at least had power. . . .
>
> That God can be known by the soul in tender personal experience while remaining infinitely aloof from the curious eyes of reason constitutes a paradox.[3]

BACK TO JOB IN ALL HIS MISERY

If nothing else, the study of Job reveals we do not fully understand God's ways. We cannot explain the inexplicable. We cannot fathom the unfathomable. So let's not try to unscrew the inscrutable.

If only the men who considered themselves Job's friends had acknowledged that. It would have been so much more comforting to Job, sitting in such enormous misery, longing for an arm around his shoulder and someone honest enough to say, "We're here, but we don't understand why this is happening any more than you do. God knows, but we're here to be with you through it. God is doing something deep and mysterious, but it is so beyond us we cannot understand it either."

May I go one step further? God doesn't have a "wonderful plan" for everybody's life. Not here on earth, for sure. For some lives His plan is Lou Gehrig's disease. For some lives (like Job's) His plan is a life of pain. For others, heartbreak and brokenness, blindness or paralysis, or congenital complications. For many, His plan is No to their requests for healing. But we don't like that. Some won't accept that. In fact, they go so far as to say, "If you believe that, you lack faith." On the contrary, if you believe that, you believe the Bible!

The God of the Bible includes the lives of people who do not get well, who do not quickly get over their problems, who do not easily overcome accidents or illnesses. God's Word pictures its heroes, warts and all. They hurt. They fall. They fail, and on occasion, by His grace, they succeed.

BILDAD'S FOOLISH MEANDERINGS

Since Bildad didn't have a clue about God's inscrutability, we should not be surprised to hear more philosophical ramblings as we return to his third round of assaults on Job. He begins by rehearsing some generalities about God. What he says is true, but as usual, it brings no comfort or consolation to Job.

> Then Bildad the Shuhite answered,
> "Dominion and awe belong to Him
> Who establishes peace in His heights.
> Is there any number to His troops?
> And upon whom does His light not rise?
> How then can a man be just with God?
> Or how can he be clean who is born of woman?
> If even the moon has no brightness
> And the stars are not pure in His sight,
> How much less man, that maggot,
> And the son of man, that worm!"
>
> Job 25:1–6

Four observations seem worth noting:

First, this is Bildad's third and last presentation. (I would add, "Thank the Lord!")

Second, this is the shortest chapter in the entire book of Job, containing only six verses.

Third, it is brief, no doubt, because there is very little left to say. Furthermore, by now I would suspect that Bildad considered Job unteachable, so why waste his "brilliant insights" on the man?

Fourth, having run out of arguments, Bildad doesn't spend any more time attempting to prove Job wrong, he simply lectures. This represents Bildad's last shot. He speaks first of God's power and greatness and then of God's justice and man's sinfulness. In so many words he is telling Job that God is all light, and he is all darkness, and that's why he's suffering. His two concluding analogies "maggot" and "worm" pretty much wrap things up.

At various times my heart truly goes out to Job. This is one of those times. Has anyone ever called you a maggot or a worm? Well, maybe someone did in a fit of uncontrolled anger, behind closed doors. Chances are good they later apologized—or should have. But in this case I think Bildad really meant it. By now he is so exasperated he has absolutely no use for Job. It seems to be his final, "Just get out of my life." It's the ultimate put-down.

There are a lot of lessons to learn from this story. One surfaces right here: Whenever you have the opportunity to be with someone in great need—even if what they're going through is the result of their own wrongdoing or failure, putting them down never helps. Tragically, that is what these men were so good at. And it only made things worse. So, is it any wonder that Job begins with a series of sarcastic verbal slams in return?

JOB'S STRONG REACTION

What a help you are to the weak!
How you have saved the arm without strength!

Job 26:2

The Hebrew seems to be saying, "How you have saved with your arm—

the one without strength." The way it has been translated into English doesn't make good sense. I believe Job is using sarcasm to seize Bildad's attention. He continues using the same style:

> What counsel you have given to one without wisdom!
> What helpful insight you have abundantly provided!
> To whom have you uttered words?
> And whose spirit was expressed through you?
>
> Job 26:3–4

Oh, Bildad! You've really got a corner on the truth! Eugene Peterson's paraphrase helps:

> Well, you've certainly been a great help to a helpless man!
> You came to the rescue just in the nick of time!
> What wonderful advice you've given to a mixed-up man!
> What amazing insights you've provided!
> Where in the world did you learn all this?
> How did you become so inspired?
>
> Job 26:2–4, MSG

By the way, the Hebrew pronouns in verses 2, 3, and 4 are all singular, so they're directed only to Bildad. When we arrive at Job 27, the plural kicks back in. But for now, these words are sent like sword thrusts. Jab . . . jab! Twist . . . twist!

What Job lacked here in tact, he made up for in total honesty. Frankly, this was no time for tact. Bildad has been brutal. It's doubtful he would even hear if Job had been soft and diplomatic. Job gets tough!

Sores will do that to you. Any nurse will tell you, especially those who work at the bedside of patients in great pain, that tact fades as pain progresses. There's something about the continuation of anguish that finally wears a soul down to raw, red reality.

Many years ago I came across this statement: "Pain plants the flag of reality in the fortress of a rebel heart."[4] Even among those who have been stubborn and rebellious, when pain hits and persists, reality comes in full measure. So it was with Job. He took off the gloves, looked into Bildad's eyes, and said it straight. The man needed that kind of response.

There's a little prayer I'd suggest you repeat each morning.

> Lord, help me today not to add to anybody's burden. Help me to bring encouragement to others. Where I can, enable me to comfort. And when I don't know, help me to admit it. When I feel sorrow and sympathy for someone, help me to say that. Help me to lift the load of the hurting, not to add to their burden.

If others are going through an agonizing experience, they need us to be of support and strength. Bildad never learned that principle; he never prayed that prayer. Too bad.

An intriguing change of roles now occurs. Instead of Bildad teaching Job, Job becomes the teacher. It's almost as if he decides, "Since you don't have any answers, let me tell you about the infinite, incomprehensible God, who hasn't revealed all the whys and wherefores of His activities."

From verse 5 through verse 13, of chapter 26, Job takes Bildad through the paces. He communicates what we would call a fascinating, cosmological explanation. Amazingly, Job starts with the departed spirits of the dead then goes all the way to the top of the universe. In a simple, straightforward manner, Job is saying, "God is in control of every bit of it. He knows about it, He understands it, He is in the midst of it and takes full responsibility for all of it. None of it is a surprise to the living God." Witness that for yourself as you read Job's presentation:

> The departed spirits tremble
> Under the waters and their inhabitants.
> Naked is Sheol before Him,
> And Abaddon has no covering.
>
> Job 26:5–6

This is a resplendent mosaic of our Lord's superiority over all. He is absolutely sovereign, even over the "departed spirits, covered by the waters, in the place of Sheol and Abaddon." He goes on . . .

He stretches out the north over empty space
And hangs the earth on nothing.

Job 26:7

Isn't this amazing? Here is an ancient piece of poetic literature full of wonderful truth. Job has not been contaminated by the evolutionary thinking of the scholars of the twenty-first century. He just believes by faith that when God put planet Earth together, He stretched it out over empty space and hung it "on nothing."

God planned it and put it all together. "In the beginning God made the heavens and the earth." How profoundly simple the first verse of Genesis is! God said "Let it be" and it became, and He hung it on nothing. This is beautiful.

Job is instructing Bildad. Whether Bildad is listening or not, who knows? But the beautiful thing is that Job has a relationship with God that Bildad never heard of. And because of that relationship, Job can rely on God for whatever he may need. There is great comfort found when we rely on God in simple faith. We trust. We stay strong. Mainly, we pray so we can make it through the challenges life throws at us. Last year a teacher sent me a very unusual response written by an applicant for a teaching position. The potential teacher delivered it to the school administration hoping to describe the dilemma of being a teacher in today's culture.

Let me see if I've got this right. You want me to go into that room with all those kids and fill their every waking moment with a love for learning. Not only that, I'm supposed to instill a sense of pride in their ethnicity, behaviorally modify disruptive behavior, observe them for signs of abuse and T-shirt messages. I am to fight the war on drugs and sexually transmitted diseases, check their backpacks for guns and raise their self-esteem. I'm to teach them patriotism, good citizenship, sportsmanship and fair play, how and where to register to vote, how to balance a checkbook and how to apply for a job. I am to check their heads occasionally for lice, maintain a safe environment, recognize signs of potential antisocial behavior, offer advice, write letters of recommendation for student employment and scholarships, encourage respect for the cultural diversity of others, and, oh yeah, always make sure that I give the girls in my class 50 percent of my attention.

I'm required by my contract to be working on my own time summer and evenings at my own expense toward advance certification and a master's degree; and after school, I am to attend committee and faculty meetings and participate in staff development training to maintain my employment status.

I am to be a paragon of virtue larger than life, such that my very presence will awe my students into being obedient and respectful of authority. I am to pledge allegiance to supporting family values, a return to the basics, and to my current administration. I am to incorporate technology into the learning, and monitor all Web sites while providing a personal relationship with each student. I am to decide who might be potentially dangerous and/or liable to commit crimes in school or who is possibly being abused, and I can be sent to jail for not mentioning these suspicions.

I am to make sure all students pass the state and federally mandated testing and all classes, whether or not they attend school on a regular basis or complete any of the work assigned. Plus, I am expected to make sure that all of the students with handicaps are guaranteed a free and equal education, regardless of their mental or physical handicap.

I am to communicate frequently with each student's parent by letter, phone, newsletter, and grade card. I'm to do all of this with just a piece of chalk, a computer, a few books, a bulletin board, a 45 minute more-or-less plan time and a big smile, all on a starting salary that qualifies my family for food stamps in many states.

Is that all? And you want me to do all of this and expect me NOT TO PRAY?[5]

Sounds like something Job would say to his alleged "friends." "You want me to do all of these things without any encouragement from you to turn to and trust in the living God?

Since you acknowledge His inscrutable workings to me, let me explain that to you! Bildad, consider the incredible, incomprehensibility, of His nature. Ponder the inscrutable power of His person, controlling those who have gone beyond the jaws of death. Give serious thought to His inscrutable creation of this earth—and His continuing handiwork.

> He stretches out the north over empty space
> And hangs the earth on nothing.
> He wraps up the waters in His clouds,
> And the cloud does not burst under them.
> He obscures the face of the full moon
> And spreads His cloud over it.
> He has inscribed a circle on the surface of the waters
> At the boundary of light and darkness.
> The pillars of heaven tremble
> And are amazed at His rebuke.
> He quieted the sea with His power,
> And by His understanding he shattered Rahab.
> By His breath, the heavens are cleared;
> His hand has pierced the fleeing serpent.
>
> Job 26:7–13

It's as if Job is saying, "Bildad, our God is in charge of all of that. He has all of it under His control!" Then he reaches the climax with this final statement:

> Behold, these are the fringes of His ways;
> And how faint a word we hear of Him!
> But His mighty thunder, who can understand?
>
> Job 26:14

Isn't that a thrilling thought? "Bildad, as magnificent as all of these things are, what I've mentioned represents only the fringes of His ways." Isn't that a great word? The fringes, the outer edges of His ways; only the quiet whispers of His mighty voice, the hushed tones of omnipotence. *Bildad—listen to me!* Who can fully understand? And to think that this Creator-God pierces through all the millions of galaxies of "the heavens" and gives His attention to this tiny green-pea planet called Earth, reaching down to folks like us, knowing even the hairs on our head. David was right: "It is too high, I cannot attain to it."

> What is man that You take thought of him,
> And the son of man that You care for him?
>
> Psalm 8:4

Perspective like that is needed when the sores on my body are running with pus and the fever won't go down. Job ends where Bildad should have begun. "Who can understand?"

Indeed, how unsearchable are His judgments and unfathomable are His ways. Now, be careful here. That does not mean He's not in touch, out of control, and He doesn't have a plan. It just means He isn't obligated to explain Himself. And because He doesn't reveal everything, we're left with three very honest words, which are helpful coming from the lips of otherwise proud people.

And what are those three words? *I don't know.*

In the final analysis, God knows, and He does all things well. He is in charge. I am the clay; He is the Potter. I am the disciple; He is the Lord. I am the sheep; He is the Shepherd. I am the servant; He is the Master. That means I am to submit myself. I am to humble myself under His mighty hand. I must be willing to adjust my life to His choices for me, to listen, to learn, to adapt to His leading wherever it may go whether I'm comfortable, happy, or healthy. That is obedience. Job by now is beginning to see it, and when he reaches the end of his brief explanation, he wisely asks, "Who can understand?"

Let's return to my opening statement: The study of Job is essentially the study of God.

> Without doubt, the mightiest thought the mind can entertain is the thought of God, and the weightiest word in any language is its word for God. . . .

A right conception of God is basic not only to systematic theology but to practical Christian living as well. It is to worship what the foundation is to the temple. . . .

It is my opinion that the Christian conception of God . . . is so decadent as to be utterly beneath the dignity of the Most High God and actually to constitute for professed believers something amounting to a moral calamity. . . .

Let us beware lest we in our pride accept the erroneous notion that idolatry consists only in kneeling before visible objects of adoration, and that civilized peoples are therefore free from it. The essence of idolatry is the entertainment of thoughts about God that are unworthy of Him. It begins in the mind and may be present where no overt act of worship has taken place. . . .

Perverted notions about God soon rot the religion in which they appear. . . . The first step down for any church is taken when it surrenders its high opinion of God. . . .

The heaviest obligation lying upon the Christian Church today is to purify and elevate her concept of God. . . . In all her prayers and labors this should have first place. We do the greatest service to the next generation of Christians by passing on to them undimmed and undiminished that noble concept of God which we received from our Hebrew and Christian fathers of generations past. This will prove of greater value to them than anything that art or science can devise.[6]

Train yourself to think theologically. Make it your determined purpose to think God's thoughts after Him, acknowledging His lofty magnificence. Teach yourself to be at ease saying the words, "I don't know."

Because Job thought correctly about God, he was able to endure, even while not understanding why. May his tribe increase.

CHAPTER FOURTEEN

A Recommitment To Things That Matter

S uffering helps us clarify our priorities and focus on the right objectives. The deeper the pain, the clearer the vision. The more we hurt,
the better we determine what really matters. During the process, we
replace knowledge with wisdom.

Each time our nation returns to another anniversary of September 11,
we pause and reflect on all that happened: The synchronized, premedi-
tated strategy of multiple murders that shocked us; the headlines and pictures that filled our newspapers and magazines for weeks; the thousands of
families who grieved the loss of loved ones. Each year we read the testimo-
nies of real people who were devastated by that series of atrocities. It isn't
uncommon for them to include words that mention some of the lessons
learned, resulting in renewed commitments to priorities.

One surviving New York cop said, "As a result of those atrocities, I will never
again take our liberty for granted." A middle-aged widow, whose husband was
killed in the World Trade Center, expressed it this way, "I now hug my children
tightly every day. I always tell them I love them every morning and every evening
before we go to bed." One forty-eight-year-old stockbroker who lost several

coworkers on 9/11 admitted, "I've decided to hold my business and my career much more loosely; my family and friends have now become more important to me." Suffering helps clear away the fog that success and prosperity create.

Pastor John Piper has written a book to fellow pastors. I love the title: *Brothers, We Are Not Professionals*. In his opening paragraph, he talks about the value of suffering.

> Sometimes massive suffering comes so close to home that for a brief season the fog of our foolish security clears, and we can see the sheer precipice of eternity one step away. The cold wobble passes through our thighs, and for a moment everything in the universe looks different. Those are good times for pastoral realism. Oh, how hollow much of our lives and ministry seem in those moments! The last thing we regret then is being less professional.[1]

I think the same is true in the business world. I cannot recall ever hearing a once-successful, professional person, now lying on a bed dying with cancer saying, "I wish I'd spent more time at the office."

If Job could speak today, he would verify all of this, urging us to pause and reasses. Once his children were taken in that freak tornado and his business went belly-up as a result of the cataclysmic series of events, his health went south, covering his body with boils, and his fever rose to dangerous levels, we never hear Job lamenting his missing the turn of a deal. He never mentions longing for a lucrative contract that would enlarge his camel-caravan business. You don't think about that when you're hanging on to life by a thread. Suffering helps us clarify our priorities.

I've lived long enough to be convinced that suffering is not an enemy. Seems strange to put it this way, but the truth is, it is a friend. Not until we acknowledge that will we glean its benefits. Job is living in the crucible. His misery in that difficult arena has forced him to focus on things that really matter.

Interestingly, he doesn't talk about those things until his friends stop talking. A week after they showed up they began to blame. They pointed fingers. They lectured, insulted, and condemned him. By the time they finally quieted down, it all began to distill in Job's mind to the point where he, in a brief interlude of time, began to see things clearly.

I have finally come to realize that one of the benefits of going through times of suffering is that my focus turns vertical. Charles Spurgeon, the great pulpiteer of London for so many years, was a flashpoint of controversy. The media of his day relished taking him on. They took advantage of a target that big. Normally he could hold his own, but there was one occasion when it began to get the best of him. All of us have our breaking point.

His wife noticed a depression that was lingering. She became concerned for him that he not lose his zeal and not miss the opportunities that were his while going through such hard times. That led her to do an unusual thing. She turned in her Bible to the Sermon on the Mount where Jesus said:

> Blessed are you when people insult you and persecute you, and falsely say all kinds of evil against you because of me. Rejoice and be glad, for your reward in heaven is great; for in the same way they persecuted the prophets who were before you.
>
> Matthew 5:11–12

In her own handwriting she wrote those words on a large piece of paper. She then taped it on the ceiling above their bed. When the preacher turned over the next morning, he awoke, blinked his eyes, and as he lay there he read those words. He read them again, aloud. He focused vertically on what God was saying, and it renewed him within. He pressed on with new passion. What a wonderful, creative idea Mrs. Spurgeon had!

When flat on our backs, the only way to look is up. It worked. He stopped licking his wounds and, like Job, he looked past all the criticism and began again to be preoccupied with thoughts of God. [2]

JOB'S VERTICAL FOCUS

As we arrive at chapter 27 of Job, his vertical perspective quickly emerges. In seven statements he refers to the name of his God no less than eleven times. (Italics are mine.)

As *God* lives, who has taken away my right
And *the Almighty*, who has embittered my soul, . . .

Job 27:2

For as long as life is in me,
And the breath of *God* is in my nostrils, . . .

Job 27:3

For what is the hope of the godless when he is cut off,
When *God* requires his life?

Job 27:8

Will *God* hear his cry
When distress comes upon him?

Job 27:9

Will he take delight in *the Almighty*?
Will he call on *God* at all times?

Job 27:10

I will instruct you in the power of *God*;
What is with *the Almighty* I will not conceal.

Job 27:11

This is the portion of a wicked man from *God*,
And the inheritance which tyrants receive from *the Almighty*.

Job 27:13

The single most important One to Job is his God. It is the Almighty. It is the Lord.

JOB'S MAIN PRIORITIES

This gives us the first of five priorities that are worth remembering. Job's priorities at this point in his life begin with his relationship with the Lord Himself.

218

Thinking God's thoughts is our highest goal. I've already referred to this in a previous chapter. I called it thinking theologically or thinking biblically. That is one of the reasons I'm such a proponent of the discipline of Scripture memorization. You cannot think God's thoughts more acutely than when you quote God's very words back to life's situations.

What comes into our minds when we think about God is the most important thing about us. And so what comes to mind when *you* think about God? I remember as a little boy thinking of God as a very old man with a long white beard, cheeks puffed out, blowing strong winds from the north. I had seen His face at school on old maps of the world.

What comes to your mind when you think about God? Do you see Him as the One who gives you breath and keeps your heart beating? Do you see Him as the One who will call everyone into judgment someday? Do you see Him as the One who watches over your children and your business? Do you acknowledge His power is greater than any power you would ever witness on this earth? Or, honestly now, is He a little remote, sort of out of touch with today's hi-tech society? Your view of God makes all the difference in how you view life.

Think of Job's situation; he is now bankrupt, childless, friendless, and diseased. Covered with boils, he is living with a high fever and constant pain. On top of that he is misunderstood, being blamed for secret sins and is now rejected by those who once respected him. How in the world does he go on? There is only one answer: His view of God keeps him going, not what others are saying. And in light of that, he recommits himself to things that matter. In a swirl of humanistic thinking, coming from Eliphaz, Bildad, and Zophar, whom Job has mentally turned off, he is now focused fully on the things of God.

In fact, he says, because he is so focused he will not pad the record; he will not speak deceitfully; he will not tell them what isn't true. He continues . . .

> For as long as life is in me,
> And the breath of God is in my nostrils,
> My lips certainly will not speak unjustly,
> Nor will my tongue mutter deceit.
> Far be it from me that I should declare you right;

> Till I die I will not put away my integrity from me.
>
> Job 27:3–5

This introduces us to Job's second priority: *Walking in integrity is the only way to live.* He refuses to skate. He's not going to fake it. He will neither lie nor deceive them. He will speak only the truth.

How refreshing and reassuring! How memorable it is to be around those rare souls who have gained control of their tongues. Job qualified. Through his afflictions he gained the upper hand over his speech. Never again would he be dominated by the strongest muscle in his body.

I had a physician tell me not to be hesitant about calling the tongue the strongest muscle in the body. "Anatomically it's true," he said. "The muscle makeup of the tongue would qualify it as certainly one of the strongest muscles, if not the strongest in the human body."

The point in undeniable. You've got a powerful muscle in your mouth. Realizing its potential impact, Job says, in effect, "My lips will be lips of integrity. I refuse to use them as vehicles of deceit."

In light of that he restates his disagreement with his critics' conclusions: "Far be it from me that I should declare you right" (v. 5). Because I believe you are wrong, for me to call wrong right is not the correct use of my tongue. That would lack integrity. "I hold fast my righteousness and will not let it go. My heart does not reproach any of my days" (v. 6). What a remarkable way to live.

We come to the third priority when we reach the central section of Job's words. He changes the subject and shifts his attention to the wicked, whom he calls "tyrants."

> This is the portion of a wicked man from God,
> And the inheritance which tyrants receive from the Almighty.
> Though his sons are many, they are destined for the sword;
> And his descendants will not be satisfied with bread.
> His survivors will be buried because of the plague,
> And their widows will not be able to weep.
> Though he piles up silver like dust

> And prepares garments as plentiful as the clay,
> He may prepare it, but the just will wear it
> And the innocent will divide the silver.
>
> Job 27:13–17

Isn't that closing comment a great line? The wicked man may have more clothes in his closet, but he'll wind up leaving them to us. Remember the materialistic line that is framed around license plates?" "He who dies with the most toys wins." The truth is: He who dies with the most toys passes them off to the righteous, and the righteous get to enjoy them! Job has come to realize this third priority: *Wrong will occur but it will not ultimately triumph.* That brings a sense of justice.

To clarify Job's realization, let me quote the last section of chapter 27 from *The Message*:

> Even if they make a lot of money
>   and are resplendent in the latest fashions,
> It's the good who will end up wearing the clothes
>   and the decent who will divide up the money.
> They build elaborate houses
>   that won't survive a single winter.
> They go to bed wealthy
>   and wake up poor.
> Terrors pour in on them like flash floods—
>   a tornado snatches them away in the middle of the night,
> A cyclone sweeps them up—gone!
>   Not a trace of them left, not even a footprint.
> Catastrophes relentlessly pursue them;
>   they run this way and that, but there's no place to hide—
> Pummeled by the weather,
>   blown to kingdom come by the storm.
>
> Job 27:16–23, MSG

Frequently I remind myself of the proverb that says,

Do not weary yourself to gain wealth,
Cease from your consideration of it.
When you set your eyes on it, it is gone.
For wealth certainly makes itself wings
Like an eagle that flies *toward* the heavens.

Proverbs 23:4–5

There go those great riches! How often have we witnessed or heard about individuals who are loaded financially. But with many of them it isn't too many years before it is gone. Those riches were like an eagle—they made themselves wings.

Rest assured, God keeps accurate records. He knows what He's about. Furthermore, He knows who is righteous and who is wicked.

It's easy to become confused if you watch too much of the evening news on television. Be very discerning about what you watch and what you read. If the source is not reliable, the information will be skewed. Thankfully there are still some in our day who think straight and aren't afraid to say so. Their words remind us that evil is evil, that wrong actions will be judged. That even though the wicked may seem to be winning, they will ultimately lose!

On the first anniversary of 9/11 I received an e-mail that falls into the category of straight-thinking, reliable information:

It is hard to believe that one year has passed since the vicious attacks on our country by radical Islamists in New York, Washington, D.C., and Pennsylvania. The word "tragedy" is being repeated endlessly today, but it is the wrong word to describe the events of that day. This was not a "misfortune" or a "turn of fate." It was a deliberate act of war that intentionally targeted Americans for death. For those who are politically correct, it was the ultimate hate crime.

The 19 hijackers on September 11 and the hundreds of others who helped implement the plan were not the products of injustice or poverty. Their acts cannot be excused by any failure of American foreign policy. They are the product of a radical vision of Islam that believes their faith is to be spread by the sword and that America and Israel, Christians and Jews, must be destroyed.

This radical Islamist vision is what explains the joy expressed by some Palestinian mothers when they are told their teenage sons strapped explosive belts around their chests, packed with chards of glass and nails, and died killing Jews at Passover dinners or in crowded cafes. It is what motivates the kidnappers of Daniel Pearl, who was tormented on videotape, forced to say, "I am a Jew," and decapitated. It is what leads the Islamic government of Sudan to kill millions of African Christians in a genocide that much of the world, including too many religious leaders in the United States, has chosen to ignore. It is why Christian churches in Pakistan have been invaded by hand-grenade-throwing thugs and why Christian villages in Indonesia and Nigeria have been attacked by Islamic mobs.

And it's why jets are flying shotgun today over Washington, D.C. and New York City and shipping containers coming into our country are being checked for "dirty" nuclear bombs or biological agents. The followers of radical Islam want to kill more of us; they want to see America destroyed. They feel no compassion. They cannot be reasoned with. They are planning, even now in the darkest of shadows, to strike at us again. That is the reality of the world we now live in and what we must keep at the center of our thinking if we are to win this war. And win it we must!

America is imperfect. All nations are in this fallen world. But America has been and still remains a beacon of hope for people around the world yearning to be free. Our impulses are decent and good. Our army has not marched through the years for conquest—it has marched to break the chains of Nazism and communism—to make other people free. We have taught our defeated enemies the essence of democracy, rebuilt their countries, and welcomed them into the family of free nations.

Now we are being tested again. May God give us the moral courage and depth of character to defend our nation and civilization against the barbarians at the gate.[3]

The nineteenth century American poet and essayist, James Russell Lowell, put it well:

> Truth forever on the scaffold
> Wrong forever on the throne—
> Yet that scaffold sways the future
> And, behind the dim unknown,
> Standeth God within the shadow,
> Keeping watch above His own.[4]

Stay on the scaffold. Keep thinking straight. Refuse to tolerate wrong! Like Job, keep forming your priorities from the Word of God. Spend less time in the papers and more time in the Scriptures. Let God dictate your agenda and help you interpret the events of our times. Become biblically correct rather than politically correct.

Suffering has enabled Job to grasp deep truths. In fact, as we arrive at his fourth and fifth priorities (Job 28) we find he has moved from the realm of mere knowledge (intellectual information) to the subject of wisdom (spiritual perception).

Job comes to three conclusions regarding wisdom. His first conclusion comes in the form of a question which appears at the end of a section full of beautiful poetry. All of this is leading Job toward his fourth priority.

> Surely there is a mine for silver
> And a place where they refine gold.
> Iron is taken from the dust,
> And copper is smelted from rock.
> Man puts an end to darkness,
> And to the farthest limit he searches out
> The rock in gloom and deep shadow
> He sinks a shaft far from habitation,
> Forgotten by the foot;
> They hang and swing to and fro far from men.
>
> Job 28:1–4

As he continues he describes man's searching for precious metals and other valuable elements.

> Its rocks are the source of sapphires,
> And its dust contains gold. . . .
> He hews out channels through the rocks,
> And his eye sees anything precious.
> He dams up the streams from flowing,
> And what is hidden he brings out to the light.

Job 28:6, 10-11

Then comes the crucial question . . .

> But where can wisdom be found?
> And where is the place of understanding?
> Man does not know its value,
> Nor is it found in the land of the living.
> The deep says, "It is not with me."
> And the sea says, "It is not with me."
> Pure gold cannot be given in exchange for it,
> Nor can silver be weighed as its price.

Job 28:12–15

Consider what he's saying, "Dig into the earth, you'll find precious jewels and metals, but you won't find wisdom. Probe into the outer spaces and the mysteries will unfold, but you'll not find wisdom. Study nature's wonders, examine all that this earth holds for you, and there will be exciting discoveries, but *you won't find wisdom!*"

This assures us that as helpful as an education may be, reading widely or traveling broadly, or even being mentored by the brightest, none of that will automatically result in wisdom. It is not found in textbooks. Or discoveries. Or inventions. Or in some guru's mind. It is here we find Job's fourth priority: *Seeking wisdom through human effort is a waste of time.*

Allow me to offer a simple definition of wisdom. *Wisdom* is looking at life from God's point of view. When we employ wisdom we are viewing life as God sees it. That's why it's so valuable to think God's thoughts after Him. You look at difficulties and tests as God looks at them. You look at family life and child rearing as God looks at them. You interpret current events as God would interpret them. You focus on the long view. You see the truth even though all around you are deception and lies.

Let's go a step further and define another scriptural term: *understanding*. What does it mean? Understanding is responding to life's struggles and challenges as God would have us respond. Not in panic and confusion. Not forfeiting those things that are valuable to us, and not by compromising our integrity. Instead, when we have understanding, we respond to life's challenges as God would have us respond. We trust Him. We believe in Him. We refuse to be afraid. We don't operate our lives according to human impulses or in step with today's politically correct culture.

How terribly important it is that we stand firm in wisdom, responding in understanding. Neither can be found by our own effort or as a result of our searching. God graciously provides both. Verse 20 asks two great questions.

> Where then does wisdom come from?
> And where is the hiding place of understanding?

Not, where can we get advice? Not, where does opinion come from? I could name a dozen sources, but most of them aren't worth listening to. Then where does this *wisdom* come from? Where can we find true *understanding*?

> God understands its way,
> And He knows its place.
> For He looks to the ends of the earth
> And sees everything under the heavens.
> When He imparted weight to the wind
> And meted out the waters by measure,
> When He set a limit for the rain
> And a course for the thunderbolt,

Then He saw it and declared it;
He established it and also searched it out.
And to man He said "Behold the fear of the Lord, that is wisdom;
And to depart from evil is understanding."

Job 28:23–28

You can earn four Ph.D. degrees and never get wisdom or understanding. You'll certainly not get a grasp of the fear of the Lord from higher learning. Even in the finest of universities, there's no course offered on the fear of the Lord. The source? God and God alone. By "fear of the Lord" I'm referring to an awesome respect for God accompanied by a personal hatred for sin. Now we can see why Solomon wrote, "The fear of the LORD is the beginning of wisdom, and the knowledge of the Holy One is understanding" (Proverbs 9:10).

This brings us to Job's fifth priority: *Cultivating a healthy and holy fear of the Lord gives us wisdom and understanding.*

ACCEPT AND LEARN FROM SUFFERING; DON'T RESIST IT

There is a man in our congregation who recently underwent brain surgery. The tumor in the frontal section within his cranium was pushing his brain back and slowly eroding his memory. Each week the growth of the tumor became more pronounced and debilitating for him. Brain surgery was the only option. I visited him in the hospital following successful surgery. A scar on his scalp stretched from his left ear across the top of his head down to his right ear. Stainless steel staples held the incision closed. He was laying there on the bed, smiling when I walked in. It wasn't long before I realized that my visiting him was for a different reason than I had planned. In going I witnessed a fresh load of wisdom. He didn't get any from me; I got it from him. He spoke of the Lord from the moment we started our conversation until I left. He mentioned insights the Lord had given. He talked about lessons he'd begun to learn. He spoke of an overwhelming sense of peace he had enjoyed from the git-go. I mean, if ever a man was fully focused on the Lord, this man was. His words flowed with a gentle tone. There was a calm pace in our conversation as he responded. He was saying, in effect, "Please don't feel sorry for me. This brain surgery has become my opportunity to trust in the Lord with my whole heart, to have Him show me some things I would have otherwise missed. He was, literally, rejoicing, as was his wife. Wisdom and understanding had completely eclipsed pain and panic.[5]

I love the way one man extols the long-term value of suffering:

> In our compassion, we don't like to see people suffer. And so our instincts are aimed at preventing and alleviating suffering. No doubt that is a good impulse. But if we really want to reach out to others who are suffering, we should be careful not to be like Job's friends, not to do our "helping" with the presumption that we can fix things, get rid of them, or make them "better." . . .
>
> So, instead of continuing to focus on preventing suffering—which we simply won't be very successful at anyway—perhaps we should begin *entering* the suffering, participating insofar as we are able—entering the mystery and looking around for God. In other words, we need to quit feeling sorry for people who suffer and instead look up to them, learn from them, and—if they will let us—join them in protest and prayer. Pity can be nearsighted and condescending; shared suffering can be dignifying and life-changing. As we look at Job's suffering and praying and worshiping, we see that he has already blazed a trail of courage and integrity for us to follow.[6]

How true! My friend in the hospital didn't need pity, he needed respect, and he got it from me that day! He has a head start on wisdom beyond many of us. So when he speaks, it is with new insight about life. He is still responding to life's challenges with joy. Both have come to him from God through the experience of suffering. The major benefit has been the rearrangement of his priorities. And to think we have been taught all our lives to fight suffering and to resist it, and whenever possible, to escape it.

Job teaches us a far more valuable lesson. The greater the suffering, the better we determine what really matters, which brings us back to where we started. Suffering helps us clarify our priorities and focus on the right objectives.

CHAPTER FIFTEEN

The Passionate Testimony of an Innocent Man

O urs is fast becoming a jaded generation. Perhaps a better word is suspicious. Once upon a time a leader was chosen because of character, and those who followed that leader respected him or her because of integrity. We simply trusted those who led us.

I remember as a little lad, hearing my father say, "We can trust him. He gave us his word." My mom and dad had some carpentry work done on our little house in East Houston back when I was a kid. I remember their talking about it at the supper table and my mother asked about a contract. My dad smiled and said, "We had a gentleman's agreement. There's no need to have a signed contract." Today those words represent a level of naiveté that's laughable.

Tragically, by the time we reached the twenty-first century we had traveled light-years beyond the simple yet sincere statement, "His word is his bond."

At the risk of being too general and simplistic with this analysis, I think much of the erosion of the public's trust can be traced back to three houses: the courthouse, the White House, and God's house.

At one time the law was upheld in the courthouse. Most attorneys walked in honesty (thankfully, some still do), and most judges had common sense along with a strong commitment to justice. Cases were taken because they were cases worth addressing, and the accused was worth defending because he or she was often innocent of the charges. There were exceptions, of course, but integrity ruled.

My heart skipped an extra beat this past week when I heard a defense attorney make a comment on a particular case of child molestation. He had just lost the case because the man was found to be guilty as charged. During the interview after that decision, the defense attorney admitted to the reporter, "I knew he was guilty. I knew it all along. My client had told me he was guilty, but after all it was an interesting case." All during the trial his defense was a sham, a charade.

Clearly, there are problems in the courthouse. But the White House? You remember trusting the president as an innocent child? Remember when you, like I, stood with our hands over our hearts and pledged allegiance to the flag of the United States of America? I remember standing barefoot in third grade saying the pledge every morning of class in the middle of World War II. I really was barefoot! (If I had my way I'd have gone barefoot all the way through high school, but they made us wear shoes once we entered junior high.) Anyway, I'm standing there and looking at the president's picture, as it's framed right next to the flag, thinking, *What a great man!* Back then, deception in the Oval Office was unthinkable. So much has changed. The Vietnam War. The endless social and racial conflicts. Watergate. Congressional scandals. The Clinton fiasco with Monica Lewinsky. Integrity in the White House? Not always. But God's house . . .

It's one thing to have Watergate—but to have Pearlygate! Not many years ago, there was a televangelist scandal that smeared its way across the work of God. All of us in ministry were hurt by it, though only a few were engaged in it. There was a time when a minister moved into the neighborhood, and people were happy to have a preacher living near. No longer. It's not uncommon for some to view a pastor with suspicion. It's heartbreaking—really. Bottom line, let's call it a breakdown of integrity.

There's an old story about a fabulously rich man who, as he lies dying, summons to his bedside his three most trusted friends: his physician, his priest, and his lawyer. When the three are assembled, he tells them, "I know they say you can't take it with you, but I'm going to try." He then distributes three identical and very thick packages, each of which turns out to contain two million dollars in cash. "I want all of you to come to my funeral," he says, "and when they put me in the ground, throw the envelopes in after me." (Your suspicious nature is already causing you to smile!)

Each friend, in turn, gives the man his word that he will do it. In due course the rich man dies. His three friends attend the funeral, and at the cemetery each tosses his package into the grave.

As they begin to walk back to their cars, the doctor reluctantly says to the other two, "My friends, I have a confession to make. Last night I was sitting in my office with the package and I got to thinking about the new wing for the sick children that our hospital is trying to build. I thought, 'This two million dollars could do a lot of good instead of ending up covered with dirt.' I knew that our dear friend, if he were in his right mind, would have preferred this charitable use of the money, so I took out the cash and gave it to the hospital for the new wing. I need to confess, the envelope I put in the grave was stuffed with old newspapers."

The lawyer lands on him in a fury, "That money," he says, "was given in trust. You were a trustee. By converting the money to your own preference or even the use of a charity, you have violated a sacred, legal duty and may have committed a felony besides."

The lawyer is still raging when the priest butts in and says, "Not so fast, my son." He then proceeds to tell his story. "I, too, have a confession to make. I was sitting in the rectory last night thinking about the church's efforts to raise enough money to endow the soup kitchen and the homeless shelter it has been running. So, I, too, struggled with the old man's request and finally decided that it was better to put the money to good use than to bury it in the ground." He quotes the parable of the talents, admitting that he, too, stuffed the envelope with newspapers and had given the cash to the soup kitchen and the homeless shelter.

By now the lawyer is nearly apoplectic. He reads both men the riot act. As an officer of the court, he says he may well have to report this breach of fiduciary duty. And apart from the law he adds, "There's a friendship to be considered. Both of you disobeyed the dying wish of our closest friend. You should have done what I did," he concluded. "In order to be absolutely certain that I carried out our friend's request with the most meticulous care, I put the cash in my office safe, and it's still there, protected from harm. Then I wrote a check for two million dollars and put it in the envelope . . . and *that* is what I tossed into the grave."

Last year I read *Eyewitness to Power* by David Gergen. The name you may not remember, but you'd know the face. He was often seen alongside people like President Nixon and later, President Ford, President Reagan, and more recently President Clinton. He was their advisor and counselor; each considered Gergen his friend. He writes not a kiss-and-tell sort of book, but a straight-from-the-shoulder volume about things he actually witnessed. The author often mentions the word integrity. When he sums up the seven characteristics that mark a president, I was not surprised to see listed first: *Leadership starts from within*. He quotes former senator Alan Simpson: "If you have integrity, nothing else matters. If you don't have integrity, nothing else matters."[1]

That explains why all of us have such high regard for Job. He was a man of integrity *before* the bottom fell out of his life, he remained a man of integrity *when* it fell out of his life, and he continued in his integrity *after* it fell out of his life. In spite of all the hardship and loss, regardless of insults, false accusations, and condemning put-downs, he never compromised his integrity. Suffering we admire, and the endurance of intensified suffering we admire even more. But the modeling of integrity through it all—we stand in admiration of that. Nothing about Job is more impressive. Job firmly states:

> Till I die I will not put away my integrity from me.
> I hold fast my righteousness and will not let it go.

Job 27:5–6

Job's problem back then, however, was like any leader's problem today; he had a jaded audience. Each viewed him with suspicion. To them his words were mere words, nothing more. No one could be going through the kind of hell he was going through physically, emotionally, domestically. Nobody would lose business, home, family, and health without being guilty of something. Something *really* secret and *really* bad. They never believed otherwise. In fact, they intensified their blame as time passed. Finally, (I would add *thankfully*), they decide to stop talking. And Job sits quietly with their words ringing in his ears. Having no defense attorney, he is left to represent his own case.

For a brief interlude (chapters 27 through 32 of the book that bears his name), Job has time to consider what they've said as he thinks through his life. The benefit of such an interlude is that he entered his thoughts into his journal. They have been preserved in the Bible. When we get to chapter 29 of his writings, we find Job looking back with some pleasant nostalgia as he remembers and as he recounts the blessings of God. What glorious days they were! If you're the type who likes outlines, including headings for the major sections, I would suggest the following:

- Job reflects on his past glory. (chapter 29)
- Job rehearses his present misery. (chapter 30)
- Job reaffirms his personal integrity. (chapter 31)

REFLECTING ON HIS PAST GLORY

> And Job again took up his discourse and said,
> "Oh, that I were as in months gone by,
> As in the days when God watched over me."
>
> Job 29:1–2

It's as if he's writing these things with a deep sigh: "Oh, I would love to know days like that again when He and I walked and talked together." Adam must have had similar feelings after the Fall. "How great it was when we walked in the cool of the evening and there was nothing between my God and me." Job continues to remember . . .

> When His lamp shone over my head,
> And by His light I walked through darkness.
>
> Job 29:3

Beautiful words, wonderful words. Job is relishing the memory of days gone by. This is not a doting parent or a languishing grandparent. This is a grown man remembering when he had his ten children with him; when he and they could visit with each other, enjoy meals together, and relax on special days of celebration with everyone around the table. "I remember when," says Job. How great it was. I love his descriptive words:

> When my steps were bathed in butter,
> And the rock poured out for me streams of oil!
>
> Job 29:6

He writes like a poet using vivid word pictures. His world was so good; life was so delightful; joy was everywhere to be found. God's grace abounded.

All of us have days we can remember when there were such great moments. Maybe in more innocent days for you. Maybe before life's harsh trials reared their heads and grew sharp horns and ugly scales. As you look back, perhaps you can recall those simple, quiet hours you spent with the Lord, when your steps seemed ordered by Him, when each dawn brought rays of fresh, new hope—just you and Him and His Word.

> When I went out to the gate of the city,
> When I took my seat in the square,
> The young men saw me and hid themselves,
> And the old men arose and stood.
> The princes stopped talking
> And put their hands on their mouths;
> The voice of the nobles was hushed,
> And their tongue stuck to their palate.
>
> Job 29:7–10

How picturesque! When folks are in the presence of someone greatly admired, they often place a hand over their mouth and stare. Young men once responded that way when they came near venerable Job.

I remember doing that. It happened during my years in training for the ministry, when I was a student at Dallas Seminary. Not only was I studying under an enviable faculty (a privileged opportunity I never took for granted), but on occasion the school would invite a respected Christian statesmen to our campus to lecture or teach a book of the Bible. I remember the first time I ever looked at Dr. Richard Seume, who was at that time a pastor in Richmond, Virginia, and a DTS board member. I can still remember his coming on the campus; his presence was like a benediction to the student body. There were others like Dr. Seume we held in highest regard. I would occasionally just want to sit near them, to watch them closely—it moved me. Younger men did that with Job.

Job would come to the city square, not in pride, but carrying out his duties, his leadership responsibilities. Younger fellows would gather to hear his wisdom. Here is a man who could be trusted with riches. He was significantly wealthy but never conducted himself as above them. How impressive to be around people like that—truly humble, yet wealthy, a man of great compassion and also great generosity. And his life was like the flowing of oil over the rocks. Flowing into others' lives. Even princes would stop and stare.

Why such respect?

> For when the ear heard, it called me blessed,
> And when the eye saw, it gave witness of me,
> Because I delivered the poor who cried for help,
> And the orphan who had no helper.
> The blessing of the one ready to perish came upon me,
> And I made the widow's heart sing for joy.
> I put on righteousness, and it clothed me;
> My justice was like a robe and a turban.
> I was eyes to the blind
> And feet to the lame.
> I was a father to the needy,
> And I investigated the case which I did not know.
> I broke the jaws of the wicked
> And snatched the prey from his teeth.
>
> Job 29:11–17

He defended the defenseless and stood in behalf of those taken advantage of. He did not forget those in great need. Furthermore, he broke the jaws of the wicked. And he championed the cause of the abused. What a model!

When the sports world lost a significant athlete not too long ago, it made the headlines. The Baltimore Colts professional football team had a quarterback named Johnny Unitas who was one of the great quarterbacks of my youth. I remember as a young man, just beginning to follow professional football, watching the man who was then called the "field general," a title once given to quarterbacks. "Johnny U" was truly a gridiron general.

He was also quite a character. I read in *Sports Illustrated* that both coaches and players stood a little in awe of him. On one occasion, he smiled and said to his coach, "Just sit back and enjoy, I won't need any help this game." That is a good quarterback. And the coach's response? "Matter of fact, we smeared 'em, and I just stayed out of the way."

Every once in a while there comes on this earth's scene certain people who capture our attention. They seem to have a command of life, and we long to be near them. Job was one of them.

> I chose a way for them and sat as chief,
> And dwelt as a king among the troops,
> As one who comforted the mourners.
>
> Job 29:25

This verse encompasses every aspect of his role in the community. He did it all—from leading the council in peaceful times to guiding the people through one crisis after another, all the while caring for the unfortunate. He inspired the whole community.

REHEARSING HIS PRESENT MISERY

"But now." That was then, this is now. Everything has changed. Perhaps Job blinks through tears as he pulls back the sleeve of his robe and exposes swollen, itching boils. His lips are cracked and bleeding. His tongue is parched. His body is gaunt. The lines on his face are longer, deeper. His hair is gone. His scalp is blistered.

> But now those younger than I mock me,
> Whose fathers I disdained to put with the dogs of my flock.
> And now I have become their taunt,
> I have even become a byword to them.
> They abhor me and stand aloof from me,
> And they do not refrain from spitting at my face.
>
> Job 30:1, 9–10

This is the same man others silently sat beside, filled with respect. No longer. Now, "I mean nothing to them. I am a diseased piece of trash. I am an object of shame." His great place of honor has eroded, his wealth only a memory.

> Terrors are turned against me;
> They pursue my honor as the wind,
> And my prosperity has passed away like a cloud.
>
> Job 30:15

He no longer has great blessings from God. Feel the ache in his words.

> At night it pierces my bones within me,
> And my gnawing pains take no rest.
> By a great force my garment is distorted;
> It binds me about as the collar of my coat.
> He has cast me into the mire,
> And I have become like dust and ashes.
> I cry out to You for help, but You do not answer me;
> I stand up, and You turn Your attention against me.
> You have become cruel to me;

With the might of Your hand You persecute me.
You lift me up to the wind and cause me to ride;
And You dissolve me in a storm.

Job 30:17–22

One night is followed by yet another miserable night. "And the benevolence that I once extended to the needy is not reciprocated. None of that comes my way." How difficult it must have been!

When I expected good, then evil came;
When I waited for light, then darkness came.
I am seething within and cannot relax;
Days of affliction confront me.
I go about mourning without comfort;
I stand up in the assembly and cry out for help.
I have become a brother to jackals
And a companion of ostriches.

Job 30:26–29

Scholar and author Roy Zuck captures the essence of Job's lamentation:

> Job concluded his plaintive rehearsal of his present remorse by stating that his joy had turned to grief (30:31). His harp and flute, instruments for expressing joy (cf. 21:12), now played only funeral dirges in accompaniment to people weeping in grief. The last five verses alternate between emotional pain (30:27, 29, 31) and physical pain (30:28, 30). The urchins mocked, spit, and attacked; God remained silent; friends were unsympathetic; and Job groaned in pain. Such was the plight of Job—the former plutocrat.[2]

Instead of respect, rejection. In place of strength and joy, his was a world of disease, humiliation, and sadness as Job writes these words with a trembling hand:

My skin turns black on me,
And my bones burn with fever.
Therefore my harp is turned to mourning,
And my flute to the sound of those who weep.

Job 30:30–31

His harp, made for celebration while people dance in the street, and the flute, with its lilting, lovely tones, now play only in a minor key. Reminds me of the lonely whine of bagpipes that were heard down the streets and in narrow alleys of New York City. On those same streets there had been dancing over our victories after world wars. On those same streets had been the lighthearted steps of those on easy street working in the financial center, not only of our nation, but of the world. But now, after 9/11, the whine of bagpipes fill the day as funeral after funeral passes by.

The scene of sadness reminds me of Psalm 137. Every psalm has its unique birthplace. This ancient song was birthed from a womb of woe. The Jews who are represented in this song are the mourning Jews who have been taken captive. The Babylonian hordes have come in and destroyed the city of Jerusalem. Zion lay in ruins, and captive Jews are on a slow march to Babylon. The psalmist composed this psalm as a funeral dirge.

By the rivers of Babylon,
There we sat down and wept,
When we remembered Zion.
Upon the willows in the midst of it
We hung our harps.
For there our captors demanded of us songs,
And our tormentors mirth, saying,
"Sing us one of the songs of Zion."

Psalm 137:1–3

Listen to the sarcasm. "Break out one of those great psalms you love to sing. Sing it for us now. Let's hear it!" At that grievous moment the psalm-ist asks:

How can we sing the LORD's song
In a foreign land?

Psalm 137:4

It's as if you and I were taken captive this next week, and marching to-ward the place where we will be imprisoned, one of our captors said, "Sing us one of those church songs. Harmonize on 'Blessed Assurance, Jesus is mine!'[3] Let's hear that one. How 'bout, 'And can it be that I should gain / An int'rest in the Savior's blood?'[4] Sing that one written by the great Charles Wesley. Sing that song. Or how about Martin Luther's victorious battle hymn: 'A Mighty Fortress Is Our God.'"[5] We'd place our instruments on the ground. It's not possible to sing the Lord's song in a foreign land.

This reminds me of an interesting phenomenon regarding great suffer-ing. I seldom hear songs in hospital rooms where those who are dying lie facing the wall. I hear prayers, but the song is silenced.

That's Job's point here. "My harp that once played those great songs our family loved to sing and my flute that accompanied their singing—no longer." His friends are unmoved. All they can think about is his guilt. "You brought this on yourself."

REAFFIRMING HIS PERSONAL INTEGRITY

Job writes on, listing one example after another that says, "Not guilty. I've reflected on past glory. I have rehearsed my present misery, but I want to tell you, I have every reason to reaffirm my present integrity. My integrity is intact." And he lists several examples.

"There have been no secret lusts, no private sex sins in my life." (That is seen in 31:1–12.) Second, "There has been no abuse of power, taking advantage of any who were in need or those who were helpless" (31:13–23). "There has been no compromise of integrity before God or man" (31:24–40). Look at the examples.

There has been no leering lust on my part.

> I have made a covenant with my eyes;
> How then could I gaze at a virgin?
> And what is the portion of God from above
> Or the heritage of the Almighty from on high?
>
> Job 31:1–2

There's been no lying.

> If I have walked with falsehood,
> And my foot has hastened after deceit,
> Let Him weigh me with accurate scales,
> And let God know my integrity.
>
> Job 31:5–6

There has been no adultery.

> If my heart has been enticed by a woman,
> Or I have lurked at my neighbor's doorway,
> May my wife grind for another,
> And let others kneel down over her.
> For that would be a lustful crime;
> Moreover, it would be an iniquity punishable by judges.
>
> Job 31:9–11

There has been no oppression.

> If I have despised the claim of my male or female slaves
> When they filed a complaint against me,
> What then could I do when God arises?
> And when He calls me to account, what will I answer Him?
> Did not He who made me in the womb make him,
> And the same one fashion us in the womb?
>
> Job 31:13–15

There has been no lack of compassion.

> If I have kept the poor from their desire,
> Or have caused the eyes of the widow to fail,
> Or have eaten my morsel alone,
> And the orphan has not shared it
> (But from my youth he grew up with me as with a father,
> And from infancy I guided her),
> If I have seen anyone perish for lack of clothing,
> Or that the needy had no covering,
> If his loins have not thanked me,
> And if he has not been warmed with the fleece of my sheep,
> If I have lifted up my hand against the orphan,
> Because I saw I had support in the gate.
>
> Job 31:16–21

There has been no materialism.

> If I have put my confidence in gold,
> And called fine gold my trust,
> If I have gloated because my wealth was great,
> And because my hand had secured so much;
> That too would have been an iniquity calling for judgment,
> For I would have denied God above.
>
> Job 31:24–25, 28

Finally, Job reaches a climax in his own defense.

> Oh that I had one to hear me!
> Behold, here is my signature;
> Let the Almighty answer me!
> And the indictment which my adversary has written,
> Surely I would carry it on my shoulder,
> I would bind it to myself like a crown.

I would declare to Him the number of my steps;
Like a prince I would approach Him.

Job 31:35–37

He longs for someone to hear him. Without legal defense he's left to defend himself in this imaginary courtroom. And those who are a part of the jury are all frowning. And Job says, "You men may think that none of this is true, but I stand on these statements. And if there's any evidence you can use against me, speak forth and let God judge." There is none. Therefore, it's as if he says at this point, "The defense rests."

THREE THEMES . . . THREE TRUTHS

You have been very patient to stay with me through this somewhat tedious chapter, and I thank you. It's not been entertaining, but hopefully it has been edifying. We've seen three themes emerge from Job's ancient pen; from each I find a truth worth remembering today.

Here's the first: *Reflecting on past blessings gives us reasons to rejoice.* Let me urge you who are parents still rearing your young to teach them how to do this by practicing it often. Suppertime is a great opportunity to reflect. It's an ideal time to look back over the day and to count the blessings, much like David did in Psalm 103. Look at the list he compiles:

Bless the LORD, O my soul;
And all that is within me, bless His holy name.
Bless the LORD, O my soul,
And forget none of His benefits;
Who pardons all your iniquities;
Who heals all your diseases;
Who redeems your life from the pit;
Who crowns you with lovingkindness and compassion;
Who satisfies your years with good things,
So that your youth is renewed like the eagle.
The LORD performs righteous deeds,

And judgments for all who are oppressed.
He made known His ways to Moses,
His acts to the sons of Israel.
The LORD is compassionate and gracious,
Slow to anger and abounding in lovingkindness.
He will not always strive with us;
Nor will He keep His anger forever.
He has not dealt with us according to our sins,
Nor rewarded us according to our iniquities.
For high as the heavens are above the earth,
So great is His lovingkindness toward those who fear Him.
As far as the east is from the west,
So far has He removed our transgressions from us.

Psalm 103:1–12

David provides a good model to follow. Pause long enough to think back. Resist all temptation to name things that did not work out well. Refuse to focus on conflicts that have not been resolved. Go to the blessings and camp there. Job did, remember? That kind of reflection lifts our spirits. Recalling only the good things of the past keeps us from becoming negative.

Now, secondly: *Rehearsing present trials forces us to swallow our pride.* If there's something we need to swallow, it's every ounce of our pride. Pride goes with a jaded culture. Cynicism and sophistication feed on it. Pride prompts us to look down on others because we have an elevated opinion of our own importance. I suggest that we rehearse the present trials we're going through and allow them appropriately to cut us down to size. Being "leveled" has its benefits.

Perhaps you are there, or you have been there recently. As a result, everything has changed for you. You once knew a delight you no longer know. Allow that to humble you. Force your pride into the backseat. Face the fact that you, like Paul who was given the thorn in the flesh, have been given this so that you would not be overly impressed with your own importance.

In fact, Paul says twice that he was given this thorn "to keep me from exalting myself." Shortly thereafter, he repeats the same words, "to keep me from exalting myself" (2 Corinthians 12:7). What better use of current trials than allowing them to humble us?

Now, finally, the third: *Reaffirming our commitment to integrity strengthens us with confidence and courage.* This is what I love most about Job: Even when he is discouraged and disappointed, he is not defeated. In fact, he has the confidence and courage to say before his God, "If this is true, if that's true, if you find any of that, just strike me down." Because he knew, deep in his heart, that his integrity was intact, he could say those words with passionate assurance.

You and I smiled earlier over the story about the physician, the priest, and the lawyer. Momentarily revisit that scene with me. I realize this is hypothetical, but be honest: Would you have tossed the envelope of two million dollars into the grave? Isn't it amazing how creative we get when there is an opportunity to put two million dollars in our pocket. We tell ourselves: "Oh, that's what he would have wanted." Or, "If he were in his right mind this is what . . . " Integrity says you keep your word. You do as you say you will do. And if you fail at that, your integrity acknowledges the failure and you make it right. Without it, we drift into compromise. With it, we stand in confidence. Integrity helps us stand fast.

Cynthia and I recently returned from a life-changing tour of the sites made famous by a small group of strong-hearted, straight-thinking men. We know them today as Reformers. They were the leaders of the Great Reformation that swept across Central Europe in the sixteenth century. Their names are legendary synonyms of courage, conviction, and relentless determination.

Jon Huss of Czechoslovakia, Martin Luther and Philip Melanchthon of Germany, Ulrich Zwingli and John Calvin of Switzerland, and John Knox of Scotland (to name only a few) were not supermen in stature or strength. Nor were they anywhere near perfect. But they were men of integrity, which included character qualities that kept them faithful. It also resulted in their being unintimidated in the face of opposition that was not only vocal, it was life-threatening. To borrow from Luther's now-famous line, each one said, in effect, "Here I stand, I can do no other," as they refused to weaken or recant. Like Job, they were misunderstood, maligned, falsely accused, and openly insulted by their critics. They represented lonely voices of truth while standing true to their convictions.

While on our tour I often lingered at a bronze statue, or stood in the pulpit where one of them once preached, wondering if, perhaps, they were strengthened to stand alone by the example left by Job in the Scriptures. Long before they lived, he testified, "Till I die I will not put away my integrity from me. I hold fast my righteousness and will not let go" (Job 27:5–6).

I also asked myself, "Would I have the courage to do what they did?" Would you?

CHAPTER SIXTEEN

Another Long-Winded Monologue

In the church I serve as senior pastor, I decided to preach through the entire Book of Job. I began the expositional series of sermons the first Sunday in March 2002. It wasn't until mid-November I delivered the final message from that same book. As I mentioned in my introduction, the congregation of Stonebriar Community Church was very patient as the series went on and on . . . and on and on! As you can imagine, there were some humorous moments during those months when folks had some fun with me about the length of the series *and* the endless theme of all the suffering and hardship and pain Job endured.

Like the letter one father mailed to me, which included a comment his daughter had made. She had asked, "Daddy, was I five or six when Pastor Chuck began preaching on Job?" When I travel, I tell people it's the only series I've ever preached where, when I announced, "This will be my *final* message on Job," the congregation gave me a standing ovation. The rousing applause was more out of relief than gratitude!

In light of all that, you can only imagine their response when the Sunday arrived—and we were months into Job with more months ahead of us before we would finish—and they read my sermon title, "Another Long-Winded Monologue." I got some classic comments on *that!* We have TV monitors in the large hallways of our church outside our worship center. They display our calendar of events for the upcoming week as well as special announcements to inform everyone of what's ahead. They also display my sermon title from one week to the next. Well! When *this* title went on display, our ushers passed along to me a few choice comments they claim to have overheard (emphasis on "claim"). After reading, "Another Long-Winded Monologue," I heard that one man shrugged and whispered to his wife, "So? What else is new?" And then there was the teenager who passed by and glanced at the monitor, frowned and said, "Oh, no . . . not again!" I told our congregation sometimes a pastor feels like the Rodney Dangerfield of the church! And when the flack gets really heavy, I've been known to quote Paul's words to Timothy out loud (with tongue in cheek), "Indeed, all who desire to live godly . . . will be persecuted" (2 Timothy 3:12).

Now, admittedly, a series on Job is long and can begin to be wearisome. A preacher learns over the years that there is just so much a person can absorb at one sitting. Young, inexperienced preachers don't know that, so they tend to say too much for too long, and the flock becomes bored and edgy. Long-winded sermons can be awfully tiring.

While he was president, Ronald Reagan, the great communicator, loved to tell the story of the young, country boy who had just finished school but had never before preached a sermon. When he arrived at this country church, he walked in and to his amazement, there was one rancher present. The church was empty except for this one man. He was sitting about halfway back on the hard pew, so the young preacher walked back there, shook his hand, and said, "Well, what do you think I oughta do?" The old rancher said, "Well, I don't rightly know son, I'm just a cowpoke. But if I went out in my field and found only one steer, I'd *feed* it." That's all the young preacher needed. He climbed up in the pulpit and delivered a sermon that went on and on and on—*and on*. Over an hour later he finally ended the marathon. He walked back to the rancher and asked, "Well, what did you think?"

"I don't rightly know, son. But I'll tell you this. If I went out in my field and found I only had one steer, I wouldn't feed him the *whole load*."

Admittedly, I preach a little too long at times, but I'm encouraged that I'm in good company. Do you remember an experience the apostle Paul had regarding a man named Eutychus? The only time he's mentioned in the Scriptures, something embarrassing happened. The setting is recorded in Acts 20.

> On the first day of the week, when we were gathered together to break bread, Paul began talking to them, intending to leave the next day, and he prolonged his message until midnight.
>
> Acts 20:7

(I have these words in the margin of my Bible alongside that verse, "God bless him!").

The story continues . . .

> There were many lamps in the upper room where we were gathered together. And there was a young man named Eutychus sitting on the window sill, sinking into a deep sleep;
>
> Acts 20:8–9

Isn't that a great way to put it? The man was slowly sinking into a deep sleep. I've seen that so many times in my ministry! (It's when they start to drool that you have to think about stopping!)

> And as Paul kept on talking, he was overcome by sleep and fell down from the third floor and was picked up dead.
>
> Acts 20:9

I love this story!

> But Paul went down and fell upon him, and after embracing him, he said, "Do not be troubled, for his life is in him." When he had gone back up and had broken the bread and eaten, he talked with them a long while until daybreak, and then left.
>
> Acts 20:10–11

This dear man just couldn't stay with it. He finally sinks into a deep sleep, falls backward down three floors and dies. Miraculously, the apostle raises him up.

Charles Spurgeon's familiar warning is worth repeating: "Remember, if we go to sleep during the sermon and die today, there are no apostles to restore us." Having written all this about preaching too long, you'll be relieved to know that my title to this chapter has nothing to do with me, personally. It has everything to do with a man named Elihu—Job's fourth "friend" who steps out of the shadows and talks much too long, saying far too little.

Eliphaz, Bildad, and Zophar have gone on and on with their caustic comments and insulting conclusions. Mercifully, as we have seen, they quit talking. No doubt they still hung around frowning at him. But they stopped flapping their lips. If you're not familiar with the story, you'd think that all sermons had ended. Not so. There's one more—*a long one!* Elihu has waited his turn. When he talks, he doesn't stop until he has delivered what amounts to six chapters in the Bible (Job 32–37). The length of these chapters in the biblical text is longer than twelve other Old Testament books and seventeen of the twenty-seven New Testament books or letters. I suppose we could say Elihu fed Job the whole load.

OBSERVING ELIHU'S APPROACH

Instead of getting bogged down in needless detail, let's begin by glancing over Elihu's words as we observe his approach.

Perhaps it will help to make a few general observations. Elihu delivers four speeches. Two of them comprise two biblical chapters that cover his initial message (chapters 32 and 33). His second speech is recorded in Job 34. His third speech is in chapter 35. Then his fourth and final speech is in chapters 36 and 37. Like many sermons we have heard, Elihu is more effective at the beginning and the ending than he is in the middle of his talk. In that section he gets a little dull and boring. In all fairness, Elihu communicates two excellent points.

First, God disciplines a person to turn him from the error of his way. That principle is as timeless as it is true. God never wastes tests. When God bears down, His goal is to turn the wayward back to Himself.

Second, God governs justly; He's fair. Another reliable fact. The major theme of all that Elihu has to say can be stated in three words: God is sovereign. He is not only good all the time, He is *in control* all the time. "Even when I'm sick?" Yes, even when you are sick. "Even when I can't understand why?" Yes, even when you can't explain the reasons. "Like this right now?" you ask. Absolutely. God is never shocked or surprised. Our lives, therefore, are never out of God's control. And furthermore, God doesn't feel obligated to explain Himself. The truth is, even if He did, most of us still wouldn't get it, because His ways are deep and His plan is profound. In hopes of driving this significant truth home, I will repeat it: God is sovereign, and He doesn't explain Himself, nor should He feel obligated to do so.

Neither Job nor the three counselors answer Elihu at any time. These six biblical chapters run uninterrupted. There's no response. There's no dialogue. From start to finish it's a monologue—a long-winded monologue at that.

Interestingly, Elihu (unlike the others) admits up front that he's angry. In fact, the biblical account states no less than four times that the man is burning with anger.

> Then these three men ceased answering Job, because he was righteous in his own eyes. But the anger of Elihu . . . burned; against Job his anger burned because he justified himself before God. And his anger burned against his three friends because they had found no answer and yet had condemned Job. Now Elihu had waited to speak to Job because they were years older than he. And when Elihu saw that there was no answer in the mouth of the three men his anger burned.
>
> Job 32:1–5

Remember when you've blurted something out in anger? Remember a few more of those times when you were "burning" with anger? During those outbursts we not only said things we wish we *hadn't* said, we said a lot *more* than we wish we would have said. But we also may have said a few things that needed to be said. In those outrages we were temporarily out of control. Keep that in mind as you read Elihu's words.

> So Elihu, the son of Barachel the Buzite spoke out and said,
> "I am young in years and you are old;
> Therefore I was shy and afraid to tell you what I think.
> I thought age should speak,
> And increased years should teach wisdom.
> But it is a spirit in man,
> And the breath of the Almighty gives them understanding.
> The abundant in years may not be wise,
> Nor may elders understand justice."
>
> Job 32:6–9

We have learned over the years that we need to respect those who are older. Elihu's words represent his feelings of intimidation. He's reluctant to speak. He even says he was "afraid" to tell them his thoughts. But he does make an accurate observation, having listened to those three gray heads who spoke earlier. He states that those who are up in years "may not be wise." He's right. The passing of many years is no guarantee that wisdom has been gleaned. A person can be old and foolish. If we find Elihu a bit of a mystery, it is because he is insightful one moment and insipid the next. He can be both pointed with insight and shortly thereafter, dull.

I think author David Atkinson's word for him is a good one: enigma.

> Elihu is rather an enigma. He blusters on to the stage as an angry young man, full of his own importance, offering to clarify the situation for Job and his friends, angry with the muddle they have got themselves into. In one respect it is rather like a comic turn, for he manages to spend a lot of time not saying very much. He covers much of the ground of the other friends while supposedly saying something new. He claims to say more than the three friends have already said, and this is certainly true at the beginning and end of his speeches. But the middle speeches are cold and disappointing—a lapse into moralism which seems very hard

on Job. Perhaps in these middle speeches Elihu is setting himself up as a sort of arbiter between Job and God. Perhaps he sees himself in a courtroom trying to argue out a case as coolly and dispassionately as he can. He is trying to set out the arguments for and against from the perspective of a detached observer. . . .

Elihu blusters away, he makes his own mistakes. But in the middle of his blustering, there are some gems, and it is these gems which are part of the preparation Job needs—and we readers need—to be ready to hear the Lord.[1]

Elihu's admission says it all: "I'm full of words" (Job 32:18). He's also full of himself. Being younger, he is rash. Being angry, he talks too long.

ANALYZING ELIHU'S MISTAKES

The man made at least four mistakes once he had the floor.

First, he took too long getting started. You know how we'll say to someone we know very well, like somebody in our family, "Please get to the point." Or, "What is it, exactly, you're trying to say?" We're pressing for the bottom line. Early on you want to say that to Elihu. "What is it? Just say it." And then when he finally does, you think, "Sorry I hurried you."

Second, he comes across as pompous. We don't read Elihu's words very long before we hear pride oozing between the lines. He leaves little room for response. He states his opinion with too much dogmatism. He sees himself as the final authority. He doesn't merely speak, he preaches. Let me give you a tip. If it's one-on-one or one-on-a-few, leave the preaching to someone else. If it's with your kids, don't preach. If it's with your spouse, don't preach. If it's at work with your boss or somebody who works for you, again, don't preach. Preaching isn't appropriate in small group settings. Elihu forgets that.

Third, he states what Job already knew. He brings nothing new to Job's attention. That's why Job never responds. He rehearses familiar information.

Fourth, he never acknowledges that he doesn't know for sure. There's something refreshing about someone who is speaking who willingly admits, "I really don't know all that I should know about this, but . . . " It's wonderful when you're around someone who has a wealth of knowledge, but you hear them admit, "I'm not the final word."

A man who meant a great deal to me during my student years (and means a great deal to me to this day) is one of my mentors, Dr. Bruce Waltke. Dr. Waltke is as fine a scholar of the Hebrew Scriptures as I have ever been around. It was my privilege to study under him the last three of my four years in seminary. What a splendid experience! I still remember taking a preparatory course in Hebrew one summer before we officially began the course that fall. He would sit on a tall stool up front as he taught. Dr. Waltke would cradle his Old Testament *Kittel Hebrew Bible* in both arms as he read from it and would occasionally sway from side to side. Sometimes I noticed, he would tear up, he would weep as he read. (I wept for other reasons as I tried to read it.) He is truly a wonderful blend: brilliant scholar and a tender heart. He not only knew the text, he understood the footnotes, knew the textural apparatus, he knew arguments for the interpretation, and yet he never came across as "the" final word.

Over thirty years ago while I was pastoring a church near the seminary, I was doing some in-depth study in Proverbs on the family—especially emphasizing the rearing of children. In my own work in the original language I came up with an interpretation that was somewhat of a maverick approach to the subject. (Imagine that!)

As I became increasingly more convinced of my position, I decided to run my unusual interpretation by Dr. Waltke. I called, made the appointment, and a few days later sat down with him in his tiny office—he was gracious to see me. "Chuck, how are you?" "Fine, Dr. Waltke." "Sit down. What's on your mind?" I said, "Well, I'm doing some work in the early part of Proverbs 22." He smiled, "Oh, one of my favorites."

So, he turned to that section in his well-worn Hebrew Bible as I explained my position after having done all my work in the text. "I just need to be sure I'm not off base in any of this." He listened and didn't interrupt as I spent about twenty minutes going over what I had come up with and why, and how I planned to apply it to the congregation.

When I looked up he had his chin resting on his hands. He was looking directly at me. I'll never forget his gentle words, "Chuck, there are no popes in the body of Christ. I'm not the final word on this. What you have concluded looks fine to me. If that's what you have determined and the Lord has shown you this interpretation after careful research, that's what you must preach." I'm telling you I could have danced out of there. His words were not only a relief, they provided a wonderful reminder that the final authority of truth does not reside in human flesh. I will never forget his comment, "There are no popes in the body of Christ."

I do not care what authority you have, how long you've studied in the field, how many advanced degrees you have earned, you are not the final word. You are still a learner. I have found the scholars who have taught me the most are the most teachable. We are all on a learning curve. I've learned some things from every pastoral intern I've mentored. Hopefully they've picked up some helpful things from me as well.

From the way he comes across, we can tell that Elihu is not a learner. Elihu's busy with that long index finger, punching it against Job's sternum. To make matters worse, chances are that he never had one boil on his body—Job's covered with them. I want to step into that scene and say, "There are no popes, Elihu. Learn from this man."

ANALYZING ELIHU'S SPEECHES

Since the man is so long-winded, I'll not try to examine every jot and tittle of his speeches. Instead, let's focus on a few things that are worth mentioning.

His first speech. If I were to sum up this first speech in a few words it would be: "God has not been silent, but His message is not as you had expected." This is underscored through much of Job 33.

He begins by confronting Job.

> Why do you complain against Him
> That He does not give an account of all His doings?
> Indeed God speaks once,
> Or twice, yet no one notices it.
>
> Job 33:13–14

In good Hebrew poetry, he says, "Once, yea twice." Sometimes it will say, "Six, yea seven." So he's saying in effect, "Here are a couple of ways God speaks to you."

First, "In a dream or a vision of the night" (Job 33:15). God speaks to you, Job, in supernatural ways.

Second, "Man is also chastened with pain on his bed" (Job 33:19). God also speaks when we're sick. When we are laid aside with anguishing pain, the Lord gets through to us. God communicates in suffering itself. As mentioned earlier, people who have gone through deep suffering have a depth of knowledge and understanding others of us lack. Why? Because they learned some profound things on the bed of affliction.

How then would Job get God's message? Elihu suggests:

> If there is an angel as mediator for him,
> One out of a thousand,
> To remind a man what is right for him,
> Then let him be gracious to him, and say,
> "Deliver him from going down to the pit,
> I have found a ransom."
>
> Job 33:23–26

Let me pause here and allow you some time to consider that. Let your mind meditate on what you just read.

Now admittedly, this may be Elihu's opinion, but it is inspired writing. It originates with the Spirit of God, and it's preserved for us in the biblical account. His reference to this particular anger is fascinating, isn't it? Could it be that in those days when God communicated through dreams and visions, when God spoke directly to individuals in a supernatural manner, there was a "mediating angel"? Apparently so.

John Hartley writes of this angel in his thorough work on Job:

> Elihu teaches that there is a heavenly intercessor who takes up the sufferer's case. This helper is an angel who functions as *a mediator* . . . one who will help whomever God is afflicting for disciplinary reasons.

He declares to that person *what is right . . . for him,* i. e., the right way for him to take, the way that will lead him out of suffering and back to God. . . .

The identity of this mediating angel is uncertain. . . . Elihu is also countering Eliphaz's position that there is no holy one to whom Job may turn for help. Elihu says that there is a special angel who works for the redemption of the afflicted. The phrase *one among a thousand* is taken by some to mean an ordinary angel, but from the way the phrase is used in 9:3 it is better understood as having very restrictive force. Therefore, this mediating angel is a very special heavenly creature. . . . In Elihu's teaching this special angel works for the restoration of those who have strayed from the right way. This means that God does not immediately abandon any of his servants who err. The converse is the truth; he labors zealously for their full restoration to faithful service.[2]

Before we proceed, a word of caution is needed. God rarely speaks these days in dreams and visions. Now that the Scriptures are complete, there is hardly a need for such. I certainly believe in the presence of angels, called elsewhere God's "ministering spirits." They carry out God's bidding. They watch over and protect us. Sometimes they even carry God's message. More often than not they are invisible. We rarely hear them, see them, or touch them, though they can manifest themselves in human form and have done so according to other Scriptures.

But in Job's era, before the Bible was complete, God frequently revealed His message through dreams and visions. Perhaps when speaking to His servants in the midst of the pain, His "mediating angel" clarified that message and assisted the sufferer in understanding it. Elihu is saying, in effect, "Job, God is speaking to you in this. Are you hearing what He has to say? God may be invisible and seem uninvolved, but He is at work." Job doesn't answer.

His second speech. This is contained in Job 34. Elihu begins by addressing everyone—Job as well as his three "friends" (Job 34:1–15). He then speaks specifically to Job (34:16–33).

Because he mentions little that has not already been said, let's cut to the chase. Job still doesn't answer the man, so Elihu, roused to anger, goes for the jugular. *The Message* conveys just how angry a speech it was.

> So why don't you simply confess to God?
>> Say, "I sinned, but I'll sin no more."
> Teach me to see what I still don't see.
>> Whatever evil I've done, I'll do it no more."
> Just because you refuse to live on God's terms,
>> do you think he should start living on yours?
> You choose. I can't do it for you.
>> Tell me what you decide.
> All right-thinking people say—
>> and the wise who have listened to me concur—
> "Job is an ignoramus.
>> He talks utter nonsense."
> Job, you need to be pushed to the wall and called to account
>> for wickedly talking back to God the way you have.
> You've compounded your original sin
>> by rebelling against God's discipline,
> Defiantly shaking your fist at God,
>> piling up indictments against the Almighty One.
>
> Job 34:31–37, MSG

Such angry and inaccurate words do not deserve Job's attention or call for an answer, so he continues to remain mute.

His third speech (Job 35). Here, Elihu builds a case against those with impure motives (Job!) and emphasizes that *that* is the reason for God's silence. As before, he concludes with harsh words directed, of course, to Job—who is still in pain! Again, from *The Message:*

> People are arrogantly indifferent to God—
>> until, of course, they're in trouble,
>> and then God is indifferent to them.

There's nothing behind such prayers except panic;
  the Almighty pays them no mind.
So why would he notice you
  just because you say you're tired of waiting to be heard,
Or waiting for him to get good and angry
  and do something about the world's problems?
"Job, you talk sheer nonsense—
  nonstop nonsense!"

Job 35:12–16, MSG

Elihu's fourth and final speech. A surprising change occurs in the closing part of Elihu's last speech. He gets back on target and delivers some reliable truth. In fact, he makes more sense and speaks with greater accuracy here than we find from any of the others who had spoken earlier. Elihu covers four important bases:

1. God protectively watches over the righteous.
2. If the righteous commit a transgression, He lets them know they've done wrong.
3. If they respond to the rod of discipline, He restores them.
4. If they persist, they will surely suffer the consequences.

Outstanding theology! Why did the man waste time and effort meandering in so many needless directions before arriving at this destination? But, thankfully, he finally got it right.

After that splendid summation, Elihu looks up and gives full attention to the Lord God. It seems as if he wants to help Job refocus—much as we do when we gather for corporate worship. Written across Job 36 and 37 could be these six words: It is all about our God!

The final speech provides a magnificent segue into the moment when God finally breaks the silence and reveals Himself to Job (chapter 38). Elihu's words enable Job to grasp a fairly good understanding of the living God. He begins by admitting he trembles when he thinks of Him:

At this also my heart trembles,
And leaps from its place.

Listen closely to the thunder of His voice,
And the rumbling that goes out from His mouth.
Under the whole heaven He lets it loose,
And His lightning to the ends of the earth.
After it, a voice roars;
He thunders with His majestic voice,
And He does not restrain the lightnings when His voice is heard.
God thunders with His voice wondrously,
Doing great things which we cannot comprehend.

Job 37:1-5

God is prominent and preeminent. He is majestic in His power, magnificent in His person, and marvelous in His purposes. How refreshing to step back in the shadows of our own insignificance and give full attention to the greatness of our God! *It's all about Him!*

How unlike the little girl walking beside her mother in a pouring rain and loud thunderstorm. Every time the lightning flashed, her mother noticed she turned and smiled. They'd walk a little further, then lightning, and she'd turn and smile. The mother finally said, "Sweetheart, what's going on? Why do you always turn and smile after the flash of lightning?" "Well," she said, "Since God is taking my picture, I want to be sure and smile for Him."[3]

We take a major step toward maturity when we finally realize it's not about us and our significance. It is all about God's magnificence. His holiness. His greatness. His glory.

In whirlwind and storm is His way,
And clouds are the dust beneath His feet.
The LORD is good,
A stronghold in the day of trouble,
And He knows those who take refuge in Him.

Nahum 1:3,7

God is transcendent. He is magnificent. He is mighty. He alone is awesome! He is all around us, above us, and within us. Without Him there is no righteousness. Without Him there is no holiness. Without Him there is no promise of forgiveness, no source of absolute truth, no reason to endure, no hope beyond the grave. Elihu turns Job's attention to this awesome God as he says:

> Listen to this, O Job,
> Stand and consider the wonders of God.
> Do you know how God establishes them,
> And makes the lightning of His cloud to shine?
> Do you know about the layers of the thick clouds,
> The wonders of one perfect in knowledge,
> You whose garments are hot,
> When the land is still because of the south wind?
> Out of the north comes golden splendor;
> Around God is awesome majesty.
> The Almighty—we cannot find Him;
> He is exalted in power
> And He will not do violence to justice and abundant righteousness.
> Therefore men fear Him;
> He does not regard any who are wise of heart.
>
> Job 37:14–18, 22–24

Nothing compares to Him. Let us never forget that! Let us worship Him and bow down before Him and exalt His name in words, in silence, and in song. As in that grand hymn:

> O worship the King, all glorious above,
> And gratefully sing His wonderful love;
> Our Shield and Defender, the Ancient of Days,
> Pavilioned in splendor, and girded with praise.
>
> O tell of His might, O sing of His grace,
> Whose robe is the light, whose canopy space!
> His chariots of wrath the deep thunderclouds form,
> And dark is His path on the wings of the storm.

Thy bountiful care, what tongue can recite?
It breathes in the air, it shines in the light.
It streams from the hills, it descends to the plain,
And sweetly distills in the dew and the rain.

Frail children of dust, and feeble as frail,
In Thee do we trust, nor find Thee to fail:
Thy mercies how tender, how firm to the end,
Our Maker, Defender, Redeemer, and Friend![4]

As we shall see in the next chapter, when God finally does speak, He answers Job out of a whirlwind. Suddenly there He is! Wouldn't it have been great for us to have been there? Whoosh! Lightning, loud thunder, mighty winds blowing dark clouds across the heavens, and out of nowhere God bursts on the scene. It must have taken Job's breath away when the Lord "answered Job out of the whirlwind" (Job 38:1).

Many years ago (I was no more than ten years old) on a still and silent morning, long before dawn, I was fishing with my father. Our little fourteen-foot fishing boat was sitting on a slick, in a small body of water just this side of Matagorda Bay. We both had our lines in the water, and neither of us was saying a word. My dad was at the stern by the old twenty-five-horsepower Evinrude, and I was up near the bow of the boat. It was one of those mornings you could flip a penny onto the surface of the water and then count the ripples. It was silent as a tomb—almost eerie.

Suddenly, from the depths of the bay near the hull of our boat, comes this huge tarpon in full strength, bursting out of the water. He does a big-time flip in the air, then plunges with an enormous crash back into the bay. I must have jumped a foot off my wooden seat, shaking with fear. My dad didn't even turn around. Still watching his line, he said quietly, "I told you the big ones were down there."

That's Elihu's message. He is here, Job! Our awesome God—all glorious above. "Job, listen. He's here. He isn't always silent. When He speaks there is no voice like His." Job's view of God may have been enlarged, thanks to his friend's final remarks.

Robert Dick Wilson was the professor of Old Testament in Semitics from 1900 to 1929 at the great old Princeton Theological Seminary, back in the pristine days when its theology was solidly evangelical. Serving on that same faculty had been B. B. Warfield, J. Gresham Machen, and other fine theologians. When Machen later left and began Westminster Seminary, Robert Dick Wilson left with him. Together, they formed the new school.

Donald Grey Barnhouse was a student at Princeton Seminary from 1915 to 1917. Barnhouse later went on to the Tenth Presbyterian Church in Philadelphia to serve as senior pastor for thirty-three years.

But before then, about twelve years after he graduated from Princeton, they invited Barnhouse to come back to the seminary and to preach in Miller Chapel. With a bit of fear and trepidation Barnhouse accepted the invitation. The day finally arrived. He noticed just before he got up to preach, Robert Dick Wilson walked in and came all the way down to the front and sat close to the chapel pulpit.

That can be intimidating, even for a preacher as strong as Barnhouse, with his old prof sitting so close. Barnhouse said later when he finished his message, Dr. Wilson walked up to him, shook his hand, and said, "If you come back, I will not come hear you preach—I only come once to hear my boys. And I come only to see if they are big Godders or little Godders." Not sure that he understood what Dr. Wilson meant by that, Barnhouse asked for an explanation.

"Oh," he said, "it's very simple. Some men have only a little God and they are always in trouble with Him. He can't do the miraculous. He can't take care of life's details. He doesn't intervene on behalf of His people. They have a little God and so I call them 'little Godders'. Then there are those who have a great and mighty God. He speaks and it is done. He commands and it stands fast. He knows how to show Himself strong on behalf of those who fear Him."

Barnhouse, anxious to know in which category he was, breathed a sigh of relief when he heard the man's final statement. "You, Donald, have a great God . . . and He will bless your ministry." He paused and looked deeply into the eyes of the young preacher, smiled, and said, just before he turned to walk out, "God bless you, Donald. God bless you."[5]

How big is your God? Big enough to intervene? Big enough to be trusted? Big enough to be held in awe and ultimate respect? Big enough to erase your worries and replace them with peace?

When your God is too small, your problems are magnified and you retreat in fear and insecurity. When your God is great, your problems pale into insignificance and you stand in awe as you worship the King.

Which are you—a little Godder or a big Godder?

CHAPTER SEVENTEEN

A Penetrating Reproof from the Almighty

G od connects with us in unusual ways. When He does, He often says the most unexpected things. If you're like me, you were taught that God's message comes in calm and peaceful settings. His tone will be gentle and quiet, like that still small voice the boy Samuel heard from his bed in the temple and the prophet Elijah heard at the mouth of the cave at Horeb. We were also told His message will be predictable. But that's not true. There are times when He gets our attention in a chaotic context. Following a close brush with death, we realize after the fact that He protected us from harm. Those messages put a chill down our spine.

That happened to Ann Chapman, employed at Michael's arts and crafts store at the Northgate Shopping Center. At 5:20 p.m. on a Wednesday afternoon the first bullet fired in a shooting spree that ultimately killed five people in Montgomery County, Maryland, cut a dime-sized hole in the display window, nicked a light fixture, pierced two poster-board signs, and hit a metal rack holding rows of minibooks. Amazingly, it narrowly missed Ann as it stopped next to a book called *Inspiration for the Heart* near *The Prayer of Jabez* by Bruce Wilkinson. The cover flap on that particular book reads, "A simple daily prayer from the heart can inspire you to seek God's constant favor, power, and protection." God's message that afternoon to Ann Chapman was anything but calm, quiet, and peaceful. In her case it came near the deadly trajectory of a bullet fired from a sniper's high-powered rifle.

God doesn't always tiptoe into our world making His presence known in a gentle manner. The prophet Nahum tells us it's sometimes "in whirlwind and storm" (Nahum 1:3). When He gave Moses the Law at Mount Sinai, that rocky mountain was surrounded by thick, heavy clouds where there were flashes of lightning and ear-splitting blasts of thunder (Exodus 19:16–19). Elijah witnessed similar scenes as did Ezekiel when the Lord made His presence known.

> The power and majesty of God are evidenced most dramatically in the forces of nature. "Whirlwind" and "storm" are often expressions of his judgment. . . . For all their grandeur, however, these mighty forces are dwarfed in the presence of the Lord, whom the highest heavens cannot contain; the tempest is but the disturbance caused as he marches by, and the dark storm clouds are merely dust stirred up by his feet.[1]

Martin Luther, while pursuing a law degree as a young man in Erfurt, Germany, was caught in a thunderous lightning storm which so frightened and humbled him, he believed God was telling Him he should not be pursuing law. He became convinced this was God's way of saying he needed to enter the monastery and serve Him for the rest of his life. Luther later testified that he sensed God's presence in that frightening storm. Against his father's wishes, he quit his law studies and became a monk. He firmly believed God was speaking to his heart in the midst of that horrendous storm. Theologians refer to that sort of visible manifestation of deity as a *theophany.*

We may be too insensitive or preoccupied to hear God's still voice, but God's soul-stirring messages are never forgotten. Many of us could testify that our lives began to be changed because of some reproof that came through an enormously significant theophany. For some it was literally a "whirlwind" experience.

It was for Job. When God broke the silence, he bolted forth "out of the whirlwind" (Job 38:1). All of us who have waited and ached so long with Job to hear God's voice, we now say with a sigh, "Finally!"

THE LORD'S FIRST MESSAGE

Once God breaks the silence, He gives two "speeches." His first message is recorded in Job 38:1–40:5. His second begins at Job 40:6. I find it interesting and surprising what God does *not* do. He doesn't give Job any *answers* to his questions. He doesn't *apologize* for having been silent so long. He doesn't offer a hint of information about the whole thing between Himself and Satan way back when it all started. Furthermore, God doesn't *acknowledge* that Job has been through deep struggles. When He finally speaks, He begins with a reproof.

By now, Job has gotten a bit independent and arrogant. You get like that when you defend yourself too long. When you've had to stand against the attacks of others, you tend to get a little cocksure.

God is going to communicate a number of things but "job one" is to get Job's heart right before Him. God always knows how to do that. If you take the time to count them, you'll find that God asks seventy-seven questions in these two speeches. His opening line is the first question Job must consider.

> Who is this that darkens counsel
> By words without knowledge?
>
> Job 38:2

The Living Bible renders it this way: "Why are you using your ignorance to deny My providence?" That is not meant to be cruel, only stop Job in his tracks. He needs a refresher course on who's in charge. He needs to realize that God's ways and works are beyond his ability to understand. Keep in mind, there's not a whole group of people standing there; it's just Job and God. So the "who" question has a simple answer!

> Now gird up your loins like a man,
> And I will ask you, and you instruct Me!
>
> Job 38:3

The singular pronouns clarify that God is not talking to the friends. He's talking directly and only to Job.

The first set of questions revolves around the single query: "Can you explain or control My creation?" It's as if the Lord is saying, "Just answer the question, Job." And that ends with a statement of *humility* which Job makes in the third, fourth, and fifth verses of Job 40.

God isn't through.

The next set of questions asks, "Can you change or subdue My creation?" And that's ended with Job's statement of *repentance*. We'll look at that in the next chapter. But for now, let's think about God's first list of questions which Job answers in utter humility. God begins His interrogation with the creation.

> Where were you when I laid the foundation of the earth?
>
> Job 38:4a

Well, obviously he wasn't anywhere around. Nobody was.

> Tell Me, if you have understanding
>
> Job 38:4

He doesn't know that answer either. Nobody does. Having gotten Job's attention, God presses the issue.

> Who set its measurements? Since you know.
> Or who stretched the line on it?
> On what were its bases sunk?"
> Or who laid its cornerstone?
>
> Job 38:6

How did all of this get fixed in space? No explanation—only one possibility—God alone.

> When the morning stars sang together
> And all the sons of God shouted for joy?
>
> Job 38:7

That must be a reference to the first stars. Those morning stars "sang together." Perhaps at creation, the stars literally sang. Maybe it's poetic writing and isn't to be taken literally. Perhaps God is telling Job that all the outer spaces were in harmony with one another. Not having been there, we don't know. Then again, He may have the angels in mind. Maybe they were the "stars" who sang at the time of creation. These angelic creatures were witnessing all of this with open mouths, staring at God's fingerwork of creation, perhaps with this incredulous look on their faces.

Quickly, God moves to the subject of the sea.

> Or who enclosed the sea with doors
> When, bursting forth, it went out from the womb;
> When I made a cloud its garment
> And thick darkness its swaddling band,
> And I placed boundaries on it
> And set a bolt and doors,
> And I said, "Thus far you shall come, but no farther;
> And here shall your proud waves stop?"
>
> Job 38:8–11

"Could you do that, Job? Were you there when that happened?" About now, for sure, Job is getting the drift of all this.

> Have you ever in your life commanded the morning,
> And caused the dawn to know its place?
>
> Job 38:12

With that holding Job in awe, God moves on to the sun—the greater light by day.

> Have you entered into the springs of the sea
> Or walked in the recesses of the deep?
> Have the gates of death been revealed to you,
> Or have you seen the gates of deep darkness?
> Have you understood the expanse of the earth?
> Tell Me, if you know all this.
> Where is the way to the dwelling of light?
> And darkness, where is its place?
>
> Job 38:16–19

Quite a set of questions, isn't it? You know what happens when you're asked questions like this? You get quiet. You're already sitting still, knowing you're in way over your head. As Job says at the end, he puts his hand over his mouth, lest he be tempted to give one answer. You are totally out of it.

It's like being in a classroom where the subject being addressed is blowing you away. And the prof is *way* ahead of you, so you duck behind the head of the person in front of you hoping he won't see you. Not only do you not know the answers, you are aware that others know you don't know, which makes you doubly silent.

The questions continue—forcing Job to realize just how many things are beyond his comprehension. God turns next to the vast dimensions of His creative work. Read slowly and try to imagine God's lecture:

> Have you entered into the springs of the sea
> Or walked in the recesses of the deep?
> Have the gates of death been revealed to you,
> Or have you seen the gates of deep darkness?
> Have you understood the expanse of the earth?
> Tell Me, if you know all this.
> Where is the way to the dwelling of light?
> And darkness, where is its place,
> That you may take it to its territory
> And that you may discern the paths to its home?
>
> Job 38:16–20

In my research I found that the deepest place in all the oceans has been discovered to be 6.78 miles. There may be deeper places, but that's as deep as has been determined as of today—a little over six-and-three-quarter miles beneath the surface.

And the expanse of the stellar spaces? You may remember it took one of our space probes twelve years to cover 4.4 billion miles, ultimately passing within 3,000 miles of Neptune's cloudbank. But that represents space travel only in our *immediate* galaxy. I'm told there are hundreds of thousands, maybe millions more. And who knows but what ours is the smallest of all those in space? It's mind-boggling.

I'm trying to picture Job. By now he is transfixed. I have the feeling all those sore boils don't seem as significant. And those dogmatic answers he had given Eliphaz, Bildad, and Zophar don't seem important anymore.

While on the subject of space, the Lord asks His servant more and more.

> Can you bind the chains of the Pleiades,
> Or loose the cords of Orion?
> Can you lead forth a constellation in its season,
> And guide the Bear with her satellites?
> Do you know the ordinances of the heavens,
> Or fix their rule over the earth?
> Can you lift up your voice to the clouds,
> So that an abundance of water may cover you?
>
> Job 38:31–33

It's like what happens to us when we visit one of those giant telescopes where we can take a look into space, witnessing realms beyond the familiar. We step back, blink, shake our head, stuff our hands in our pockets, and get quiet. We don't turn around and start instructing the person who runs the observatory. The enormity of it all makes us feel incredibly insignificant; we're microscopic specks when compared to the telescopic vastness of outer space. It's especially enormous because the One who could answer every question is talking to Job. He not only created it, He set it all in motion and keeps everything moving in clockwork precision.

And if that isn't enough, God introduces the animal kingdom. He specifies both four-footed and winged creatures. Let's roam through these descriptions as if visiting the local zoo. Try to imagine Job as he entertains each question!

> Can you hunt the prey for the lion,
> Or satisfy the appetite of the young lions,
> When they crouch in their dens
> And lie in wait in their lair?
> Who prepares for the raven its nourishment
> When its young cry to God
> And wander about without food?
> Do you know the time the mountain goats give birth?
> Do you observe the calving of the deer?
> Can you count the months they fulfill,
> Or do you know the time they give birth?
>
> Job 38:39–39:2

> Who sent out the wild donkey free?
> And who loosed the bonds of the swift donkey,
> To whom I gave the wilderness for a home
> And the salt land for his dwelling place?
>
> Job 39:5–6

> Will the wild ox consent to serve you,
> Or will he spend the night at your manger?
> Can you bind the wild ox in a furrow with ropes,
> Or will he harrow the valleys after you?
>
> Job 39:9–10

> The ostriches' wings flap joyously
> With the pinion and plumage of love,
> For she abandons her eggs to the earth
> And warms them in the dust,

And she forgets that a foot may crush them,
Or that a wild beast may trample them.

Job 39:13–15

Do you give the horse his might?
Do you clothe his neck with a mane?
Do you make him leap like the locust?
His majestic snorting is terrible.
He paws in the valley, and rejoices in his strength;
He goes out to meet the weapons.
He laughs at fear and is not dismayed;
And he does not turn back from the sword.

Job 39:19–22

Is it by your understanding that the hawk soars,
Stretching his winds toward the south?
Is it at your command that the eagle mounts up
And makes his nest on high?
On the cliff he dwells and lodges,
Upon the rocky crag, an inaccessible place.
From there he spies out food;
His eyes see it from afar.
His young ones also suck up blood;
And where the slain are, there is he.

Job 39:26–30

Why? I can hear you ask that question. (That was my first reaction when I read all of this.) "Why?" I asked myself, "What in the world does a visit into outer space or a trip to the zoo have to do with comforting Job with those boils all over his skin? All God needed to do was go "zap" and He could have taken them all away. Instantly and forever they'd be gone. But He didn't do that.

Author David Atkinson helps us understand.

Why, we need to ask, does God spend all this time talking about the skies and the stars and the animals? Surely there is a more appropriate topic of conversation for someone who for some weeks has been going through an appalling sense of isolation?

It is, of course, only when a depressed person has the safety and reassurance of another's presence that conversation can happen. Now that Job knows he is not alone, it is appropriate for God to talk—and perhaps to distract Job from his misery, certainly to give him new perspectives on his situation. . . .

It is as though the Lord God is taking a walk through his creation—a walk through the Garden, perhaps, as the storm becomes still—and is inviting Job to accompany him: Do you see this? Do you recognize that? . . .

Let me amaze you, says God, by the complexity and intricacy of it all! From the foundation of the earth (38:4), when the morning stars sang together and all the sons of God in the heavenly court shouted for joy (38:7), that joyous celebration of the Creator has been sung ever since. Consider the sea, held back from its chaotic power (38:8–11), the skies, the deep, the light, and the darkness (38:12–21). . . .

Think of the animals too! Can you hunt prey for the lioness (38:39)? Who provides for the ravens (38:41)? What about the life-giving power of birth—for the mountain goats (39:1); the wild asses (39:5); the wild oxen (39:9)?

Come round with me, Job: see these things; wonder at them; enjoy them. You cannot control them, but they are under my control, says God. . . .

"You are never what you ought, till you go out of yourself and walk among them." That is perhaps why God takes Job on this tour—to show his majesty in his works: to take Job out of himself, to distract him from his misery, to broaden his horizons to the creative and life-giving majesty of God, and especially to enable him to see himself in a new setting.

Job, this is where your heart will find rest: in finding your own place within the panorama of God's purposes for his world. Can you lift your eyes from the ash heap, and see the glory of God in his creation?[2]

It seems that the Lord is helping Job get beyond his immediate world of hurt—his ever-present counselors with their never-ending criticism and blame. By doing this, He is preparing Job's heart, if you will, for a whole new understanding of His ways, for a willingness to forgive those men of their harsh words, and for the ability to recover and go on without bitterness or other inner scars.

The ash heap may be an appropriate place on which to sit if we are in mourning, but it is no place to stay if we wish to feel better. Sometimes we will most help distressed people—help them draw nearer to God, from the depths of depression—not by teaching them doctrine, or by preaching our best sermon, or by showing them the error of their ways, but by walking with them round the garden, by taking them to see a waterfall or a sunset, by helping them recover an enjoyment in the world. Such steps are not always practicable, of course. But in so far as we can enable depressed people to see themselves in a new setting, and to recover a place of security and belonging within the rich panorama of God's creation, we are helping them.[3]

JOB'S HUMBLE RESPONSE

There is no question: Job gets it.

Then Job answered the LORD and said,
"Behold, I am insignificant; what can I reply to You?
I lay my hand on my mouth.
Once I have spoken, and I will not answer;
Even twice, and I will add no more."

Job 40:3–5

If you take the time to analyze those words, you'll see that Job has three responses. The first is a response of *humility*. The second is a response of *relief*. And the third is a response of *surrender*. That's all God wanted to hear. And what an important change for Job! Without realizing it, he had become this independent, determined, self-assured apologist defending himself. Without saying so, he'd begun to appear as if he had his arms around the providence of God.

His first response is verse 4, "*I am insignificant.*" Many of those who have been schooled in the fine points of psychology will reject this response. They will say we should be encouraged to realize how important we are, how valuable we are to God, what a significant place we fill in this world. They would counsel, "Don't think or say, 'I am insignificant.'" Before we're tempted to go there, take note that God doesn't reprove Job for saying he is insignificant or unworthy.

The Hebrew term for *insignificant* means "light in weight" in contrast to the term translated "heavy."

> "Unworthy" translates . . . "light in weight," as opposed to . . . "heavy/worthy/honorable." With a rhetorical question of his own, Job replied that he could not answer any of the questions. In a gesture of submission and surrender he covered his mouth. . . .
>
> Job had outtalked Eliphaz, Bildad, and Zophar; but in the presence of God he was dumbfounded, that is, dumb and confounded.[4]

We'd put it this way: "I'm a lightweight." Frankly, it's true. It is an appropriate term for Job to use after being asked so many things he couldn't answer, and shown so much he didn't understand. In unguarded humility the man admits, "I'm insignificant."

His second statement is *"What can I reply to You?"* I see that as an expression of *relief*. God didn't want answers, He *knew* the answers. He knows all of them! He wanted Job to acknowledge, "I don't know any of the answers. And if I don't know about those things, as objective as they are, how could I ever fully understand the profound mysteries surrounding my world?" By acknowledging that, quiet relief replaced troubling resistance.

My point here—and this is terribly important: When we are broken and brought to the end of ourselves, it is not for the purpose of gaining more answers to spout off to others. It's to help us acknowledge that the Lord is God, and His plans and reasons are deeper and higher and broader than we can comprehend. Therefore, we are relieved from having to give answers or defend them.

Job's third response is a statement of *surrender*. "I put my hand on my mouth," verse 4 concludes. I dare not say more. I've said enough—actually too much—already.

LEAPING FROM JOB'S DAY TO OUR DAY

Job's response prompts me to think of what this says to our twenty-first-century world. What needed messages it offers to our times! I find at least three of them between the lines of Job's response.

The first: *If God's ways are higher than mine, then whatever He allows I bow before Him in submission.* The result of that attitude is *true humility.* Submission to the Father's will is the mark of genuine humility. And all of us could use a huge dose of that. How unusual to find a humble spirit in our day, especially among the competent, the highly intelligent, the successful.

Here's the second: *If God is in full control, then however He directs my steps, I follow in obedience.* What *relief* that brings! Finally—I can relax, since I'm not in charge.

I was speaking at a pastors' conference at Moody Bible Institute in Chicago not long ago. The most vivid memory of that conference was the large sign up front. It was hung above the platform for all in attendance to read each time we came together. In big, bold letters it read:

RELAX EVERYBODY, FOR ONCE YOU'RE NOT IN CHARGE.

The auditorium was full of pastors—fifteen hundred in all! And each one of us is usually in charge (we think), only to show up at this conference and be reminded to relax—we're *not* in charge. It was an encouraging relief for everybody in attendance.

That's the sign God stretched in front of Job. "You're not in charge of anything, Job; this is My responsibility. You're my servant—I'm your Master. I know what I'm doing." Since God knows what He's doing, however He directs my steps, I simply follow. What an encouraging relief that brings!

Here's the third: *If God has answers I lack, then whenever He speaks, I listen in silence.* In the process of listening, I learn. Learning requires our slowing down, patiently waiting for God to work, staying ready to listen as He instructs us in His ways. You and I are not by nature humble, submissive, and quiet. We much prefer being in charge, in control, and barking out orders. For sure, we don't like to wait. We want what we want when we want it.

Four-year-old Timmy was buckled up in the backseat with his older brother and sister as the family was making a long trip. About every other mile he would ask, "Are we almost there, Daddy? Have we almost gotten there? Are we about there, Mommy?" Exasperated, his mother turned and said to Timmy, "Timmy, no! We're not *almost there.* It will take a *very long time* before we're there!" Time passed in silence. Timmy could stay quiet no longer. So he changed his question: "Mommy, when we get there will I still be four years old?"

"Lord, hurry up! Come on now!" We'd rather rush than wait. We'd rather get forgiveness than permission. We'd rather resist than obey. We would rather talk than listen. We would rather be in charge than submit.

Because those things are true, we need the reminder of this Puritan prayer:

> When thou wouldst guide me I control myself,
> When thou wouldst be sovereign I rule myself.
> When thou wouldst take care of me I suffice myself.
> When I should depend on thy providings I supply myself,
> When I should submit to thy providence I follow my will,
> When I should study, love, honour, trust thee, I serve myself;
> I fault and correct thy laws to suit myself,
> Instead of thee I look to man's approbation, and am by nature an idolater.
> Lord, it is my chief design to bring my heart back to thee.
> Convince me that I cannot be my own god, or make myself happy,

nor my own Christ to restore my joy, nor my own Spirit to teach,
   guide, rule me.
Help me to see that grace does this by providential affliction, for when
   my credit is god thou dost cast me lower, when riches are my idol
   thou dost wing them away, when pleasure is my all thou dost turn
   it into bitterness.
Take away my roving eye, curious ear, greedy appetite, lustful heart;
Show me that none of these things can heal a wounded conscience, or
   support a tottering frame, or uphold a departing spirit.
Then take me to the cross and leave me there.[5]

I can't conclude this chapter without adding some gut-wrenching reality. It will take conscious effort on our part to change. You may have become difficult to live with. If that is true, those closest to you are running out of ways of saying the hard thing. My hope is that your reading this chapter will help you turn a much-needed corner. And I do need to warn you: If you *do* get serious about changes and begin to implement some of them, it will shock those folks who have been trying to get your attention.

In his fine volume, *True North,* fellow pastor Gary Inrig quotes Tom Anderson, whose story describes the reason for my warning.

I made a vow to myself on the drive down to the vacation beach cottage. For two weeks I would try to be a loving husband and father. Totally loving. No ifs, ands, or buts. The idea had come to me as I listened to a commentator on my car's tape player. He was quoting a biblical passage about husbands being thoughtful of their wives. Then he went on to say, "Love is an act of the will. A person can choose to love." To myself, I had to admit that I had been a selfish husband— that our love had been dulled by my own insensitivity. In petty ways, really chiding Evelyn for her tardiness; insisting on the TV channel I wanted to watch; throwing out day-old newspapers before Evelyn had a chance to read them. Well, for two weeks all that would change.

   And it did. Right from the moment I kissed Evelyn at the door and said, "That new yellow sweater looks great on you." "Oh, Tom, you noticed," she said, surprised and pleased. And maybe a little shocked.

After the long drive, I wanted to sit and read. Evelyn suggested a walk on the beach. I started to refuse, but then I thought, Evelyn's been alone here with the kids all week and now she wants to be alone with me. We walked on the beach while the children flew their kites.

So it went. Two weeks of not calling the Wall Street investment firm where I am a director; a visit to the shell museum, though I usually hate museums; holding my tongue while Evelyn's getting ready made us late for a dinner date. Relaxed and happy, that's how the whole vacation passed. I made a new vow to keep on remembering to choose love.

There was one thing that went wrong with my experiment, however. On the last night at our cottage, preparing for bed, Evelyn stared at me with the saddest expression.

"What's the matter?" I asked her.

"Tom," she said, in a voice filled with distress, "do you know something I don't?"

"What do you mean?"

"Well . . . that checkup I had several weeks ago . . . our doctor . . . did he tell you something about me? Tom, you've been so good to me . . . am I dying?"

It took a moment for it all to sink in. Then I burst out laughing. "No, honey," I said, wrapping her in my arms, "you're not dying; I'm just starting to live!"[6]

That is my hope for you as a result of seeking these new dimensions through Job's eyes. The fact is, your attitude is a choice you make each day. And if it takes a walk through the zoo or out among the stars, take it. Whatever it takes to convince you what a "lightweight" you really are and, yes, how much your world still revolves around you. God is doing everything possible to get your attention. Isn't it about time you listened and changed? It starts with making a few significant choices.

Begin today. Who knows? You may find you're just starting to live.

CHAPTER EIGHTEEN

Full Repentance for All the Right Reasons

I t is difficult to cultivate a humble heart in a contentious culture. Put another way, a repentant spirit is rarely found in a litigious society. How seldom we hear "I am wrong; I am truly sorry; will you please forgive me?" As opposed to that, how often we hear, "I will sue you! I'll take you to court!"

The following is a classic example of how our world thinks. It is not only a true story, it was the first-place winner of The Criminal Lawyers Award Contest in the year 2002.

A Charlotte, North Carolina, lawyer purchased a box of very rare and expensive cigars, then insured them against fire, among other things. Within a month, having smoked his entire stockpile of these great cigars and without yet having made even his first premium payment on the policy, the lawyer filed claim against the insurance company.

In his claim, the lawyer stated the cigars were lost "in a series of small fires." The insurance company refused to pay, citing the obvious reason: that the man had consumed the cigars in the normal fashion was obvious.

The lawyer sued and won!

In delivering the ruling the judge agreed with the insurance company that the claim was frivolous. The judge stated, nevertheless, that the lawyer held a policy from the company in which it had warranted that the cigars were insurable and also guaranteed that it would insure them against fire, without defining what is considered to be unacceptable fire, and was obligated to pay the claim.

Rather than endure a lengthy and costly appeal process, the insurance company accepted the ruling and paid $15,000 to the lawyer for his loss of the rare cigars lost in the "fires."

NOW FOR THE BEST PART . . . After the lawyer cashed the check, the insurance company had him arrested on 24 counts of AR-SON! With his own insurance claim and testimony from the previous case being used against him, the lawyer was convicted of intentionally burning his insured property and was sentenced to 24 months in jail and a $24,000 fine.[1]

Try to teach your children the importance of walking humbly with God with stories like this swirling through the media. Is it any wonder the words "I repent" are rarely heard these days?

Maybe that's the reason my head snapped back when I jumped ahead in the story of Job and read his words, "I retract, and I repent in dust and ashes" (Job 42:6). Eugene Peterson's rendering provides verbal expressions Job probably had in mind: "I'm sorry—forgive me. I'll never do that again, I promise! I'll never again live on crusts of hearsay, crumbs of rumor."

If you check the context in which Job made that statement of repentance to God, you'll find that nothing has yet changed for him. He's still bankrupt; he's still without his family. He's still covered with sore boils, and those three self-righteous critics, yea four, are still frowning nearby, still convinced he's getting what he deserves. That makes Job's attitude of repentance all the more authentic. It would have been much easier to fall down in utter submission before God if he were now healed and relieved, and if those four critics had been put in their place. But with *none* of that turned around, Job bows before his Lord and sighs, "I retract . . . I repent." No question about it, that represents full repentance for all the right reasons.

John Hartley puts his finger on the essence of Job's humble response:

> Job abases himself and recants, confessing himself to be no better than the *dust* and *ashes* on which he has been sitting. Job has come to a true assessment of himself before the holy God. . . . Job both renounces all false pride and concedes that God has been true to justice in allowing him, the noblest sheikh, to be brought so low that he has had to sit outside the city on the ash heap. The term *recant (niham)* means to turn from a planned course of action and take up a new course. It implies the strongest resolve to change direction, but not an attitude of remorse. It is affirmative action based on conviction. In recanting Job surrenders to God the last vestige of his self-righteousness, i.e., he withdraws his avowal of innocence. From now on he will locate his self-worth in his relationship with Yahweh, not in his own moral behavior or innocence.[2]

We're witnessing in Job the personification of an humble and contrite heart. Speaking of that, consider the words of David following the misery he endured in the backwash of his adultery with Bathsheba. In his brokenness following repentance, David wrote a song, realizing the wrongness of his actions, a song that found its way into the Bible. Today we know it as Psalm 51. It contains David's feelings surrounding his repentance.

He begins,

Be gracious to me, O God, according to Your lovingkindness;
According to the greatness of Your compassion blot out my
    transgressions.
Wash me thoroughly from my iniquity
And cleanse me from my sin.
For I know my transgressions,
And my sin is ever before me.
Against You, You only, I have sinned
And done what is evil in Your sight,

So that You are justified when You speak
And blameless when You judge.

Psalm 51:1–4

There's no hiding his transgressions, no blaming someone else. There is only open confession flowing from his repentant heart. Speaking of that, he asks the Lord:

Create in me a clean heart, O God,
And renew a steadfast spirit within me.

Psalm 51:10

He doesn't expect the people around him to understand or to take pity on him. He owns full responsibility for his actions. He's getting everything right with God, which is where repentance begins. David's words provide some helpful insights about true repentance:

The sacrifices of God are a broken spirit;
A broken and a contrite heart, O God, You will not despise.

Psalm 51:17

Look closely. Repentance provides two sacrifices God finds pleasure in: a broken spirit and a contrite heart. Turn these words over in your mind. While doing that myself, I came up with five characteristics of a broken spirit and a contrite heart.

First, *a contrite heart nurses no grudges.* A contrite heart never says, "If it hadn't been for what she . . ." or "If he hadn't done . . ." or "Because I was raised like I was raised . . ." No. A broken spirit blames no one.

Second, *a contrite heart makes no demands.* It obligates no one else to do *anything.* Others' responses aren't a part of our agenda when we're truly repentant.

Third, *a contrite heart has no expectations.* I don't expect good treatment. I don't expect people to understand or to forgive me. That may happen in time, but it's not something the contrite heart expects.

Fourth, *a broken spirit offers no conditions.* No ifs, no maybes, no buts, no bargains.

Fifth, *a broken spirit and contrite heart anticipate no favors.* I don't anticipate as a result that you will do something gracious for me. I'm on my own before my God. By repenting, I'm acknowledging the wrongness of my actions, my attitudes, my words with no anticipation of applause or a nod of understanding from others.

When these things transpire in full repentance, there is no room left for bitterness.

WHAT PROMPTED SUCH REPENTANCE?

Now, let's look back into the biblical record and see if we can find what prompted such a repentant spirit in Job. We're going to discover that God got Job's full attention. It's as if He places both His mighty hands on Job's shoulders and looks him in the eye. This is followed by two unforgettable examples that communicate a message Job will never forget.

God's Hands on Job's shoulders

Before looking at the biblical basis for my word picture, let me mention something we've all gone through as parents. What I'm about to write may not be "politically correct," but it is the truth. Parents *know* it's the truth. There are times that nothing works better with our small children than placing both of our hands on their shoulders and speaking firmly as we look them in the eye. Exasperated over their words or attitudes or misdeeds, we put both hands on their shoulders, and we speak slowly and firmly. During those few moments we admonish them to "straighten up" or "watch your mouth" or "correct that negative attitude!" Amazing how well that works!

In a similar way, I'm suggesting here that the Lord takes Job by the shoulders and gives him a firm talking-to. And what is it He is saying to His servant? Something along these lines: "Job, listen to me. I am God. You are My servant. I am your authority. I am in charge. I'm the Potter, you're the clay, remember? I'm molding and shaping you—you *will* be shaped. It's important that you fully understand, Job, you are not on My level. You are My servant—you are not God." God is setting His servant straight!

Read these words from *The Message* and see if you don't agree:

> I have some more questions for you,
> and I want straight answers.
> Do you presume to tell me what I'm doing wrong?
>   Are you calling me a sinner so you can be a saint?
> Do you have an arm like my arm?
>   Can you shout in thunder the way I can?
> Go ahead, show your stuff.
>   Let's see what you're made of, what you can do.
> Unleash your outrage.
>   Target the arrogant and lay them flat.
> Target the arrogant and bring them to their knees.
>   Stop the wicked in their tracks—make mincemeat of them!
> Dig a mass grave and dump them in it—
>   faceless corpses in an unmarked grave.
> I'll gladly step aside and hand things over to you—
>   you can surely save yourself with no help from me!
>
>   Job 40:7–14, MSG

Obviously, Job can't do any of the above. Compared to the Lord God, he could never "show his stuff;" he would have no success making "mincemeat" of the wicked.

Let's go back to God's intervention for a moment, okay? Putting all this into today's domestic setting, it's as if God says, "Let me make something real clear to you, Son. As the father, I'm the one who earns the living in this home. If you're in charge and you earn the living, then you need to go where I go and work where I work. You need to face the pressures I face, then make the decisions I make. You take care of the mortgage. You handle the leadership in this family. You make the plans. You make certain they are carried out correctly. I ask you: "Are you able to do that?" Obviously, the son has to say, "No sir, I can't do that." "You're right, son, you're not the dad. That means you answer to me. Now, let me assure you *I will love you forever,* but you *will not rule this home.* That's my role. Do you understand that?"

Job is beginning to get it. But sometimes kids need examples to help convey the message. So, God gives him a couple of unforgettable illustrations.

God mentions two powerful animals

Something makes me think Job was a real lover of the animal world, perhaps a serious student of nature. So, knowing that, the Lord chose a couple of animals. First, the Behemoth, next, Leviathan. Now, why on earth would God choose *these* animals? Stop and think. These two animals are at the top of the food chain. Neither is intimidated. They can take care of themselves in the wild. Most every other animal bows to them, and if they don't, they pay a terrible price, usually with their life.

The Behemoth represents the hippopotamus. I understand that this huge creature is far more dangerous and deadly than most of us realize. The Leviathan is an ancient word for the crocodile. We'll look at the Leviathan shortly. But before we consider either one, let's understand that both of these beasts, though they are intimidating to you and me, were made by God. Because that is true they are continually subservient to their Creator. They have the natures and instincts He gave them. They do the things He created them to do. The implied message behind all this? If you're unable to handle these creatures, obviously you're not on My level. And if you, in fact, are fearful of them, then you would certainly not qualify as their Maker. First, let us consider the hippopotamus in a little more detail.

> Behold now, Behemoth, which I made as well as you; He eats grass like an ox.
>
> Job 10:15a

Notice the opening. "You're both creatures, very different. It walks on all fours; you walk erect on two legs. It eats grass and vegetation like an ox; that's not your diet." He then mentions the strength of this enormous beast:

Behold now, his strength in his loins
And his power in the muscles of his belly.
He bends his tail like a cedar;
The sinews of his thighs are knit together.
His bones are tubes of bronze;
His limbs are like bars of iron.

Job 40:16–18

That last vivid statement probably means he's chief or the mightiest among the animals. Other animals, when they see him, move away from him. God has placed him at the uppermost level of authority in the animal kingdom.

He is the first of the ways of God;
Let his maker ring near his sword.
Surely the mountains bring him food,
And all the beasts of the field play there.
Under the lotus plants he lies down,
In the covert of the reeds and the marsh.
The lotus plants cover him with shade;
The willows of the brook surround him.
If a river rages, he is not alarmed;
He is confident, though the Jordan rushes to his mouth.
Can anyone capture him when he is on watch,
With barbs can anyone pierce his nose?

Job 40:19–24

In ancient days, to capture and/or kill one of these gigantic creatures, you'd have to pierce the nose or plug it up so that he'd have to open his mouth to breathe. And at the moment he opens his mouth, the hunter would thrust a handmade spear into its throat, killing him. How rare would that be! Job is listening. He is getting the point: "Even one species of animal life is enough to make you back down, Job. You're no match against something this overpowering. If I, the Lord, am powerful enough to create and subdue a creature this strong and intimidating, I'm deserving of your trust, your submission, and your worship."

While Job is beginning to grasp all that, the Lord moves quickly to the Leviathan.

> Can you draw out Leviathan with a fishhook?
> Or press down his tongue with a cord?
>
> Job 40:1

We who love to fish realize that we usually select the hook size depending on the size of the fish's mouth we're hoping to catch. Larger hook—larger fish. Smaller hook, obviously, smaller mouth or smaller fish.

In light of that, "Can you draw out a Leviathan (or a crocodile) with a fish hook?" This creature is fierce. Look at all the "can yous" and "will yous" that follow:

> Can you put a rope in his nose
> Or pierce his jaw with a hook?
> Will he make many supplications to you,
> Or will he speak to you soft words?
>
> Job 41:2–3

Literally these are all absurd word pictures. Will that beast speak soft and tender things? Did you ever have a crocodile look up and whisper soft little words and loving comments? There's some divine humor here. God goes on, overdrawing the word pictures:

> Will he make a covenant with you?
> Will you take him for a servant forever?
> Will you play with him as with a bird,
> Or will you bind him for your maidens?
>
> Job 41:4–5

How's that for a humorous thought? It's the idea of putting a leash around him, for your daughters to enjoy as a pet and take to school with them. Picture a delightful eight-foot-long pet croc they're enjoying. The idea makes us laugh. It's supposed to. It's ludicrous. Completely absurd. God goes on and on until He comes to the climax of the example and states:

> Behind him he makes a wake to shine;
> One would think the deep to be gray-haired.
>
> Job 41:33.

The Lord's point is clear: "I *alone* control this beast in the swamp, Job!" Now I realize, when I refer to the croc as a beast to be feared, I'm working against what you've seen on television. I'm referring to this weird guy from Australia—the one with a very small brain who swims with these suckers and thinks they're the most wonderful creatures imaginable. You've seen his programs—they make me shudder! Late at night he's out in his little dinghy, and he slips over the side into the swamp as he says with a big smile, "I've lived all my life for this moment." I'm thinking, *You may be living your last* hour, *you klutz!*

And then he slides beneath the murky water, and he swims along until he spots a twelve-footer, and says something like, "Oh, look at those claws. They're beautiful!" But when I look at the claws, I think, "They would tear you apart, you dork! Get out of the water!" The guy is a taco shy of a Mexican meal. He will *never* make it to old age!

You know what makes it worse? The guy married a woman who likes messing around with them too! She's also a floor short of a full elevator ride. I mean, she finds 'em and grabs 'em and hugs 'em. (There's something sick about that whole thing.) To make matters worse, I'll bet neither one of those Aussies ever read Job 41!

God is making it clear that the crocodile is not made to be a pet. It lives in the swamps and it is ferocious. It is bloodthirsty. It is brutal. It is a killer, but again it is completely submissive to its Maker.

The crocodile cannot operate outside specific parameters, the limits that God has established for the reptile. It does exactly what it was created to do. It swims because God made it an excellent swimmer. And it feeds on a meat diet because God gave it that appetite. He did it all. He made it all. He owns it all.

Glance back at God's earlier reminder. He puts all of this in perspective:

> Who has given to Me that I should repay him?
> Whatever is under the whole heaven is Mine.
>
> Job 41:11

There's another direct eye-to-eye statement: "Job, you're Mine. You are clay in My hands. I'm doing a great work, and you are to trust Me in the mystery of it all."

HOW DID JOB RESPOND?

Job listens all the way through this most unusual message. As God gets to the end of His second speech, He underscores His major point:

> He looks on everything that is high:
> He is king over all the sons of pride.
>
> Job 41:34

I don't know if he did, but Job could very well have put his hands up in the air and blurted out: "I've heard enough. I got it. *I got it,* Lord!"

Remember Job earlier had said, "If only He would come and talk with me. I would plead my case before Him." The implication seems to have been, "He owes me a hearing. After the way I've lived and all that I have gone through, the least He can do is present Himself before me." Stop, Job! We don't give God the script. It's not our prerogative to dictate the parameters of God's plan or state the details of God's response. That's not ours to do, since everything under heaven is His. Job sees all that now and repents.

His submissive response is magnificent! Job answered and said,

> I know that You can do all things,
> And that no purpose of Yours can be thwarted.
>
> Job 42:2

"Whether it's creating and growing the hippo or giving the crocodile its strong will and ferocious nature, or any creature of the forest and the jungles, in the air or under the surface of the seas, or even whether it's a man or woman, no purpose of Yours can be thwarted."

Reminds me of King Nebuchadnezzar's words after his years of insanity, after he finally came to his senses.

> All the inhabitants of the earth are accounted as nothing,
> But He does according to His will in the host of heaven
> And among the inhabitants of earth;
> And no one can ward off His hand
> Or say to Him, "What have You done?"
>
> Daniel 4:35

That's true submission. "O God, I may be a king on this earth, but I now acknowledge Your sovereign authority. I don't even breathe without Your giving me breath. I can't move without Your giving my muscles, my bones, my nerves that ability. All heaven and earth is Yours. You own it all and nothing of Yours can be thwarted." That's Job's attitude.

In utter humility, Job goes further:

> Who is this that hides counsel without knowledge?
> Therefore I have declared that which I did not understand,
> Things too wonderful for me, which I did not know.
>
> Job 42:3

"I've come to the end of my understanding and I leave it at that. My very existence is Yours, O God. It's Yours to unravel the mystery, to track the labyrinthine ways, to handle the profound, to know the reasons behind the inexplicable events of my life." In full surrender he backs off and bows down.

This is Job's way of acknowledging his inability to understand why, with no further argument, harboring no bitterness. There is no thought of *How dare you do this to me?* What do we see in Job? A broken and contrite spirit.

> I have heard of You by the hearing of the ear;
> But now my eye sees You;
> Therefore I retract,
> And I repent in dust and ashes.
>
> Job 42:5–6

If there ever was a streak of pride or rebellion in his heart, it was now gone. Gone forever.

Cynthia and I were once close friends with a wonderful Christian family—a dad and mom and three sons. The oldest son was greatly gifted intellectually and musically. Along with being a fine young scholar, he was also a splendid violinist.

Earlier in his high school years, the father had some trouble with the boy's spirit of submission. But you know how you'll do with your gifted children, you'll give them room, you cut them a little too much slack. A proud streak accompanied the boy's independent spirit.

Upon graduating from high school the young man chose a prestigious school on the West Coast—very expensive but an excellent university known for its academics. The physician father paid the full tuition, and the boy began his first year many miles from home. Wasn't long before the kid started running around with a tough crowd. He continued his musicianship, played violin in the school's orchestra, and did well, academically. But while he was out there, he cultivated an even more surly, rebellious spirit.

After completing his freshman year he returned home, bringing his proud independence with him. It wasn't long into the summer before his mom and dad and the two younger brothers realized they had a real hellion living under their roof. The conflicts intensified. His arrogant, stubborn, and meanspirited attitude disrupted the family harmony. Late one afternoon the father had had enough.

He called the boy into his study, closed the door, pointed to the large leather chair, and said firmly, "Sit down." He then delivered a speech the boy would never forget. "Everything you own is mine. I bought every stitch of clothing you wear and everything that hangs in your closet. Your car out there in the driveway is mine; I paid for it. The money in your pocket came from my account. I want you to empty your pockets and your wallet on my desk. Leave everything that is mine in this house, and I want you to get out. Leave all your clothing, give me the car keys, and oh, by the way, also leave your violin. I bought that instrument too. You leave everything that you have been using, which I am now claiming. You may keep the clothes on your back and the shoes on your feet, but that's it. There's the door. Leave now.

"When you decide to change your attitude and come back into this home as a family member with a cooperative, submissive spirit, you need to know we will accept you and we'll welcome you back as a part of our family, but not until! I love you and always will, but you're not the boy we raised, and I'm not putting up with it one minute longer."

The father later told me that the boy stood to his feet, put all his money on the desk, walked to the door, and left everything without saying one word. He proudly walked to the sidewalk out front, took a left and got about three blocks down the street. The dad then added, "He got a liberal arts education between the front door of our home and the curb about three blocks away."

He said he stood down there motionless with his hands in his empty pockets thinking everything through as night was falling. He thought about all he would be facing, the street life he knew nothing about, and every-thing he was leaving—all the things back home he needed and longed for. He remembered his father's strong rebuke and also his promise to accept him back with an attitude of repentance. When it was almost dark, he turned around, walked back home with his head down, and knocked on his own front door. Dad opened the door with Mom standing near, and the other boys behind her. Then came the words, "I am wrong. I am sorry. I realize I need you, and I want all of you to know that I'm sorry. I love you." They reached out and embraced him. (Probably the brothers had been thinking, "Who's gonna get his room?" You know how brothers are.) But as I recall the story, that same evening, there was a big dinner together and great joy. His repentance changed everything.

Do you know what Job finally realized? It is all about God, not me. Job got it! And what does that mean?

- God's purpose is unfolding and I cannot hinder it.
- God's plan is incredible and I will not comprehend it.
- God's reproof is reliable and I dare not ignore it.
- God's way is best and I must not resist it.

Have you learned those things yet? Have you come to realize your business is about your God. Your family is about your God. Everything you claim to possess, He owns. Every privilege you enjoy is granted by His grace. None of it is deserved. Job got all that . . . the question is, *have you?* Tragically, many don't get it until faced with impossible moments. God has ways of leveling His own.

How satisfying a submissive life can be. The blend is beautiful to behold: a strong-hearted person, who is surrendered and humbled with a "broken and contrite spirit"—entertaining no grudges, making no demands, having no expectations, offering no conditions, anticipating no favors, fully repentant before the Lord God. And the marvelous result? The Lord begins to use us in amazing ways. Why? Because the world doesn't see that unique combination very often.

Job finally sees God for who He really is, and he fully repents. The result is one blessing after another, as we shall soon see. In fact, double blessing upon double blessing comes his way. Once God placed His mighty hands on the man's shoulders, Job finally got it.

Is somebody trying to get your attention these days? Have you decided you're not going to sit there and take it any longer? Have you gotten about three blocks away? Before walking one more step, stop and think.

Learn a lesson from a once-rebellious freshman. Turn around. Come on home.

CHAPTER NINETEEN

Finally . . . Justice Rolls Down

T here is something deeply satisfying about justice. We love it when right is rewarded and wrong is punished. The old axiom, "Justice is truth in action" explains our love for it; what is fair finally occurs.

No one is better at justice than the Living God, who is not only all-knowing, He is completely fair and absolutely righteous. When His justice finally arrives, it was worth the wait. That wait can seem interminably long. But never doubt it: Regardless of how long or short the wait—the Lord is just. Even though all God's accounts are not settled at the end of each month, *they will be settled.* Justice is an essential ingredient of His character; He not only will not ignore it . . . He cannot.

Travel back with me for the next few minutes to an ancient era when religious indifference was commonplace. Back in those years of Jewish history, kings and prophets were known in the land. Externally there was material wealth and military might, but inwardly there was idolatry, political corruption, and social evil. Nevertheless, religious activities continued on in a ritual-like manner, which the Lord despised. He announced His displeasure through the lips of His prophet, Amos, who boldly declared:

> I hate, I reject your festivals,
> Nor do I delight in your solemn assemblies.
> Even though you offer up to Me burnt offerings and your grain offerings,
> I will not accept them;
> And I will not even listen to the sound of your harps.
> But let justice roll down like waters
> And righteousness like an ever-flowing stream.
>
> Amos 5:21–24

The Lord had gotten "sick and tired" (as we would say) of their hollow religious meetings, their busy conventions and conferences, their empty-hearted offerings, even their noisy, upbeat songs. He wasn't about to put up with the sham much longer; His fuse was now frighteningly short. Don't miss those four powerful words toward the end of His announcement: "Let justice roll down. " Indeed, it did.

It is that which makes the climax of Job's life so satisfying. This dear man, who never deserved the suffering he endured, is dealt with justly. And those who made his life so miserable weren't overlooked either. The God of Justice finally steps up, bringing great rewards and restoration to the righteous, and strong discipline on the unrighteous.

A QUICK REVIEW

Job finally got it. He finally realized that God's plan is profound, that His reasoning is right, and that His ways are higher than he could ever understand. With that, Job waves the white flag of surrender and says in complete sincerity, "I retract and I repent. I've said things I shouldn't have been saying, I talked about things I knew nothing about, I became self-righteous in my own defense. Lord, please know that my heart is Yours. I humble myself before You. I place myself at Your disposal. Your purpose is right; Your plan is incredible; Your reproofs are reliable; Your way is best."

That did it. When the Lord heard the deepest feelings of Job's contrite heart, when the Lord witnessed the humility of his broken spirit and the openness and teachability of Job's soul, mercy kicked in, and justice rolled down. There is even "poetic justice" as the Lord decides to use Job in the process of bringing those other men to justice. We will soon see how He does that. But before we go there, this is a good place to insert an insight worth remembering.

You will be amazed at how the Lord will use you in others' lives once you adjust your life to His ways. You will be many things for them: a reproof, a refuge, a point of hope, a reason to go on, a source of strength, a calming influence, and so much more. It's wonderful to realize (to your surprise) how He chooses to use you as a vehicle to help restore those who've strayed so far. This often includes those who hurt *you* in their straying.

JUSTICE IN RELATION TO JOB'S FRIENDS

Once the Lord hears His servant's statement of repentance, He then turns His attention to the three friends. Before going into this episode, we need to understand why Elihu is omitted. Probably because Elihu, the last of the friends, was more right than wrong. He was more on target than the first three had been, though his perspective needed some minor adjustments and his pride needed to come down a few notches. Not being as guilty as Eliphaz, Bildad, and Zophar, he fell into a different category. Perhaps the Lord dealt with him later, choosing not to include that confrontation in the sacred record.

I'm not saying that as a result of your repentance you will be free of any further trials. Nor am I suggesting that difficulties will immediately leave you and you'll never again know what it is to be depressed or discouraged. You're only human. I'm saying the lifestyle you've *been* living will not be the way you *will begin to live* when you focus on the truth that life is all about your God. Job sees it.

These other men didn't. They're standing in the shadows, still frowning with their arms folded, wondering why divine lightning isn't striking Job, why the Lord isn't vindicating their words and rewarding them for what they did. Are they in for a surprise!

It came about after the LORD had spoken these words to Job, that the LORD said to Eliphaz the Temanite, "My wrath is kindled against you and against your two friends, because you have not spoken of Me what is right as My servant Job has."

Job 42:7

Stop. I know you want to rush on and see those men get clobbered, but wait. Go back and take another look at God's opening words.

I love it that the Lord says to the three, "My wrath is kindled against you! You made me angry. Your words were wrong words. Your actions were wrong actions. I hold you accountable for what you did!" You know why I appreciate that being a part of the narrative? Because I was reared in a religious context so strict, everyone was told Christians should never be angry. "If you are angry, you are *sinful*. Furthermore, you need to confess that you got mad." We're never commanded in Scripture to refrain from any expression of anger, only from *staying* angry (Ephesians 4:26–27). If the Lord can say His wrath is "kindled" against these men who did and said what was wrong, surely there's a place for justified anger in us.

The Lord Jesus vehemently sent the moneychangers who were desecrating the temple out of that sacred place, you'll recall. He plaited strips of leather together, weaving them into a whip(!) and drove them out like you'd drive stubborn oxen. You can't tell me He smiled and gently said, "Now gentlemen, I'm a little uneasy about what I'm seeing here. When you have time would you please clean up your mess and quietly exit?" (Wouldn't you love to see a picture of what really happened? The sleeves of His robe rolled up, swinging that whip in righteous indignation! Those Pharisees didn't know whether to spit or open their phylacteries when they saw Him rushing toward them.) It was anger in the best sense of the word. Something's wrong if you *don't* get mad over stuff like that!

Please understand, however, the Lord's words against these three friends do not represent a temper tantrum. It's not a sudden overreaction as He pitches a fit. No, this has been a long time coming, remember. He's seen it all, heard every harsh word. He's been standing back, waiting for the right moment. Finally He reaches the full length of His tether, saying, "My wrath is kindled."

The reason for such anger is given here at the end of verse 7 (identical words are repeated at the end of verse 8). Look closely: "Because you have not spoken of Me what is right, as My servant Job has."

Why were they wrong? Don't miss this: In their effort to uphold God's justice, they ignored His mercy and limited His sovereignty. They went too far. They insisted that human suffering is always the result of sinfulness, and that boxed God in. Furthermore, they lacked mercy in their words. As we've stated several times, sinfulness is not always the reason people suffer. It is *a* reason on occasion, but it's not the only reason. That's where they missed it.

Remember their thinking? (How can you forget!) They claimed Job had some secret sin. They claimed Job had done wrong and hidden his transgressions. They considered Job a hypocrite. If he would only come to terms with all that and deal with it, then he'd be healed. Wrong analysis, said the wrong way with wrong attitudes. Bottom line, they didn't represent God as they should have: "You have not spoken of Me what was right as my servant Job has."

That, by the way, says volumes to those of us who are communicators, counseling, teaching, and preaching the Word of God. God cares very much that He is presented in an accurate, fair, and appropriate manner. With mercy. For the right reason. In love.

The Lord not only confronts their doing wrong, He does something about it. He doesn't say, in anger, "Now then—get out! Or, "Go to your room! You're finished!" That would not be merciful, nor would it afford an opportunity for them to be restored—and *restoration* is always the goal following repentance. Mercy comes on the heels of justice. As the prophet Habakkuk prays, "In wrath remember mercy" (Habakkuk 3:2).

"Now, therefore," here comes the mercy. It's as if God says, "You have done wrong, you've not done as my servant Job has done. Now therefore, here's what you are to do to make things right." The plan for their restoration is articulated.

> Now therefore, take for yourselves seven bulls and seven rams, and go
> to My servant Job, and offer up a burnt offering for yourselves, and
> My servant Job will pray for you. For I will accept him so that I may
> not do with you according to your folly, because you have not spoken
> of Me what is right, as My servant Job has.
>
> Job 42:8

A restoration game plan that includes offering up seven bulls and seven rams in a burnt offering seems strange to us today. But it wasn't at all strange back in the Old Testament days when the faithful came to God seeking forgiveness. Animal sacrifices were part of the process if they hoped to find forgiveness and relief from their guilt. Sometimes the animal's blood would be poured out on an altar. Sometimes they would place the entire carcass of the animal on the altar (as in this case), and the fire beneath the carcass would consume it. As the smoke from the burnt offering floated upward, it would come before God as "a sweet smelling aroma." Sounds very strange to us because we don't live in that era. We have never seen such a thing. But in those days, that's how God's anger was assuaged. Burnt offerings accompanied by prayer resulted in Divine forgiveness. Please note—Job was to pray for them. Since his heart was right (and theirs was not—not yet), God would accept his prayer on their behalf.

LET'S GO A LITTLE DEEPER

The one who was *offended*, Job, receives the offering of the *offenders*, the three friends. Really the ultimate offended One is the Lord God Himself who had been so grossly misrepresented.

> And my servant Job will pray for you.

I love it that the offended now prays for the offenders. The Lord clearly states, "For I will accept him." The Hebrew says, "I will lift his face up that I may not do with you according to your folly." Meaning, "That I may not give you what you deserve."

Did you miss something? If you take the time to read the biblical account, you'll see that God gives Job the same title four times: "My servant" (Job 42:7–8). What an honorable title. He had it before the suffering began (Job 1:8), and he has it still. Job's heroic endurance resulted in his keeping the same title in God's estimation. Talk about justice rolling down, Job must have been deeply gratified to hear these words spoken in the ears of those who had spent so many days putting him down: "My servant Job has spoken what is right."

The next scene must have been equally gratifying. Here are these men who earlier stood over Job as judges, now getting the required animals and bowing before the Lord with their offerings, waiting for Job to pray for them. Isn't this a great scene? We've been waiting *so* long to see it! And how healthy it was for those three to make it right, not only before God, but with Job! It is good for us to confess our wrongdoing to those we have offended. It is right for us to say by our actions we have done what is wrong as we seek forgiveness.

Job obeys the Lord once these men had done their part. "Eliphaz and Bildad and Zophar went and did as the Lord told them; and the Lord accepted Job" (Job 42:9). They did it rather quickly. There was no arguing, no wrestling, no reluctance. Furthermore, they did *exactly* as the Lord required. And so did Job. Graciously, he prayed for each one. There's no bitterness on his part. He doesn't say, "Okay, kneel down. You guys have put me through hell. I'm gonna see what you look like when you're humbled. Kneel down there—get on your faces!" There's none of that. Remember? *A contrite heart makes no demands of others.*

What a grand scene! You know what's happening? Sins are being forgiven. Guilt is being removed. Harsh feelings are being forgotten. Grudges are being erased. That's what happens when justice and mercy are blended.

How beautifully this portrays what happened at the Cross. That's why the death of Christ is called efficacious. It is *effective*, because God's justice against sin was once and for all satisfied in the *death* of the Lamb. And as a result, God's mercy is released in the *forgiveness* of those who trust in the Lamb. And we are then set free. Free at last!

Frederick Faber put it this way.

> There's a wideness in God's mercy
>   Like the wideness of the sea;
> There's a kindness in His justice
>   Which is more than liberty.[1]

In the next generation William Newell wrote a song we've sung throughout our growing-up years as Christians. It says the same thing in different words.

Years I spent in vanity and pride,
    Caring not my Lord was crucified,
Knowing not it was for me He died
    On Calvary.

By God's Word at last my sin I learned—
    Then I trembled at the law I'd spurned,
Till my guilty soul imploring turned
    To Calvary.

O the love that drew salvation's plan!
    O the grace that bro't it down to man!
O the mighty gulf that God did span
    At Calvary.

. . . .

Mercy there was great and grace was free,
    Pardon there was multiplied to me,
There my burdened soul found liberty—
    At Calvary.[2]

Ultimate justice rolled down at the Cross. When it came, it came with mighty waves of mercy, freeing us forever from the guilt of our own sin. How good is that!

For Job, it's about to get even better.

JUSTICE IN RELATION TO JOB'S LIFE

Job's full reward will wait till the next chapter, but let's take a quick peek through the tent flap here.

> The LORD restored the fortunes of Job when he prayed for his friends,
> and the LORD increased all that Job had twofold.
>
> Job 42:10

Isn't that just like our faithful Lord! Here is tangible proof that He is the best at justice. After all those hot, painful days. After all those long, restless nights. After all those condemning lectures he's had to endure. After all his own hours of grief and confusion, misery and waiting. After the loss of everything and the haunting memory of burying all his wonderful children. Finally, at long last, justice rolls down. And Job, broken in his own repentance, contrite of heart, having his face lifted up on behalf of his friends, witnesses their being restored because of God's mercy. At that moment his eyes meet the Lord's and he hears something like—"Hey, Job. Come over here to Me. It's time for your reward: Everything is going to be twice as good."

- Suddenly the boils are gone, leaving no scars.
- Suddenly the fever breaks as a cool breeze refreshes him.
- Suddenly the friends are smiling and applauding.
- Suddenly he's able to return home, and the homestead he builds is twice the size!
- And suddenly one morning, some time later, his wife giggles over breakfast, leans on his shoulder, and whispers with a smile, "I'm pregnant."

One of the hidden hints of Job's joys needs to be mentioned. Job prayed, not for himself and not for his own restoration of fortune. He prayed for those men who had wronged him. He'd forgiven them! His getting everything back twofold wasn't like his winning the divine lottery where he lucked out. He had no plans. He had no knowledge of how the story would end. Remember, a contrite heart has no expectations. All he knows is that the Lord says, "You pray for these friends. I'll lift up your face as you do that. The three humbly come in and offer their sacrifices." Job obeys by praying for his friends. The Lord is so pleased, so honored by Job's quiet obedience in doing it right, He says, "Now, come over here, Job. Let me tell you what I will do for you: I will increase everything twofold!"

You know what else is wonderful? Satan's silence. All of this is like, "In your face, Satan!" The Adversary stands silent in defeat. Satan has now witnessed the truth of what God had told him: "Consider my servant, Job. He has integrity. Though you may not kill him, you may touch him—he is in your power, only spare his life, but he will never curse Me." That prediction was proven true. Hence, Satan's silence and Job's rewards.

AND WHAT DOES THIS SAY TO US TODAY?

I find at least two enduring truths for us as I think through at these closing scenes in Job's story.

First, forgiveness is worth asking for. If there's something that has come between you and your heavenly Father, why wait at a distance? Come. Talk openly with Him. He loves to hear the unguarded confessions of His children. He takes delight in our humble admission of wrong. Just tell Him. As we have seen, He will never turn you away. Forgiveness is worth the asking.

Second, justice is worth waiting for. As I said at the beginning of the chapter, God is a God of justice. He will faithfully bring it to pass—if not now, later. If not later, in eternity. God will make it right. His fairness is part of His veracity. God, who patiently allowed this most unusual experiment with Job to run its course, has now brought it to completion. His servant has been rewarded. These friends have been brought to their knees. Best of all, Satan has been silenced and proven wrong (again!). And the Lord is still enthroned, in charge, and fully glorified.

I have no way of knowing what your situation is right now. I don't know what you're wrestling with or who has wronged you. Nor do I know how severe life has been for you. But I do know this: Life has not been easy. Your tests have probably not been as severe as Job's, but I'm sure they have been difficult, maybe the worst you've ever known in your lifetime. You may find yourself in prison. You've been wronged, and it's never been made right, and justice is on hold.

There is a reason for the delay. Perhaps it is to give you time to examine your own life. Is there a wrong you need to confess, an offense you've caused but never attempted to reconcile? May I urge you to set aside your pride and step back into that unfinished business and take care of things now? You would be amazed how relieving it will be to draw in that anchor so you might get moving in the right direction.

It might very well be that your willingness to forgive and move on is all that is necessary to prompt the Lord to let His justice roll down. So, what are you waiting for?

CHAPTER TWENTY

And Job Lived Happily Ever After . . . Or Did He?

S ince our earliest years we have been fascinated by stories. When we were very young, our stories were filled with imagination, which became for us a world that was larger than life. The main characters were often animals that talked and laughed, sighed and cried. And most of them lived in a fantasyland that captured and held our attention, filling us with excitement and wonder.

Those stories started the same way: "Once upon a time . . . " And we were off into lands of kings and queens, princes and knights, good and evil, as well as love, romance, and marriage. What wonderful stories! After all the twists and turns, wrong is defeated. Goodness prevails as peace returns, and the same six words announce the ending we children loved to read: "And they lived happily ever after."

Cinderella did. So did Sleeping Beauty and Prince Charming. Even the Beast and Beauty lived happily ever after. As we grow older our cynicism mixed with reality makes us frown and ask, "How could they, since they remained in an imperfect world? Happily ever after? Get real!"

Remembering these stories reminds me of the little four-year-old who rushed into the kitchen all excited about the story she had heard in daycare. It was about this beautiful young woman, the princess, who fell fast asleep. Along came a handsome prince who kissed her—and she suddenly awoke! "And do you know what happened next?" asked the perky preschooler.

"Why yes—they lived happily ever after," said her mother.

"Oh, no—*they got married!*"

In childhood innocence, the little girl made the right distinction between a fairy tale and reality. It's not easy for most of us to do that. We keep thinking it's going to happen. We keep forgetting.

When we build a new house—we think it will be our "dream house," but it's not. Shortly after we move in, some of the electric plugs don't work, the garage door malfunctions, the roof has a leak, the wood flooring upstairs starts to squeak, and invariably one of the toilets keeps getting stopped up.

We get a new job—we think it will be the most fulfilling experience of our career. We forget that we have to bring ourselves with us when we show up to begin. And many of the people we work with are a lot like those we left behind. And the boss isn't perfect, and the health benefits aren't all that great.

How about a new car? It smells wonderful. The paint finish is fabulous, and it runs beautifully—until next Monday morning when it won't start. Or until the guy parked next to you at the mall opens his door too far and leaves the mother of all door dings on the fender of your new red chariot.

One more comes to mind. A new baby! Remember thinking how great it would be to start your family, to have that adorable little chunk of love cooing at you from her crib in the newly decorated nursery? Then the baby finally arrives—after thirty-seven hours of labor. She refuses to breast feed, and has colic so bad she doesn't sleep through the night for eighteen months, and . . . and . . .and . . . In thirteen years she wakes up a teenager. Let's not go there.

In moments like that, you want to have a book burning of every volume that includes a story where *anybody* lived happily ever after! So, farewell fantasyland. It's not a perfect world. Not even those great characters who appear on the pages of the Bible lived happily ever after.

Are you ready for this next statement? Not even Job!

Before we're tempted to place him on a downy mattress surrounded by a big stack of fluffy satin pillows in an ideal setting of pristine beauty and perfect peace, we need to remind ourselves, Job doesn't suddenly go to heaven. He is still firmly fixed on planet Earth for the rest of his years, which were many. Well, wasn't he wonderfully rewarded? Yes, he was. Didn't he receive from God *twice* what he had before the bottom dropped out? Indeed. And how about his family—didn't he have ten more kids? See what I mean?

THERE'S GOLD IN THOSE FIERY TESTS

Before we return to the last chapter of Job's journal, let's do a quick replay of his third reply to Eliphaz. I'm referring to those words I urged you to memorize in the central section of Job 23. I think you will see these words through new eyes now that you realize how the story led to Job's full recovery. But, back when his body was covered with sores, back when his friends were still against him, when he was still bankrupt sitting in a garbage dump at the outskirts of the city, Job had the temerity to say, "But He knows the way I take; when He has tried me, I shall come forth as gold" (Job 23:10).

Look at that one more time. The H is capitalized since the pronoun is referring to the living God. Job makes three statements based on faith in the midst of his suffering. All three are about his God.

First: I know that God knows my situation. "He knows the way I take."

Second: I believe it is God who is testing me. "When He has tried me."

Third: I believe that after the trials have ended, He will bless me in a unique way. In fact, I will emerge a better man. There will be goldlike blessings that will emerge following this affliction. Quite a remarkable statement if you ask me. Realistic too. He doesn't deny the trials, but there's hope beyond them. God knows. God will reward. That is what we find when we get to the last chapter of Job's life.

Wouldn't it be great if we could be in Job's position at the end of the book without going through what he did through the book. How good would it be to gain his knowledge without all the suffering. Impossible! Stay realistic and realize that cannot happen. It takes fire to refine gold.

Before I proceed into chapter 42, I want to talk about going through the fire. Just as we are different in our appearance and in our background and in our levels of maturity and chronological age, so we experience different tests. For all you know, the person living in your neighborhood is going through one of the deepest times of her or his life. As we've considered several times in this volume, that may be where *you* are today. Fires rage. This vile world is no friend to grace, which means you may be in the heat of it. You may have run right up against the toughest test you've experienced so far.

I hope these two words will not seem hollow or pious when I write them: *Take hope.* Take hope that this is not going on without God's awareness. The Lord God knows the way you take, and it's not without purpose. After the fiery trial, you, too, will come forth as gold. You are being refined by the test He's allowed, and you are being reshaped in the process—purified and humbled. Better times are coming. If not soon, and if not later on this earth, they will come when you stand before Him and He distributes the "gold, silver, and precious stones." It will then be worth it all. Many of Job's rewards came while he was still alive on planet Earth. Yours may await you in Glory. Either way, God knows. God always remembers. God will reward.

JOB'S FOUR GREAT REWARDS

After the long, arduous wait, Job became the personal recipient of four goldlike blessings from the hand of God. As I point them out, my prayer is that you might take hope where you find yourself today. Your rewards will be different, of course, because no two trials are identical. But these are his:

The first of the four blessings is this: *Job's possessions are doubled.*

The Lord restored the fortunes of Job when he prayed for his friends. The latter part of the verse explains what that means: "And the LORD increased all that Job had twofold" (Job 42:10).

There are times it is not wise and appropriate to take a verse absolutely literally, but this is one of those times we should. Pay close attention to what is said in verse 10: Everything doubled. His land, as well as his possessions on that land. A larger home was able to be built rather than the one half that size they lived in before. We are also told about the multiplication that occurred among his animals with the passing of time: "The LORD blessed the latter days of Job more than his beginning" (Job 42:12).

If you return to Job 1:3, you will read what Job originally owned. He had 7,000 sheep and he winds up, (Job 42:12 tells us) with 14,000. So his flocks grow as he feeds them and breeds them. Their numbers increase to twice the size flock. There's plenty to eat. And there's also plenty of land to graze in, so the sheep grow in number to 14,000.

And remember the caravans that Job had in his enterprising business? That business doubles. He no longer has 3,000 camels, but 6,000. What a sight that must have been! Camels were the freight trucks of Job's culture—they carried the load in the caravans. That segment of his business doubles. And he's now got 1,000 yoke of oxen to work the fields.

He must have been able to see out of every window of his home luscious, green, and colorful plants and the growth of all his crops. He's even got 1,000 female donkeys. So the man has twice as much as he had before. Not instantaneously, but over the passing of a few years, his possessions grew. Candidly, Job had more than enough. Much more. He was rich before; now he is enormously wealthy!

There are times when the Lord chooses to bless certain individuals with much more than is enough. What we must learn is to let it be. If envy is your besetting sin, I urge you to break yourself from one of the ugliest habits among Christian people! I'll completely honest with you, I hear it frequently. The great temptation is to remind the Lord of how faithful *you* have been when you see a neighbor or a friend whose business grows when yours doesn't. Why not rejoice with those who are rejoicing? Please stop trying to outguess the Lord in such matters.

It is both unfair and inaccurate to assume that most wealthy individuals have not earned their riches or did not receive them from the hand of God. Some of God's dearest saints are eminently wealthy. So? I say again— let it be. If you are one of them, you hardly need the reminder that you didn't create it yourself. It came because of His grace. Use it appropriately. Give generously. Walk in humility. And if He chooses not to bless you as He has blessed another, respect and appreciate His choice rather than resent it. Let's applaud Job for being a recipient of God's prosperous favor. He has "come forth as gold," having been tested and found faithful.

There's a second reward that comes in verse 11. *His relatives and friends emerge.* Some of you have a twisted sense of humor (a little like mine, I'm sorry to say), and you think like I do. I can imagine a cartoon where Job looks up and sees all his friends and relatives showing up, and he blurts out: "Where in the world were you guys before you were told I won the lottery?" Some wag once said, "You have two ways of knowing how many friends you have: Win the lottery or own a pickup."

> Then all his brothers, and all his sisters, and all who had known him
> before, came to him, and they ate bread with him in his house; and
> they consoled him and comforted him for all the evil that the LORD
> had brought on him. And each one gave him one piece of money, and
> each a ring of gold.
>
> Job 42:11

But this was no lottery. God simply decided to unload enormous monetary blessings on Job. One day Job looked up and he was surrounded by *all* his brothers and *all* his sisters. Interesting, they're never mentioned until now. They weren't around several weeks ago when Job's days were dark and difficult. Actually, we don't know that for sure. If they *were*, they said nothing and neither their names nor their words are recorded.

But now everybody showed up: all his brothers, all his sisters, all who had known him before. You know whom I would include? Because they're now forgiven, let's not forget Eliphaz, Bildad, Zophar, and Elihu. Why not? They're not blacklisted, are they? If we read the earlier part of Job 42 correctly, they're forgiven after Job prays for them. That means they're restored. So why not include them as part of the great reunion?

Notice what all these people did when they came together. They came to him, and they ate bread with him in his house. They also consoled him and they comforted him for all the adversities that the Lord had brought on him. What a great family-and-friends reunion! What a great feast they must have enjoyed together! How many stories were told. What joyful laughter filled the rooms. Job hasn't laughed for months, so he must have made up for lost time. Finally, the man's pain is gone for good. What seemed like a death sentence has ended. Finally, home is home once again! I love it that they comforted and consoled him. Maybe he had a few deep scars remaining from the sores. Perhaps they asked to see them. He may have told them about the night he lost all hope of making it. Maybe he had to pause and wipe away a few tears. Those are the things that make a reunion meaningful and memorable.

Each one gave him one piece of money and a ring of gold. Isn't that intriguing? Maybe this was early on, and he hadn't yet begun to build back his business. Perhaps they wanted to participate in helping him get back on his feet. Remember, he had lost it all. Maybe he had to take all of the rings he had before and sell them to live on. They wanted to be sure he had a few nice things as well. Or, it could be they were housewarming gifts welcoming him to a new home that he had just finished, and they were happy for him. I so appreciate it that they all got together and took turns affirming this dear man who had endured such pain and loneliness.

In a fast-paced world like ours, it's easy to lose our roots. To begin living just for ourselves. Not Job's kin! They may have been gone, but they got back in touch with him. They had a lot to talk about. You know who had a lot to talk about? Job and his wife. In many a home where physical affliction hits hard, there's a separation that occurs. Distance grows as love erodes. Some marriages can't make it, as the wife moves in one direction and the husband drifts in another.

You've got to hand it to Job and his wife. They stuck it out. They pulled together. She's not painted in a good light by many of my fellow preachers, I'm sorry to say. I still think there were great qualities in that lady. Let's face it: She stays with him all the way. As confused as he was, she watched her husband dwindle to a shell of what he had once been. Must have been terribly difficult, but she was there. She hung in there. You know what this says to us married folk? Of course you do.

You have a child that can't keep up with other children at school? Perhaps there was brain damage at birth so there's a problem with retardation, or your child has a lengthening disease that is taking its toll. Please stay together. Hang tough. Job's wife was right there. They had a lot to talk about as they'd turn in at night with all the lamps out. There was something deeply satisfying, knowing they had stayed together through all the anguish.

This brings me to the third reward that came his way: *Job's children are all replaced.* "He had seven sons and three daughters" (Job 42:13). Try to picture some of this. It had to have included some hilarious moments. They're both gettin' up in years, okay? And one day, out of the blue, she says to Job, "You're not gonna believe this, but I think I'm pregnant." He goes, "Say what?" Let's just say they're both seventy. Start there. Here's Job laughing with his wife over the fact she's going to have a baby. She goes up in the attic and takes some maternity clothes out of mothballs, and says, "Well, I guess I can fit back into that." No just once, not twice. We're talking *ten more pregnancies*. So for the next twenty-five years and more they're rearing children again. That'll keep you young, huh?

There are ten more children. He and his wife are given the strength and ability to reproduce regardless of their ages (we're never told exactly what it is), and to rear another houseful of kids. When you stop to think about it, they get to enjoy the blessings of parenting with the wisdom of grandparents. You can't beat that combination.

How often we have said, "I *so* wish I'd known then what I know now. I would have been a much better parent." Well, they have the chance for fulfilling every parent's wish. They don't make the mistakes they made the first time, and certainly not as many of them.

> He named the first Jemimah, and the second Keziah, and the third Keren-happuch. In all the land no women were found so fair as Job's daughters.
>
> Job 42:14–15

There were seven sons and three daughters. We read a little about the girls here, nothing about the boys. We are given their names, Jemimah, Keziah, and Keren-happuch. I checked the meaning of their names. Doesn't seem to be that much significance in those names.

But we are told something significant about the daughters themselves. They must have been lovely young ladies. "In all the land no women were found so fair as Job's daughters." You know part of the reason? They were raised right. Their character had been carefully cultivated. The beauty of the life of faith had been nurtured within each daughter. What a treasure! They had gained a wisdom and insight, knowledge and understanding, from wise parents, ahead of their years. We also read "their father gave them inheritance among their brothers" (Job 42:15). How unusual for daughters in ancient times to enjoy an inheritance!

But keep in mind, this is *before* the Mosaic Law. Under the Law we read that the inheritance went to a daughter only if there were no sons (Numbers 27:8). Living before the law of Moses, these three daughters received an inheritance along with their brothers. So there's no favoritism, boys and girls alike were equally nurtured and loved.

Now the fourth reward is mentioned. This one has to do with Job's later years: *the blessing of a long and satisfying life.*

> After this, Job lived 140 years, and saw his sons, and his grandsons, four generations. And Job died, an old man and full of days.
>
> Job 42:16–17

Let's again assume that Job is about seventy by the time his healing and recovery of strength come. He's lived a full life already. Now we read that he lives 140 years *after* the trials. Job enters a second full phase of life with a lifespan of 210 years. How great that must have been for him! Among his many delights, "He saw his sons, and his grandsons, and great grandsons."

I count four, maybe five generations: Job, sons, grandsons, great-grandsons, perhaps even great-great, depending on where the generations would start. What a sweet way to summarize his later years: He "dies an old man and full of days." *The Living Bible* renders this, "Then at last he died an old, old man after living a long, good life."

ENCOURAGEMENT FOR THE AGING

Not enough is said in our era about those who are aging. They often represent an overlooked body of people, even though there are now more in this particular category than ever before in the history of humanity. So we linger here not only to have a little fun with it, but to draw some encouraging lessons from it. This is a man who has seen a lot of life.

It was said of Abraham,

> Abraham breathed his last and died in a ripe old age, an old man and
> satisfied with life; and he was gathered to his people.
>
> Genesis 25:8

Probably a reference to joining his people in the afterlife. We would say, in heaven. It was said of David, "Then he died in a ripe old age, full of days, riches and honor" (1 Chronicles 29:28).

Job is not dying a struggling, cranky, broken old codger whom no one enjoyed being around. This man is seeing his children, his grandchildren, his great-grandchildren. He is reliving the joys of his renewed life as he stays involved with them, passing along many of the things that he has learned.

The patriarchal formula "old and full of years," is expressive of a completely fulfilled life. What an enviable way to reach the end! He didn't "live happily ever after," since that's not possible. But what pleasures were his to enjoy! This old world is full of depravity. We cannot eradicate or escape a sin-cursed nature. We must deal with a hostile nature in others (and ourselves!) that is less than desirable. But there can still be satisfaction. There can be fulfillment in old age. Furthermore, there can be continuing purpose and deep contentment in later years.

As I completed preaching a message on this section of Scripture back in 2002, an older lady came to me and said, through tears, "I can't remember when a sermon has meant more to me." She added, "Sometimes it feels like folks our age are just about forgotten."

That memory prompts me to pass along some encouraging advice to you who have older parents still living and older family members still around: Remember them. Take care of them. Love them. If they're away, write to them. Call them. Keep up a dialogue through e-mails. Continue to nurture that relationship.

Age is not kind to the human body or to the cultivation of relationships. Let's learn from Job's later years the value of cross-generational involvements. Admittedly, no one else can make an individual be fulfilled and feel satisfied, but we can certainly help the journey be a little more enjoyable.

And now—a little advice to you who are feeling overlooked and forgotten. There's a Jewish proverb that says, "For the ignorant, old age is as winter; for the learned, it is a harvest." As age stacks up, you will find that because you have kept yourself alert and alive, you will continue to see life through new eyes. Step up! Stay engaged in life! Don't succumb to feelings of self pity! "As soon as you feel too old to do a thing, go out and do it. As soon as you feel critical, say something kind in a kindly way. As soon as you feel neglected, send a cheery note to a friend."[1]

As the years begin to accumulate we find ourselves saying, "Stop worrying. It's okay. Don't get worked up over that!" I say that on occasion to one of our now-adult kids who is in a dither over one of their children who go half-crazy at times. I say, "It's okay; it's just a phase. (It's been going on for about four years, but it's a phase.) Don't sweat it. It's okay." One of my roles, I now realize, is being an encouragement to our kids and grandkids.

Henry Thoreau once wrote, "None are so old as those who have outlived enthusiasm." Isn't it wonderful to be around older people who are still contagiously enthusiastic? Isn't it great to see them have goals and dreams and tangible pursuits that have them excited from the time they awaken until bedtime? Folks like that are *contagious*.

General Douglas MacArthur wrote this great statement on his seventy-fifth birthday:

> In the central place of every heart there is a recording chamber; so long as it receives messages of beauty, hope, cheer, and courage, so long are you young. When the wires are all down and your heart is covered with the snows of pessimism and the ice of cynicism, then and then only are you grown old.[2]

My continuing close relationship with Dallas Theological Seminary is wonderfully satisfying. I'm not referring only to being around young students. You have no idea unless you're where I am as often as I am, the pleasure that I get from being with some of the same men who were among my mentors. These are who took their time to teach me when I was younger. What a great group of aging men! They're still walking with God. It's *wonderful* to see seventy-five, eighty, a few ninety-year-olds still loving Jesus. Still writing great works. Still reading. Still challenging me to stay strong. (I love it when they call me Sonny.) A couple of years ago, Dr. Walvoord and I were talking. He said, "Young man, back when I was your age . . . " I smiled and thought, "What a great compliment!"

Someone said, "Remember older people are worth a lot more than younger folks. They have silver in their hair, gold in their teeth, stones in their kidneys, lead in their feet, and natural gas in their gut."[3] We're worth a lot!

TIPS FOR STAYING YOUNG

I'd like to offer several tips on how to stay young. These are originals. Nobody gave them to me. I've sort of discovered them as life has unfolded over the past ten or fifteen years. I don't care what your age is. You'll be here someday. And when you are, you'll need to review these. You want to stay young? Remember five things.

Number one: *Your mind isn't old, so keep developing it.* Watch less television and read more. Spend time with people who talk about events and ideas rather than sitting around a shop talking about people and how sorry this young generation has become. Nobody wants to be around a crotchety old person who sees only the clouds and talks only about bad weather.

One comedian has said his daddy is so ready to die he won't even buy green bananas. That's a dreadful way to live. Dare the aging process, buy a whole *bunch* of green bananas. And while you're at it, get out there and plant a few small oak trees.

Number two: *Your humor isn't over, keep enjoying it.* I love being around older people who still see the sunny side of life. They see funny things happening. They can tell a great story. They enjoy a loud belly laugh. You look *fabulous* when you laugh. And it takes years off of you. Helps remove some of the lines on your face. Speaking of that, glance into a mirror. Maybe *you* would do well to cultivate a better sense of humor. Fred Allen used to say if you don't laugh out loud enough, it will go down and spread your hips.

Number three: *Your strength isn't gone, keep using it.* Don't let yourself get out of shape. Stay active. Eat right. Watch your weight. Guard against becoming isolated and immobile. And while I'm at it, quit addressing every ache and pain. Quit talking about how weak you're getting and how others will have to do this for you. Jump in there. *You* keep doing it.

A physician friend of mine for so many years, made the mistake of telling an eighty-four-year-old woman who had just finished running her five miles that morning, "Listen, you need to take it easy. You don't have to run five miles." She had come in for her annual checkup. Following her regular workout a week-and-a-half later, she died. He said to me at her memorial service, "I'll never again tell a patient to *take it easy.*"

Step up! Take the stairway. Don't always take the elevator. Exercise. Stay limber. Walk out into life and travel. Take some risks. Accept the challenges that opportunity throws at you. Say yes as often as you can. You'll become increasingly more in demand. Your strength isn't gone, unless you are telling it to leave.

Here's a fourth: *Your opportunities haven't vanished, so keep pursuing them.* There are people all around you who could use an encouraging word, an affirming note, a phone call that says, "I love you and believe in you and I'm praying for you." So go there. Opportunities to help others have not vanished. Don't allow yourself to get so fearful that all your drapes stay closed and all three of the locks on your doors stay locked. If you're not willing to risk, you'll begin to live in the terror of someone's taking advantage of you. What a dreadful existence! Without removing any of the essential needs for safety, don't live your life suspicious of others, thinking only of the dangers. If you do, you'll never leave your neighborhood. Opportunities haven't vanished, keep pursuing them with vigor.

Fifth is obvious: *Your God is not dead, keep serving and seeking Him.* The living God is ageless. The Lord Jesus Christ is timeless and ever relevant. Continue to enjoy some time alone with your Lord. It's important!

Job pulled through all of this and lived on—another 140 years. And I read nothing of his being set aside. Ten kids will do that to you, if nothing else. That'll keep you hoppin'.

I appreciate this prayer, which I have repeated many times:

> Lord, thou knowest better than I know myself, that I am growing older, and will someday be old.

Keep me from getting talkative, and particularly from the fatal habit of thinking I must say something on every subject and on every occasion.

Release me from the craving to try and straighten out everybody's affairs.

Keep my mind free from the recital of endless details—give me wings to get to the point.

I ask for grace enough to listen to the tales of others' pains. They are increasing, and my love of rehearsing them is becoming sweeter as the years go by.

I dare not ask for improved memory, but for a growing humility and a lessening cocksureness when my memory seems to clash with the memories of others.

Teach me the glorious lesson that occasionally I may be mistaken.

Keep me reasonably sweet. I do not want to be a saint—some of them are so hard to live with—but a sour old woman (or man) is one of the crowning works of the devil.

Make me thoughtful, but not moody; helpful, but not bossy.

With my vast store of wisdom, it seems a pity not to use it; but Thou knowest, Lord, I want a few friends at the end.

Give me the ability to see good things in unexpected places, and talents in unexpected people. And give me, Lord, the grace to tell them so.[4]

You have lived long enough to know that there is no one more trustworthy than the Lord Himself. Continue cultivating a meaningful relationship with Him. Seek Him diligently and often. Stay active in serving Him. This is one of the best reasons for staying involved at your local church. What avenues of service there are for those who are available, whose attitudes are positive, and whose minds stay active and alert.

I wish for you a full life, like Job's. Marked not by living happily ever after (an impossibility), but truly satisfied, fulfilled, challenged, useful, godly, balanced, and *joyful*.

Yes, for sure, joyful. And don't forget—reasonably sweet.

CHAPTER TWENTY-ONE

What Job Teaches Us about Ourselves

Children have a way of saying things that often make us smile. They don't mean to be funny, but more often than not, they are. This usually happens when they're answering questions—serious questions. As they give their opinions, we can't help but laugh.

Take for example the subject of love and marriage:

- "How do you decide who to marry?"
  Kristen, Age 10: "No person really decides before they grow up who they're going to marry. God decides it all way before, and you get to find out later who you're stuck with."

- "How can a stranger tell if two people are married?"
  Derrick, Age 8: "You might have to guess, based on whether they seem to be yelling at the same kids."

- "What do you think your mom and dad have in common?"
  Lori, Age 8: "Both don't want any more kids."

- "When is it okay to kiss someone?"
  Pam, Age 7: "When they're rich."
  Curt, Age 7: "The law says you have to be eighteen, so I wouldn't want to mess with that."

- "Is it better to be single or married?"
  Anita, Age 9: "It's better for girls to be single but not for boys. Boys need someone to clean up after them."

- "How would you make a marriage work?"
  Ricky, Age 10: "Tell your wife that she looks pretty, even if she looks like a truck."[1]

Some of the notes that have been handed (or e-mailed) to me about my sermons on Job have been *hilarious!* One child asked her daddy if their pastor's *name* was now Job. Another ten-year-old kept giving me pictures he had drawn depicting the scenes I described in one sermon after another. (You should see some of those boils!) Finally, as I got near the end of the book, he stopped drawing. No more pictures, but I did get a small two-sentence note, which read "Can you find another subject? I've run out of ideas." Gotta love that honesty.

This is a good time for me to commend you for staying with me this far. Bless you! By now you know two things for sure: First, this isn't shallow entertainment, an easy story to stay interested in. Second, there's a reason there aren't many books written on Job.

It may not be very exciting, and it certainly isn't a simple plot to unravel, but what Job lacks in popular appeal he makes up for in realism. The long hallways of a leukemia ward in a hospital may not be exciting or creative, but each room contains people asking the same questions and wrestling with the same issues as Job. Exciting and entertaining it isn't, but substantive and real? *In spades!*

What happens in places like that and in books like this is you find yourself paying less attention to the temporal and the externals. You give increasingly more attention to the eternal. To what is going on deep within.

Soul-searching replaces channel surfing. You start asking questions that are hard to answer. You think a lot deeper about the things all of this is teaching you. We've come to that place in this book. What *does* Job teach us about *ourselves?* In my final chapter we'll consider what Job teaches us about our God.

My primary goal in this chapter may surprise you. It is neither to inform nor reprove—you've had enough of both in the previous twenty chapters. And I certainly don't need to repeat the details of the story. I've done that so often you are probably starting to feel like the pianist rehearsing familiar scales to the monotonous tick of a metronome. My goal is to intensify your enthusiasm for life—to move you from a day-by-day toleration of the status quo mentality to a renewal of your drive to really come alive. The word is *passion*.

Benjamin Zander, professor at the New England Conservatory of Music, illustrates what I'm hoping to accomplish.

> A young pianist was playing a Chopin prelude in my master class, and although we had worked right up to the edge of realizing an overarching concept of the piece, his performance remained earthbound. He understood it intellectually, he could have explained it to someone else, but he was unable to convey the emotional energy that is the true language of music. Then I noticed something that proved to be the key. His body was firmly centered in the upright position. I blurted out, "The trouble is you're a two-buttock player!" I encouraged him to allow his whole body to flow sideways, urging him to catch the wave of the music with the shape of his own body, and suddenly the music took flight. Several in the audience gasped, feeling the emotional dart hit home, as a new distinction was born: The *one-buttock* player. The president of a corporation in Ohio, who was present as a witness wrote to me: "I was so moved that I went home and transformed my whole company into a *one-buttock* company."
>
> I never did find out what he meant by that, but I have my own ideas. . . .
>
> I met Jacqueline DuPre in the 1950s, when I was twenty and she

was fifteen, a gawky English schoolgirl who blossomed into the great-est cellist of her generation. We performed the Two Cello quintet of Schubert together, and I remember her playing was like a tidal wave of intensity and passion. When she was six years old, the story goes, she went into her first competition as a cellist, and she was seen run-ning down the corridor carrying her cello above her head, with a huge grin of excitement on her face. A custodian, noting what he took to be relief on the little girl's face, said, "I see you've just had your chance to play!" And Jackie answered, excitedly, "No, no, I'm just about to!"

Even at six, Jackie was a conduit for music to pour through.[2]

Put bluntly, my hope is to help you become a "*one-buttock* player" on life's keyboard, not satisfied with pounding out another year of dull, predictable notes and chords, but throwing yourself full-bore into the symphony!

SEVEN LESSONS WORTH REMEMBERING

> There was a man in the land of Uz whose name was Job; and that man was blameless, upright, fearing God an turning away from evil.
>
> Job 1:1

We soon discover Job and his wife had seven sons and three daughters. His possessions were great, with thousands of sheep and camels, along with half a thousand oxen and donkeys. In fact, the word was out on this man: He was "the greatest of all the men of the east" (Job 1:3). There was no one better known and probably no one wealthier. Job had it made.

Without his knowing it, a dialogue took place in the invisible world above. As the Lord and Satan had their strange encounter, the subject quickly turned to this well-known earthly individual. The Lord calls Satan's atten-tion to his exemplary life, and Satan responds with a sinister sneer. "Of course, who wouldn't serve You the way You've prospered and protected him. Take away all the perks and watch what happens; the man will turn on You in a flash." God agrees to let the Adversary unload on Job.

And so, in today's terms, the Lord bet him that would never happen. Philip Yancey refers to that agreement as the "divine wager." Satan instigates a sudden and hostile removal of all the man's possessions, leaving him bankrupt. Within a matter of minutes, everything he owned was gone.

This brings us to the *first* of seven lessons worth remembering: *We never know ahead of time the plans God has for us.* Job had no prior knowledge or warning. That morning dawned like every other morning. The night had passed like any other night. There was no great angelic manifestation—not even a tap on his window or a note left on the kitchen table.

In one calamity after another, all the buildings on his land are gone, and nothing but lumber and bodies litter the landscape. It occurred so fast, Job's mind swirled in disbelief. Everything hit broadside . . . his world instantly changed.

You and I *must* learn from this! We never know what a day will bring, good or ill. Our heavenly Father's plan unfolds apart from our awareness. Ours is a walk of faith, not sight. Trust, not touch. Leaning long and hard, not running away. No one knows ahead of time what the Father's plan includes. It's best that way. It may be a treasured blessing; it could be a test that drops us to our knees. He knows ahead of time, but He is not obligated to warn us about it or to remind us it's on the horizon. We can be certain of this: Our God knows what is best.

Read the following scriptures slowly and thoughtfully:

> I know, O Lord, that a man's way is not in himself,
> Nor is it in a man who walks to direct his steps.
> Correct me, O Lord, but with justice;
> Not with Your anger, or You will bring me to nothing.
>
> Jeremiah 10:23–24

> "For I know the plans that I have for you," declares the Lord, "plans for welfare and not for calamity to give you a future and a hope. Then you will call upon Me and come and pray to Me, and I will listen to you. You will seek Me and find Me when you search for Me with all your heart."
>
> Jeremiah 29:11–13

The mind of man plans his way,
But the LORD directs his steps.

Proverbs 16:9

Man's steps are ordained by the LORD,
How then can man understand his way?

Proverbs 20:24

"For My thoughts are not your thoughts,
Neither are your ways My ways," declares the LORD.
"For as the heavens are higher than the earth,
So are My ways higher than your ways
And My thoughts than your thoughts.

Isaiah 55:8–9

Be anxious for nothing, but in everything by prayer and supplication
with thanksgiving let your requests be made known to God. And the
peace of God which surpasses all comprehension, will guard your hearts
and your minds in Christ Jesus.

Philippians 4:6–7

Consider it all joy, my brethren, when you encounter various trials,
knowing that the testing of your faith produces endurance. And let
endurance have its perfect result, so that you may be perfect and complete, lacking in nothing.

James 1:2–4

Therefore humble yourselves under the mighty hand of God, that He
may exalt you at the proper time, casting all your anxiety of Him,
because He cares for you.

1 Peter 5:6–7

Did you do as I asked? Did you read each one slowly and thoughtfully?

The ultimate plan our Lord has for us is not a calamitous, fatalistic, heartbreaking, life-ending set of events, designed to weaken and destroy our faith. On the contrary, it is a plan that is "for our welfare . . . to give us a future and a hope," writes the prophet Jeremiah. But that doesn't mean it will be easy or comfortable. Because He is a God of the unexpected, it will be surprising! It will be different than you or I would have ever pondered or planned, or for that matter, preferred. Therefore, to increase your passion for life, I have some pretty simple advice: Be ready for anything. And I do mean anything.

One of my friends at our church told me that one of his longtime friends who had a well-paying job at EDS, got notice from the National Guard that he was being called up. No heads-up warning. This meant an immediate change of lifestyle. He had to leave his excellent occupation in order to serve in the guard. He and his wife (and several kids) needed to sell their lovely home. She was forced to adjust to a completely different world without the constant companionship and support of her husband. Who knows where they will have to live, what schools the children will be attending, or how safe he will be during his tour of military duty. It came like a bolt out of the blue.

We have no guarantee that life will rock along for us as it has this past year. What you enjoy today as a result of your good job and great health, you may not be enjoying this time next year or six months from now. This isn't designed to frighten you; it's designed to help prepare you for a whole new way of thinking. Our times are in *His* hands. Have you ever meditated on that thought, I mean *really* believed it?

Job's response, you will recall, is absolutely remarkable.

> Then Job arose and tore his robe and shaved his head, and he fell to
> the ground and worshiped. He said,
> "Naked I came from my mother's womb,
> And naked I shall return there.
> The LORD gave and the LORD has taken away,
> Blessed be the name of the LORD."
>
> Job 1:20–22

Here's a *second* lesson worth remembering: *A vertical perspective will keep us from horizontal panic.* Don't misunderstand Job's response to the devastation. Job didn't escape into some mental state of denial. He faced the music—somber and sad that it was. He was so overwhelmed by all the loss he tore his robe. He was broken and saddened and grieved over the death of his kids. That's why he shaved his head and later sat in ashes. In fact, these reactions assure us he refused to escape emotionally through denial. But don't miss his ultimate response. He fell to the ground and worshiped.

His vertical perspective is clear and undaunting. Nothing that happens on the horizontal plane will cause this man to panic. It's as if Job is saying, "I had. I enjoyed. I was blessed. I'm now without those benefits. They're no longer a part of my world. I'm heartbroken over the loss of my family. But the same God who gave all of this by His grace, is the God who in His sovereign will has chosen to take each one away. I honor and praise Him. May His name be forever exalted!"

Much earlier in this book I quoted the profound words of Francis Andersen. Time has a way of erasing important thoughts which should be retained. Since one of the secrets of memory is review, allow me to repeat several lines worth a second look.

> Job finds nothing wrong with what has happened to him. At this point Job's trial enters a new phase, the most trying of all. . . . He never curses God, but all his human relationships are broken. His attitude is the same as before (1:21). It is equally right for God to give gifts and to retrieve them; . . . it is equally right for God to send good or *evil*. . . . Such positive faith is the magic stone that transmutes all to gold; for when the bad as well as the good is received *at the hand of God*, every experience of life becomes an occasion of blessing. But the cost is high. It is easier to lower your view of God than to raise your faith to such a height.[3]

When life trucks along comfortably and contentedly, in good health and with a happy family . . . my, my! How high our view of God can be!

How thrilled we are with all those wonderful verses of Scripture. How we hang on the words of the pastor's sermons. And how fervently we sing the songs of celebration. But let hardship arrive or let our health take a nosedive, how quickly our song is silenced, how cynical our attitude, how sour our faith becomes, and how quickly we're tempted to lower our view of God. The man is correct. It's easy to question God when hard times replace good times. A strong vertical perspective fans the flame of passion.

Well, it only got worse. Job does not sin or blame God, which frustrates Satan but does not surprise our God. He knew Job would continue in his integrity.

As the next day dawns Satan comes out swinging. The Lord asks, "Have you noticed my servant, Job?" It must have been a great moment when the Lord could point to Job who has demonstrated no break in his faith, no doubt in His trust, and Satan has to face the music. Refusing to accept defeat, the Accuser flashes that cynical sneer once again:

> Satan answered the LORD and said, "Skin for skin! Yes, all that a man has he will give for his life. However, put forth Your hand now, and touch his bone and his flesh; he will curse You to Your face." So the LORD said to Satan, "Behold, he is in your power, only spare his life."
>
> Job 2:4–6

You know all too well what happened. As soon as he got the green light:

> Satan went out from the presence of the LORD and smote Job with sore boils from the sole of his foot to the crown of his head.
>
> Job 2:7

Job is leveled to the ground, literally. His pain is beyond description. His fever is raging. He can't eat, can't sleep, and there's no sign of relief. His misery knows no bounds. Watching him suffer is more than his wife can endure. Seeing him sitting there in the ash heap, she can stay quiet no longer. She allows herself to say the unthinkable.

> Do you still hold fast your integrity? Curse God and die!
>
> Job 2:9

She loved him, never doubt it. The sickness hasn't made her love him less. Her compassion overruns her better judgment, and in that unguarded moment she gives herself the freedom to verbalize an alien thought. "If you will curse God He will take you on home. You and I both know this act will swiftly end the suffering." (Can you imagine the breathless anticipation of Satan at this moment?) Job may be in misery, but he has enough presence of mind to detect heresy when he hears it.

> But he said to her, "You speak as one of the foolish women speaks.
> Shall we indeed accept good from God and not accept adversity?"
>
> Job 2:10

That statement provides us with a *third* lesson: discernment. *Discernment is needed to detect wrong advice from well-meaning people.* Those words whispered in his ear came from his wife! She's loved him through ten births. She's loved him through the rearing of all their children. She's loved him from the lean, early days in business through the years of great prosperity where they could at last enjoy some relief. This woman loved him when he was a nobody, and she continued to love him when he became a household word in every home of the East. Job has known her love through all the years, but that has not blinded him from realizing her counsel is wrong. "Though spoken by one who loves me and wants what is best for me, I dare not heed her advice."

Consider her counsel long enough to understand how far off she was. She is questioning what God had admired, and she is encouraging what Satan had predicted. Think about it. God had said to Satan, "He still holds fast his integrity." And she's suggesting, "Job, no longer sustain your integrity."

Satan had said, "He will curse You to Your face." And she says to the man she loves, "Job, just curse God."

The devil was on tiptoe, urging, "Yes! Yes! Do it!" And you know his demons were at work trying fervently to weaken him. But Job stands firm. He discerns the error and flat-out rejects it.

Job knew he could not, in good faith, follow her advice, no matter how well meaning she was. His response reveals his inner discipline. His words are bold and blunt:

> He told her, "You're talking like an empty-headed fool. We take the good days from God—why not also the bad days?"
>
> Job 2:10, MSG

What great theology! "God isn't our God only when times are good. Our faith in Him isn't limited to those days He blesses us. We don't claim Him as our Lord only when we get what we want. He's our God even when adversity strikes. He is Lord of good days and bad days. He didn't leave us the day I started suffering!" Job was right on. Talk about a passion!

Consider a *fourth* lesson: *When things turn from bad to worse, sound theology helps us remain strong and stable.* It is a sign of maturity that Job, after suffering such a barrage of cataclysmic events, would be thinking so clearly, so correctly without wavering. No uncertainty. The man did not entertain her suggestion for a moment. "You speak as a fool" was his immediate reaction. "Surely you know by now these lips cannot curse God. Death is in His hands, not mine. When He's ready to take me, He'll take me." How could Job do it? He was grounded in his knowledge of God. In times like that, sound theology is invaluable.

Reminds me of a Charles Schultz cartoon I saw several years ago. Remember "Peanuts"? Linus with his blanket is standing at the picture window in the family room. Standing beside him is Lucy, who, of course, is in charge. They're watching it rain, and it is coming down in sheets. They can hardly see the trees in the backyard. Linus sighs, "My, look at all that rain. If this keeps up it's going to flood this whole area, maybe the whole *world.*" Lucy answers without hesitation, "That will never happen! It says in Genesis 9, verses 7 to 17, that God will never again flood the earth. And He's put a rainbow in the sky to prove that His promise is true." Linus looks at her, shakes his head and says, "You've taken a big load off my mind." She responds immediately, "Sound theology has a way of doing that."

Maybe her husband's retort took a big load of Mrs. Job's mind. How memorable it is when the one who is suffering can teach the one who is well. Sound theology provides a foundation like nothing else. Quick reminder here: Be careful that you never substitute psychological gobbledygook for good biblical theology. Work hard at not weakening your theological foundation by double talk. Don't go there. It will backfire on you when you least expect it.

On my birthday I got one of my favorite kind of greeting cards—one of those funny Far Side cards. There's a guy hanging by his collar on the limb of a tree. His feet and legs are dangling about two feet off the ground. He's limp and helpless, as his camera hangs loosely from his neck. Two huge bears are off to the side discussing his fate. One bear says to the other, "His name's Bradshaw. He says he understands I came from a single parent den with inadequate role models. He senses that my dysfunctional behavior is shame-based and codependent and he urges me to let my inner cub heal." A little pause for thought, then he concludes: "I say we eat him."

Stick with sound theology. Steer clear of pop psychology with its confusing nomenclature. It seems reasonable at the moment, but when you need something of substance it will neither stabilize nor strengthen you. A life of passionate enthusiasm needs to stay grounded on granitelike theological truth.

Finally, Job's friends show up. That's when things turned south. But you wouldn't know that right away. At first they seemed like reasonable and caring men.

> Now when Job's three friends heard of all this adversity that had come upon him, they came each one from his own place, Eliphaz the Temanite, Bildad the Shuhite and Zophar the Naamathite; and they made an appointment together to come to sympathize with him and comfort him.
>
> When they lifted up their eyes at a distance and did not recognize him, they raised their voices and wept. And each of them tore his robe and they threw dust over their heads toward the sky.
>
> Then they sat down on the ground with him for seven days and seven nights with no one speaking a word to him, for they saw that his pain was very great.
>
> Job 2:11–13

This introduces us to a *fifth* lesson worth remembering: *Caring and sensitive friends know when to come, how to respond, and what to say.* I so wish that Eliphaz, Bildad, and Zophar had simply stayed silent, remained near to comfort Job and his wife, brought a bowl of soup or broth, and a cool cup of water when needed. These men qualified on the first two, didn't they? They knew when to come to Job. Soon as they got word of his devastating circumstances, they dropped everything and came to his side. And at least, initially (for seven days) they responded the right way. They simply sat alongside. No doubt they hurt for him, prayed for the man and his wife, and hoped to sympathize and comfort.

We who have been hospitalized know the joy of looking across the room and seeing the faces of a couple or three friends. What comfort to know they cared enough to be near. Down deep inside, we're grateful they're not saying much. They're not in our face "preaching" to us or trying to explain why we're suffering. They're just staying near. Love brought them, compassion flows from them, and gentleness draws you to them.

But the wheels started coming off the cart when those same men broke the silence. They felt the need to open Job's eyes and spell out the reasons for his afflictions. Perhaps they meant well when they started, but their "good advice" quickly eroded. They rebuked him. They questioned his motives. They probed ever deeper for hidden, secret sins. The damage they did was unconscionable.

All of us who desire to live life with passion need to spend some time evaluating our compassion. You and I will sometimes find ourselves in the role of a caring friend, hopefully a sensitive friend. Everyone who is hurting needs a friend—a friend outside the family. They don't need many, only a few faithful friends. These are the ones who bring comfort and a sensitive spirit to the hurting. They are rare, and their reassuring presence is invaluable. We need friends who love us genuinely and on occasion, friends who confront us wisely.

David comes to mind. Early on, not long after being anointed as the future king of Israel, the young giant-killer finds himself hunted and haunted by King Saul who became insanely jealous of him. Saul's son, Jonathan, hears the inappropriate comments his father makes about David. He knows that they are inaccurate, prejudiced, and extreme. He senses real trouble brewing in his father's heart. Overnight, Jonathan takes up the cause of David and becomes David's closest friend. He seeks him out wherever David is hiding. He won't let David suffer alone. He listens. He reassures. He understands. He offers words of hope and encouragement. That's the role Jonathan filled. "He loved him as he loved his own life" (1 Samuel 20:17).

As time passes, both Saul and Jonathan die violent, tragic deaths. David becomes the king, and many years later he plunges into a snake pit of carnality, adultery, murder, and shameless hypocrisy. Not surprisingly this took a terrible toll on his leadership. Out of the shadows emerges another faithful friend, Nathan, who is equally sensitive and caring. Nathan's role is different from Jonathan's. Nathan is used by the Lord to confront his friend and to help restore his integrity. Nathan arrests David's attention and turns his heart back to God in true repentance. Everyone needs a *Jonathan.* Everyone needs a *Nathan.* Whichever role we play, it's important to remain caring and sensitive. To know when to come, to know how to respond, and what to say when we speak.

Overwhelmed by his situation, Job ultimately lets it all out. He can hold it in no longer. He opens his mouth with outbursts of frustration. He curses the day he was born. He goes back nine months earlier and despises the moment he was conceived. Everything pours out in a stream of excessive words.

> Let the day perish on which I was to be born,
> And the night which said, "A boy is conceived."
> May that day be darkness;
> Let not God above care for it,
> Nor light shine on it.
> Let darkness and black gloom claim it;
> Let a cloud settle on it;
> Let the blackness of the day terrify it.
>
> Job 3:3–5

He then curses the fact he didn't die at birth.

Why did I not die at birth,
Come forth from the womb and expire?
Why did the knees receive me,
And why the breasts, that I should suck?
For now I would have lain down and been quiet;
I would have slept then, I would have been at rest.

Job 3:11–13

With that, he dumps out the rest of his frustration:

For what I fear comes upon me,
And what I dread befalls me.
I am not at ease, nor am I quiet,
And I am not at rest, but turmoil comes.

Job 3:25–26

Those are the exclamations of a man who has come to his wits' end:
He's lost everything. His health is now gone, bringing indescribable pain,
and the suffering doesn't end. The kids are still dead. There's not enough
money to provide for what's needed. His surroundings are atrocious. His
wife is there, albeit disillusioned, urging him to pack it in. *That's enough!*
Even a man of integrity has his limits. Job must have finished his verbal
eruption with his head in his hands, heaving audible sobs.

That's when the friends turned to vultures and began their feeding frenzy.
Such inappropriate reactions provide us with a *sixth* lesson: *It's easy to be
Monday-morning quarterbacks when we encounter another's outburst.* Admittedly, it is not easy to hear the kind of things Job blurted out. Not being
in his place, not feeling his pain, not knowing his thoughts or his fears—
not really—it is the most natural response imaginable to react:

"I would never say that—*and he shouldn't!*"

"I would never do what he's done—*and he shouldn't!*"

"I would always say and do this—*and he should!*"

And all of that leads to "Job, don't say that. You are really going to
regret it!" But the fact is, *he* is the one going through it. *He* is the one in

the heat of the battle. *He* is there; they are not. They just *thought* they knew what they'd say or do.

Monday-morning quarterbacks think, *I would never react like that. I would never say such a thing to God.* And then the clincher: *This is how I would respond. I mean how could she call herself a* Christian *and act like that? Why, if I were the Lord, I'd discipline her for that.*

Monday-morning quarterbacks are notorious for knowing everything! And pointing out *every* mistake. (We don't even wait until Monday morning!) "Don't throw that pass, you idiot! They've got the split end covered! They're gonna intercept if you throw it—don't (Interception) No! When are you gonna *get a life?*" as we yell at the game on television. And most of us have never been a quarterback. We've certainly never had three or four six-foot-nine-inch, 370-pound linemen with blood in their eyes and fangs sticking out of their lips running full speed in our direction—grinning. And we say, "Don't throw that thing, you dodo! Don't throw it! If I were there, I wouldn't have thrown it. I'd take a hit."

Uh, yeah . . . sure.

Stop that nonsense. Let's agree to allow our Job-friend the space to unload without getting our lecture. It will help if we remember things we shouldn't have said. We, too, have said things that were wrong or inappropriate. We, too, have responded incorrectly when the heat was on. We, too, have run off at the mouth. We, too, have thrown verbal interceptions. When we did, we didn't need someone to tell us we blew it. Within seconds we realized it. We may even think at the time we're doing it, *I'm gonna regret this.* But we still do it.

You'll need this lesson. You'll need this principle especially if you're a spiritual leader, you teach the adult Bible study, you're a counselor at a church, or you're a pastor on the staff. The world is too full of dogmatic "I told you so" or "You really shouldn't" or "You ought to." Just be quiet. Pray silently. Try hard to imagine the pain.

Eliphaz lands on him with both feet. Fists are swinging—round one, round two, round three, punching at Job. Then Bildad hits him. Then Zophar beats up on him. Not one of those guys has *ever* gone through anything like Job is going through. So, they pour out all their "good advice." Friendships will not stand the strain of too much "good advice" for very long.

We hardly need to be reminded that Job ultimately sees the error of his way. And what does he do? He openly acknowledges it: "I retract and I repent" (Job 42:6). What a great man! He suffered through all of this for who knows how long. Weeks? Maybe months? Too long! Finally, after proving himself a man of heroic endurance, the Lord calls Job His "servant" (four times). He then rebukes the friends who had made such a mess of the situation.

> It came about after the LORD had spoken these words to Job, that the LORD said to Eliphaz the Temanite, "My wrath is kindled against you and against your two friends, because you have not spoken of Me what is right as My servant Job has."
>
> Job 42:7

As we saw previously, the Lord abundantly rewarded His servant for his sustained integrity as well as his submissive spirit. But mainly, God honored Job because of his faithful endurance, which provides our *seventh* and final lesson worth remembering: *The cultivation of obedient endurance is the crowning mark of maturity.* A major goal of wholesome, healthy Christians is the hope of reaching maturity before death overtakes us. I will tell you without hesitation that one of my major goals in life is to grow up as I grow older. A commendable etching on a gravestone would be: "Here lies a man who kept growing as he kept aging." Growing up and growing old need to walk hand in hand. Never doubt it: Maturing is a slow, arduous process. Job accomplished it; he reached that goal. Small wonder we read that he died an old man and full of days. He lived the rest of his years (140 more) full of enthusiasm and passion. What an *enviable* way to finish one's life.

When trouble comes we have two options. We can view it as an intrusion, an outrage, or we can see it as an opportunity to respond in specific obedience to God's will. This is that rugged virtue James calls "endurance."

Endurance is not jaw-clenched resignation, nor is it passive acquiescence. It is "a long obedience in the same direction." It is staying on the path of obedience despite counterindications. It is a dogged determination to pursue holiness when the conditions of holiness are not favorable. It is a choice in the midst of our suffering to do what God has asked us to do, whatever it is, and for as long He asks us to do it. As Oswald Chambers wrote, "To choose suffering makes no sense at all; *to choose God's will in the midst of our suffering makes all the sense in the world.*" [4]

WHAT A WAY TO GO

Where are you today? Where is your journey leading you? More importantly, which option have you chosen? Are you viewing your trial as an outrage or an opportunity? Try hard not to forget the list of seven lessons Job teaches us about ourselves. Do you keep a journal? If you do, I've got a practical suggestion. Go back through this chapter and transfer the seven lessons onto a page of your journal. Think through your current situation and apply whichever ones are appropriate. Return to that page every month or so. It will make an enormous difference. As you grow older you will keep growing up. And, instead of simply reading about the life of Job, you will begin *living* that kind of life.

That makes all the sense in the world.

CHAPTER TWENTY-TWO

What Job Teaches Us about Our God

Clear communication is essential. The right people need to communicate the right things to the right recipients. When those three ducks aren't lined up, things backfire.

A couple from Minneapolis decided to enjoy a long weekend in sunny Florida to thaw out during a particularly frigid winter. Because both had busy careers, they found it impossible to coordinate their travel schedules. They decided that the husband would fly to Florida on Thursday, and she would travel down there the next day. Upon arriving as planned, he checked into the hotel. Once in his room he opened his laptop to send his wife a brief e-mail back in Minneapolis. However, he accidentally left off one letter in her e-address, and sent his message without realizing his error.

In Houston, a widow had just returned from her husband's funeral. He had been a minister of the gospel for many years when he was suddenly "called home to glory" following a heart attack.

Lonely, hoping to find comfort in condolence messages from a few relatives and friends, the widow sat down to check her e-mail. Upon reading the first message, she fainted and fell to the floor. Her son rushed into the room, found his mother unconscious, then glanced at the computer screen which read:

> To: My loving wife
> From: Your departed husband
> Subject: I've arrived!
>
> I have just arrived and have been checked in. Everything went very smoothly after my departure. I also verified that everything has been prepared for *your* arrival tomorrow. Looking forward to seeing you then.
>
> Hope your journey is as uneventful as mine.
>
> P. S. It sure is hot down here.[1]

Miscommunication can lead to serious misunderstanding. That goes for biblical truth too. When accurate information is deposited into the ears of someone who may be unable to understand it, confusion occurs—especially if the recipient doesn't understand the context in which the Scriptures were written.

Cynthia and I have some very good friends, a couple who, several years ago with their young son, were enjoying the Christmas holidays together. The father decided shortly after the holidays ended that the three of them would read the Bible through during the next year. They would do this as a family. So each morning or evening, the three of them would sit down together and continue their journey through the Scriptures.

They got under way, of course, in the Book of Genesis. It wasn't long before they read that Adam and his wife were both naked and were not ashamed. The boy frowned, looked down, and listened in silence. And a little later, Adam had relations with his wife, and it says she then gave birth to their son. Not many paragraphs later, the older son murdered the younger brother. And then in the fifth chapter, Adam again had relations with his wife and she bore another son named Seth. Their son, by now is sitting with his head constantly bowed. All that led into the story of Noah and the Great Flood that brought worldwide destruction. But the story of Noah, you may recall, ends in a shameful way where he gets drunk, uncovers himself in his tent, and his son walks in on his father's nakedness. Noah dies in a context clouded by sin, shame, and failure.

A couple of days later they were reading in chapter 19 of Genesis on Sodom and Gomorrah. That did it! Their son spoke up, "Stop! Daddy, should I be listening to *all of this stuff?*"

You and I know there wasn't anything wrong with what was being read, but in the ears of a child he couldn't help but wonder, "What is this stuff in the Bible all about?"

New believers can have the same reaction. Truth from the Scriptures can become confusing for them, especially when God is involved in unusual events. Can't you imagine a young believer, not knowing much about our heavenly Father asking, "Why would a good God allow His chosen people, the Jews, to live 400 plus years in Egyptian bondage? Why would a good God do that? Why would a loving God encourage the destruction of *all* the Canaanites when Joshua and his fellow Hebrews invaded the land, starting in Jericho? How could it be that *every one of them* was to be killed? And how could a holy God call David, "a man after My own heart" even though he was later guilty of adultery and murder, and was, in fact, a polygamist? And talk about confusing: How could a compassionate, loving God stand back and permit an upright, faithful man like Job to suffer like he did?

Misunderstanding causes many not to trust God. If He is so full of compassion and justice, if He wants us to call on Him when we are in need, why would He *ever* approve of something as cruel as Satan's mistreatment of Job? Tough questions.

Maybe we should let Job speak for himself. What does *he* think? Since he's the one who went through it all, it makes good sense to back off and learn what *Job* would teach us about God.

Rather than turning this final chapter into a lengthy and complicated theological treatise based on numerous sections of the Book of Job, I think it would help if we limited our thoughts to the last chapter. As I did in my previous chapter, I have seven specific lessons that I think Job would teach us about our God if he were alive today. Thankfully, his inspired words are preserved for all to read. Through Job's pen we're able to understand our God even better.

SEVEN LESSONS ABOUT OUR GOD

Job sat silently through God's extensive message. It begins in chapter 38, and He doesn't finish until the end of chapter 41. Amazingly, He never answers Job's questions. He doesn't come near those issues. Instead, you'll recall He escorts Job around the universe and into the sea, introducing him to several of the animals of the field and birds of the air. Though God doesn't answer Job's questions, before the end of the book, the man with the boils is bowing in submission before Him. The One who permitted, in fact personally *approved*, what happened to His servant Job, offers no answers to the man's specific questions. And yet, I repeat, Job humbly submits. Surely he learned some things about God that we need to know. While we, like Job, will not have all (or even *most*) of our questions answered, we have much to learn from God's servant. I will do my best to communicate clearly. All I ask is that you give this last leg of our journey your full attention.

> Then Job answered the Lord and said,
> "I know that You can do all things."
>
> Job 42:2

The first lesson Job teaches us: *There is nothing God cannot do.* Having heard and having realized the unlimited power of his infinite God, Job states his realization in the simplest of terms, "You can do all things." In other words, God is "omnipotent." The first part of that interesting word, *omni* means all. And of course, *potent* means powerful or effective. God is all-powerful. This affirms that He has no limitations, needs no approval, faces no obstacle that hinders His activities in any way. His actions run their course without resistance. The works of our heavenly Father are always and completely effective.

Theologically stated:

> Since He has at His command all the power in the universe, the Lord
> God omnipotent can do anything as easily as anything else. All His
> acts are done without effort. He expends no energy that must be re-
> plenished. His self-sufficiency makes it unnecessary for Him to look
> outside of Himself for a renewal of strength. All the power required to
> do all that He wills to do lies in undiminished fullness in His own
> infinite being.[2]

Though somewhat technical wording, I find those amplifying comments
helpful. The point is clear—God's power is infinite and independent, self-
energized, and never depleting. He creates from nothing without any de-
crease of energy. He sustains all life without needing any assistance. He gives
life and takes life. He raises from the dead those He wishes to raise without
any resistance. And He withholds the most powerful creature ever created
(Satan himself) with no struggle, without restraint. Nothing stands in God's
way. Nothing hinders God's work. Nothing alters God's plan. He alone deserves the description, "awesome."

We've cheapened that word by overuse. We've applied it to virtually
everything we find intriguing. Sound systems are now *awesome*. Video games
are *awesome*. Back when they built them, the early Datsun Z-car was ad-
vertised as an *awesome* automobile. I can remember going to the show-
room and looking at it. The longer I looked at it the less *awesome* it was. It
had four wheels like every other car. It had two doors, a steering wheel, a
dashboard—all standard stuff. It was tiny! In fact, smaller than all other
cars I was able to squeeze into. It didn't have an *awesome* engine, even
though the advertisements kept saying, "It is *awesome!*" Hardly. Only our
omnipotent God is *awesome*.

Four times in the Scriptures (Jeremiah 32:17, Jeremiah 32:27, Luke 1:37,
Luke 18:27), we read that nothing is impossible with God. Now *that* defines *awesome*.

We find a second truth worth remembering as we read the end of Job's
opening sentence.

And that no purpose of Yours can be thwarted.

Job 42:2

And what is this lesson? *It is impossible to frustrate God's purposes.* In Job's words we find the term *thwarted.* God's priorities are never thwarted. The Hebrew term is from the verb that means "to cut off." "No purpose of Yours can be cut off." God's purpose can't be blocked, restrained, or stopped. God's intentions can neither be altered nor disrupted. What He purposes will transpire without delay, without hindrance, and without fail. Everything that happens on this earth falls within the framework of exactly what God has purposed. Yes, *exactly.* None of what occurs is a last-minute, stopgap response, therefore He is *never* surprised. Whatever occurs is unfolding precisely as He has planned it in His omniscience. With Him, things that occur on earth are never out of control.

Let me remind you of the words of an ancient king who recovered from insanity and realized that the living God was having His way in his life.

All the inhabitants of the earth are accounted as nothing,
But He does according to His will in the host of heaven
And among the inhabitants of earth;
And no one can ward off His hand
Or say to Him, "What have you done?"

Daniel 4:35

"No one can *ward off his hand*" is another way of saying, "No purpose of God can be thwarted." No one can cancel the Lord's agenda. No one can restrain Him or hinder His plan from running its predetermined course. Please do not be afraid of this great doctrine! If you're like me, you will learn to find comfort in it.

Job has not come back from insanity, but he has endured a maddening, long episode of loss and humiliation, grief and physical/emotional pain. He has been leveled to the role of a homeless man, having once been the greatest of the men of the East. Job is on the other side of all that, and is just now beginning to realize (get this) *without any of his questions answered,* that he is at the mercy of his great God whose purpose cannot be frustrated. He is still the One who does all things well. His submission resulted from that realization. Without having an explanation to his why questions, Job knows he can trust his God.

Which brings us to a *third* lesson worth remembering: *God's plans are beyond our understanding and too deep to explain.*

> Who is this that hides counsel without knowledge?
> Therefore I have declared that which I did not understand,
> Things too wonderful for me, which I did not know.
>
> Job 42:3

In other words, "I babbled on about things far beyond me, made small talk about wonders way over my head" (MSG).

It took humility to say that.

If you were to ask me to give you the core message of the Book of Job, I'd have you read Job 42:3. Job's story is about coming to an understanding that God's plans are beyond our understanding and too deep to explain.

Do not be hesitant to admit that there are times we are downright *disappointed* with God. I mean, after all, we have done what is right, and we have done it for all the right reasons; yet look at what has transpired! How could He have permitted such a thing? Because God has revealed Himself as good and fair, compassionate and loving, we anticipate His responding in ways that fit His character (as we understand it). But, He doesn't "come through."

Philip Yancey addresses this forthrightly and honestly.

> I can think of several helpful things God could have said: "Job, I'm truly sorry about what's happened. You've endured many unfair trials on my behalf, and I'm proud of you. You don't know what this means to me and even to the universe." A few compliments, a dose of compassion, or at the least a brief explanation of what transpired "behind the curtain" in the unseen world—any of these would have given Job some solace.

God says nothing of the kind. His "reply," in fact, consists of more questions than answers. Sidestepping thirty-five chapters' worth of debates on the problem of pain, he plunges instead into a magnificent verbal tour of the natural world. He seems to guide Job through a private gallery of his favorite works, lingering with pride over dioramas of mountain goats, wild donkeys, ostriches, and eagles, speaking as if astonished by his own creations. The beauty of the poetry at the end of Job rivals anything in world literature. Even as I marvel at God's dazzling portrayal of the natural world, however, a sense of bewilderment steals in. Of all moments, why did God choose this one to give Job a course in wilderness appreciation? Are these words relevant?

In his book *Wishful Thinking*, Frederick Buechner sums up God's speech. "God doesn't explain. He explodes. He asks Job who he thinks he is anyway. He says that to try to explain the kind of things Job wants explained would be like trying to explain Einstein to a littleneck clam . . . . God doesn't reveal his grand design. He reveals himself."

The message behind the splendid poetry boils down to this: *until you know a little more about running the physical universe, Job, don't tell me how to run the moral universe.* "Why are you treating me so unfairly, God?" Job has whined throughout the book. "Put yourself in my place."

"NO!" God thunders in reply. "You put yourself in *my* place! Until you can offer lessons on how to make the sun come up each day, or where to scatter lightning bolts, or how to design a hippopotamus, don't judge how I run the world. Just shut up and listen."

The impact of God's speech on Job is almost as amazing as the speech itself. Although God never answers question one about Job's predicament, the blast from the storm flattens Job. He repents in dust and ashes, and every trace of disappointment with God is swept away.[3]

Perhaps God doesn't explain Himself because knowing and understanding His way may not help us all that much. Stop and ask yourself: Does knowing why really help? Is the pain removed by knowing the cause? Ours is a world filled with devastating catastrophes, random shootings by hidden snipers, jets crashing into tall buildings, deliberately poisoning elderly people at rest homes, serial rapists and murderers, mothers who kill all of their own children, droughts and famines, wives in automobiles who run over their husbands, priests who molest innocent little boys, preachers who are fraudulent and phony, CEOs who take unfair advantage of their employees. The list doesn't end. How could God permit such things? Would it really help to know why? In a fallen world full of depraved people who act out their worst thoughts, would it change the wrong?

I'll go a step further. Maybe God doesn't explain Himself because we're incapable of comprehending His answers. Since He lives in an existence that is completely unlike ours and in a realm far beyond our comprehension, ours being tactile and limited by space and time, within the rigid boundaries of all the physical laws, how could we possibly understand? None of our limitations apply to Him, so what would enable us to grasp His plan?

What bothers us is that He doesn't act like *we* think He *ought* to act. He doesn't do what our earthly dads would have done in similar circumstances. While I'm at it, where was He when His own Son was crucified? To the surprise of many (most?), He was there all the time working out His divine plan for our salvation. As the process was running its course, Jesus' own disciples didn't get it—they were the most disillusioned people on the planet. Do you remember what they were thinking? They were wondering how in the world they could have believed in a hoax. From their little-neck clam perspective, their Master's death didn't make any sense.

Do you know what Job finally sees? Job sees God and that is enough. He doesn't see answers. He is to the place where he doesn't *need* answers. He has gotten a glimpse of the Almighty and that is sufficient.

There is a *fourth* lesson worth remembering. *Only through God's instruction are we able to humble ourselves and rest in His will.*

> Hear, now, and I will speak;
> I will ask You and You instruct me.
> I have heard of You by the hearing of the ear;

> But now my eye sees You;
> Therefore I retract,
> And I repent in dust and ashes.

Job 42:4–6

Take special notice of Job's words. He does not reply, "I've got an argument here." On the contrary, He says," I retract and repent." There's no divine force. There's no threatening rebuke from God. "Job, if you don't get down on your knees and beg for mercy from Me, I'm going to finish you off!"

No. In gentle, resigned submission Job rests his case in the Father's will. He says, "You instruct me and as a result of Your instruction, I will willingly submit and accept it." Do you know what I love about Job's attitude? (Read this very carefully.) There is an absence of talk about "my rights." There is not a hint of personal entitlement. There is no expectation or demand. There's not even a plea for God to understand or to defend him before his argumentative friends. Furthermore, there's no self-pity, no moody, depressed spirit. He is completely at rest. His innermost being, at last, is at peace.

You may say, "Well, if God has blessed me like He blessed Job, I'd say that too." Wait. He hasn't yet brought relief or reward. The man is still covered with boils. He still doesn't have any family. He's still homeless. He's still bankrupt. With nothing external changed, Job says quietly, "Lord, I'm Yours."

I asked you to read Peter's counsel in the previous chapter. Please do so again:

> Therefore humble yourselves under the mighty hand of God, that He
> may exalt you at the proper time, casting all your anxiety on Him,
> because He cares for you.

1 Peter 5:6–7

Focus on the timing. Humble yourself not *after* He exalts you, but humble yourself *now*. Don't wait. Pull back, stop the arguing, and rest in Him. It is remarkable how He will quiet your spirit and transport you to a realm of contentment you've never known before, even with

348

most of the answers missing. The philosophers of this world demand answers. The believer who has now learned through this kind of cataclysmic experience to trust, regardless, demands nothing. And the worries slowly fade away, one after another.

Remember my earlier comment about true repentance? A contrite heart makes no demands and has no expectations. That's Job—right here, right now. It's a beautiful sight. I need to add, Job has no corner on contentment. It's yours to claim.

We're ready for a *fifth* lesson: *When the day of reckoning arrives, God is always fair.* Do you remember another previous comment? All God's accounts are not settled at the end of the month. We've arrived at the place we've been waiting for. Let's call it the "Accounts Settlement" desk of God. Patiently and with long-suffering God has been observing everything, taking note of who is saying what. Not one idle word slips His attention. He not only knows what was said by whom, He knows why. He knows who spoke truth and who didn't. He deals with wrongdoers at His "Accounts Settlement" desk. He blesses those who have walked with Him. He forgives those who bring their offerings and humble themselves before Him. God restores. God rewards. God heals. God honors Job who prayed for his friends with an open heart. God noticed it all. I suggest you underscore Hebrews 6:10 in your Bible: "For God is not unjust so as to forget your work and the love which you have shown toward His name, in having ministered and in still ministering to the saints." Eugene Peterson in *The Message* renders those first words "God doesn't miss anything."

Some who read my words have been terribly abused. You have been victims of the worst kind of mistreatment. You have been taken advantage of by someone you trusted. You have been abandoned by your mate. You have been treated unfairly. Someone has ripped you off. You've lost a fortune through a fraudulent scheme. Every one of us could give stories of abuse and neglect, misrepresentation and unfair treatment. It's never been made right. And so, please return to this great truth: God does not forget. He just doesn't adjust His plan to our timetable. His "Accounts Settlement" desk doesn't operate on a nine-to-five schedule: He doesn't handle our case when we want it handled. I wanted God to zap Eliphaz the very moment he said that first insulting word to Job. He's waited through all the sarcastic speeches, stayed silent through all the insults. Finally, He says, "Eliphaz, Bildad, Zophar, you have been *wrong*."

Job has waited all this time to be vindicated. Remember how it came up? Without fanfare:

> The LORD said to Eliphaz the Temanite, "My wrath is kindled against you and against your two friends, because you've not spoken of Me what is right as my servant Job has."
>
> Job 42:7

God heard! Yes, He heard! He didn't say anything at the time, but He heard it all. He is not unjust to forget one idle word. And I can assure you, He did not overlook one wrong act committed against you. He has a perfect plan. His plan is unfolding. When His timetable says, "Now," justice will roll down, and His "Accounts Settlement" desk will take swift action.

God's arrangement of things is not a frustrated plan. God is not sitting on the edge of heaven, biting His nails, wondering what He's going to do about our world. He knows exactly what He's going to do and when He's going to do it. Job sees that clearly—now. He realizes, finally, that God doesn't miss anything.

The *sixth* lesson is wonderfully encouraging: *No one can be compared to God when it comes to blessings.*

> And the LORD accepted Job. The LORD restored the fortunes of Job when he prayed for his friends, and the LORD increased all that Job had twofold. Then all his brothers and all his sisters and all who had known him before came to him, and they ate bread with him in his house; and they consoled him and comforted him for all the adversities that the LORD had brought on him. And each one gave him one piece of money, and each a ring of gold. The LORD blessed the latter days of Job more than his beginning; and he had 14,000 sheep and 6,000 camels and 1,000 yoke of oxen and 1,000 female donkeys. He had seven sons and three daughters.

> In all the land no women were found so fair as Job's daughters; and
> their father gave them inheritance among their brothers.
>
> Job 42:9–13, 15

Did you read that too quickly? The end of verse 9? Mark it. "The Lord *accepted.*" And then, "The Lord *restored.*" End of verse 10, "The Lord *increased.*" Beginning of verse 12, "The Lord *blessed.*" Those are words of grace, statements of divine favor. Let them hit with full impact:

Accepted.

    Restored.

        Increased.

            Blessed.

Because of the fallout of our cynical society, you and I are being programmed to rush by words of grace and blessing and to hurry on to words that are negative. They bring us down. Killings in the workplace. Mold in your house. Weather disasters. Fractured families. Beetles in trees. Forest fires. High rate of divorce. Economic woes. Acts of terrorism. The homeless. Fallen ministers. Broken hearts. Mistreatment of children. Wife abuse. Chemical dependence. Deadbeat dads. Premature deaths. Fraudulent builders. Rising unemployment. Scandals among CEOs and famous athletes. On and on. That's what fills the evening news.

We never hear: "Now, tomorrow night we'll report only good news." Instead, it's "Stay tuned if you think *that* report was bad, in a moment we'll have a full exposé."

I mean, even the weatherman predicts "partly cloudy." He never says, "Mainly sunny tomorrow." It's always a 20 percent chance of rain. He never says, "It probably won't." And furthermore, he's usually wrong (talk about job security). Enough of all that!

Who does God bless? Job! This lesson we learn from Job is *great* news! You haven't forgotten that Job cursed the day he was born, have you? Or that he resented the fact he didn't die when he was placed on his mother's breast? He was also the one who said, "I am not at ease. I am not quiet." In other words, "I resent what has happened." That's the same Job who is wonderfully blessed at the end of the book. Why? Grace, grace, grace, grace, grace!

We don't get grace—we just don't get it. You work hard, you get a promotion. You work harder, you get a bigger promotion. You work super hard, you run the company. Then you can take advantage of people who work and work hard and work super hard. That's the way a fallen world thinks. Grace comes along and says, "You're sick today? I'm going to bless you mightily. You're not doing too well? I'm going to bless you greatly. You blew it? You're repentant? I'm going to bless you." Because grace doesn't wait for works to catch up.

One of my major messages is about grace. You might think, because I preach about grace that I have a fabulous life.

Before you settle in too comfortably on that thought, let me share a page out of my very normal life with you. I went to the grocery store the other day. One of the things on my list was a dozen eggs. My goal was to get them in the cart, paid for, and home in the refrigerator before Dr. Ken Cooper caught me buying them. So I quickly put the bags into the grocery cart, transferred them to the car, and made a superhuman effort to carry all six bags into the house at once. It's that old economy of motion thing—it should only take one trip for a real man. Why make three trips successfully, when one very impossible trip will do it? (I am told this is a right brain–left brain–male thing.)

By now you probably have the picture. Somewhere in the process of holding on to six bags, I had to figure out a way to insert the key in the lock on our door, open the door quickly, turn off the alarm, all while simultaneously juggling the six bags. I can now testify there is not a way to do that! Murphy's law tells us that something has to give. And if something has to give, which bag do you think that would be? Right! The bag with the dozen eggs. I was feeling terribly sorry for myself as I worked on the gooey mess on the floor, but I finally got up enough of the yucky stuff to walk across the floor without sliding. Hurdle number one!

I reached into the refrigerator to put away the pitiful remnant of the original dozen eggs, and assuming the egg tray in the refrigerator is empty, I was not as careful as one should be if one still has eggs in that tray. Once again, THREE-EGG OMELETTE ALL OVER THE FLOOR! Did I tell Cynthia this is a new method of cleaning the floor prescribed by Heloise?

Did I let it dry and see if it would chip off? Being the dutiful husband that I am, I couldn't tell a lie. Besides, none of that would fly with my wife, so I decided to do the honorable thing and clean up the mess.

But, lo! There was still an egg left in the tray. I had saved that one egg. So, I gingerly and tenderly reached for the precious, remaining egg. AND IT BROKE IN MY HAND AND RAN DOWN TOWARD MY ELBOW! I LOST IT! I TOTALLY LOST IT!

My wife heard the commotion, came into the kitchen, and asked, "Is there something wrong? Can I help?" Not good timing! However, I replied, in a moderately irritable tone of voice, "NO, I'VE GOT IT!"

So, I cleaned it all up. You know what? I didn't deserve to live through the night. But guess what? I woke up the next morning *wonderfully* blessed. Why?

Grace, grace, marvelous grace. The Book of Job teaches about grace. When He blesses Job He doesn't bless a perfect man; He blesses an imperfect man. If he were perfect he wouldn't be repenting. If he had said the right thing, he wouldn't be retracting. When are we going to get it? Because of His grace, God wonderfully blesses us. He does it better than *anyone!*

Job is beside himself. The boils are gone. Next thing he knows there's a knock on his door, and there's a couple of guys who need work. They know three other guys who need employment. Before you know it, he's got enough money, so he hires them. And he looks up to see the camels coming back. The men he hired are building his buildings, and a new house is being rebuilt. And the wife says to him one morning, "We're starting over!" She does it ten times. (Stop, Lord, stop. That's enough.) You know the rest.

> After all this Job lived 140 more years, and saw his sons and his grandsons, four generations. And Job died, an old man and full of days.
>
> Job 42:16–17

Let the music begin! Job's later years are wonderfully fulfilling, which brings us to the *seventh* lesson. Here we go. *Only God can fill our final years with divine music that frees us to live above our circumstances.* God's unmerited favor frees us. It enables us to live fully for Him.

Job finally grasps the truth, which frees him up. He is freed from the prison of fears. Freed from the tiny cell of limited thinking and negative attitudes. He's freed from grudges. He's freed from the need to know why. He's free! Free at last, thank God Almighty, he's free to live another 140 years enveloped in the music of the Master. Kids, grandkids, great-grandkids all around him. It's so wonderful he can hardly remember all the boils that plagued him so many years ago. What a way to go! It's the kind of music only God can bring.

Some his age were struggling with dementia. Some were battling increased loss of memory. A few of his peers were physically unable to keep up, feeling shelved when they were once engaged in life. Not Job. He finished well, living his life full of days, excited about tomorrow, preoccupied with divine music that set him free.

Remember the award-winning film, *The Shawshank Redemption*? It's a great film because it makes you think. It also lifts you beyond the prison cells of those men. Tim Robbins plays the part of a free-spirited man named Andy. He is with other struggling prisoners, all of whom are fighting against brutality to hold on to their humanity. He spends his days carving chessmen from stone. He petitions the state for books for the prison library so he can help inmates earn their high school diplomas. These are just a couple of the ways that Andy held on to his humanity.

One other creative idea cost him two weeks in solitary confinement, you may remember. He gains access to the prison's public address system and plays a record of great operatic music for all the prison to hear for the first time. As the classical music streams through the cells, the washrooms, and across the prison yard, the inmates stop and stare transfixed.

The actor, Morgan Freeman, a friend of Andy's and narrator of the story, says these words about that moment.

> I have no idea to this day what those two Italian ladies were singing about. Truth is, I don't wanna know. Some things are best left unsaid. I'd like to think they were singing about something so beautiful it can't be expressed in words and makes your heart ache because of it. I tell you those voices soared, higher and farther than anybody in the great place dared to dream. It was like some beautiful bird flapped

into Alexander's cage and made those walls dissolve away. And for the briefest of moments, every last man at Shawshank felt free.[4]

That's what the music of God does for us when we end our lives well. Like Job, we are free at last.

Our journey with Job has come to an end, but our friendship will continue for a lifetime. Job dies an old man and full of years. He truly came to know the living God, not in spite of his pain, but *because* of it. The pain drove him to his knees where he ultimately surrendered himself before his God. In complete trust, he rested in Him.

I invite you to trust Him right now in the prison of your circumstances. Let God be God. Remind yourself faithfully and regularly you are not in charge. Limited, sinful, needy, and incapable of freeing yourself, I invite you to the Cross. That's where your burdens are rolled away and where His music begins. Come to Him today. Let the music begin. It's a love song that invites you in.

Thank you, Father, for Your faithful presence.

Thank You also for Your mysterious ways.

We entrust to You the lessons we have just begun to learn.

Thank You for our friend whom we've met in the pages of this book . . .

for the things he has taught us.

Most of all, thank You for the heroic endurance he has modeled.

Thank You for Your grace, which lifts us above and beyond prison walls

and gives us a song to sing— a song that frees us from sorrows and from ourselves.

In the matchless name of Christ our Lord.

Amen.

CONCLUSION

S uffering not only impacts a person, it touches all who are in that person's family. And, depending on how extensive the trouble, that family is never quite the same.

George MacDonald writes eloquently of this:

> Sometimes a thunderbolt will shoot from a clear sky; and sometimes in the life of a peaceful family, without warning of gathered storm, something terrible will fall. And from that moment everything seems changed. That family is no more exactly what it was before. Better it ought to be, damaged it may be.
>
> The result depends on the family itself and its response to the invading storm of trouble. Forever after, its spiritual weather is altered. But for the family who believes in God, such rending and frightful catastrophes never come but where they are turned around for good in that family's life and in other lives they touch."[1]

For twenty-two chapters we have witnessed not only a man whose life was struck by such a "thunderbolt," but also a family—Job's family. We have seen the damage those "frightful catastrophes" brought on him and on them. Their story has touched our lives deeply, and therefore we are grateful it has been preserved in the Scriptures for our benefit and the benefit of others in generations to come. The pain he endured—they endured—has become a platform of hope on which we can stand, preparing ourselves to face some "invading storm of trouble" that may now be gathering, which is yet to fall.

In my concluding words I wish to address the very real issue of a family's being impacted by such "thunderbolts" from a clear sky. Without going into any of the specific details, I can testify to the truth of MacDonald's words. My own family and I have been struck time and again by trials fitting that description during the past decade. They have hurt and wounded us, bringing changes we would never have expected. Not wanting to sound melodramatic, I would add that we have seriously wondered at times if we could survive the invasion of yet another storm . . . and then another would strike, hitting us hard, making us reel under the terrible blast.

Perhaps that explains why I was drawn so magnetically and personally into the story of Job. I immediately identified with the rapidity and the devastation of the assaults, though, certainly, not to the level he suffered. Nevertheless, ours have been deep and frequent blows. They have forced us to do the very things I have urged you to do as you've read through these chapters.

You may remember several of them: Maintain integrity no matter what happens; accept the challenge to change; keep a clear vertical perspective; think theologically; refuse to question the sovereign purpose of God; submit to His will, regardless; don't expect to understand His mysterious ways; count on the justice of the Lord to roll down in His time; humble yourself under His mighty hand; be assured that He misses nothing; rest contentedly in His plan; remember that some day yet future He will abundantly reward.

These are not mere theoretical guidelines gleaned from the life of Job; they are the foundational principles that have kept the Swindolls on our feet for years! We are only human—we have no supernatural abilities in ourselves. Like everyone else on this earth, we are imperfect, limited in understanding, and deficient in our own strength. And so, in the writing of this book, my family and I have gained fresh hope to go on.

Like you, we have no way of knowing what tomorrow may bring . . . but if it is anything like the past, more storms will come. They will drive us to our knees once again, forcing us to trust Him even though we cannot understand why He would permit such a thing to occur. Like Job, we believe in Him with all our hearts, we want to walk in obedience before Him, and we desire nothing more than to bring greater glory to His name.

This much the Swindoll family members know—and we have Job to thank for it:

> "He knows the way we take;
> When He has tried us, we will come forth as gold.
> Our feet have held fast to His path;
> We have kept His way and not turned aside.
> We have not departed from the command of His lips;
> We have treasured the words of his mouth
> More than our necessary food."

Our lives are in His hands. If our future includes further "frightful catastrophes," by His grace we will weather those storms with heroic endurance. And if the way our family responds touches other lives for good, including yours, that will be sufficient reward.

ENDNOTES

INTRODUCTION

1. Peter H. Gibbon, *A Call to Heroism* (New York: Atlantic Monthly Press, 2002), 184. Used by permission.

CHAPTER ONE:
SETTING THE STAGE FOR DISASTER

1. Thomas Carlyle, "Heroes and Hero Worship, Lecture II, May 8, 1840, The Hero as Prophet. Mahomet: Islam," Public domain.
2. Eugene H. Peterson, "Introduction to Job," from *The Message* (Colorado Springs, CO: NavPress, 2002) 839. Used by permission.
3. Michael Easley, e-mail to Chuck Swindoll, February 26, 2002, "CVN-74 NIGHT SHIFT." Source Unknown.
4. J. Vernon McGee, *Job* (Nashville, TN: Thomas Nelson Publishers, 1991), 14.
5. Francis I. Andersen, *Job: Tyndale OT Commentary Series* (London: Inter-Varsity Press, 1976.), 80. Used by permission of InterVarsity Press, P. O. Box 1400, Downers Grove, IL 60515. www.ivpress.com.

CHAPTER TWO
REELING AND RECOVERING FROM DEVASTATING NEWS

1. Lisa Beamer, *Let's Roll* (Wheaton, IL: Tyndale House Publishers, Inc. 2002). Used by permission.
2. Henry Wadsworth Longfellow (1807–1882), *The Ladder of St. Augustine*. Public domain.
3. Philip Yancey, *Disappointment With God* (Grand Rapids, MI: Zondervan Publishing House, 1988), 163-164. Used by permission of The Zondervan Corporation.
4. Gustave Doré, *Job Hearing of His* Ruin (woodcut circa 1860). Public domain.
5. Alexander Whyte (1836–1921), *Old Testament Characters, Vol. 1* (London, England: Oliphants Ltd., 1952), 379. Public domain.
6. Ray Stedman story as told to Dr. Charles R. Swindoll.
7. Francis I. Andersen, *Job: Tyndale OT Commentary Series* (London: InterVarsity Press, 1976), 89. Used by permission of InterVarsity Press, P. O. Box 1400, Downers Grove, IL 60515. www.ivpress.com.

CHAPTER THREE
SATAN VS. JOB . . . ROUND TWO

1. Ray C. Stedman, "The Johnny Gunther Story," as told in *Adventuring Through the Bible* (Grand Rapids, MI: Discovery House Publishers, 1997), 245. Used by permission of Discovery House Publishers, Box 3566, Grand Rapids, MI 49501. All rights reserved.
2. Warren Wiersbe, *Be Patient* (Colorado Springs, CO: Chariot Victor Publishing, A Division of Cook Communications, 1991), 19.
3. Robert Alden, *The New American Commentary* (Nashville, TN: Broadman & Holman Publishers, 1993), 67–68. Used by permission.
4. Francis I. Andersen, *Job: Tyndale OT Commentary Series* (London: InterVarsity Press, 1976.), 93–94. Used by permission of InterVarsity Press, P. O. Box 1400, Downers Grove, IL 60515. www.ivpress.com.
5. *Ibid*, 94. Used by permission.

CHAPTER FOUR
JOB'S ADVICE TO HUSBANDS AND FRIENDS

1. Alexander Whyte (1836–1921), *Old Testament Characters* (Grand Rapids, MI: Kregel Publications, 1990) 379. Public domain.
2. Source unknown.
3. John Eldredge, *Wild at Heart* (Nashville, TN: Thomas Nelson Publishers, 2001) 137. Reprinted by permission of Thomas Nelson, Inc. All rights reserved.
4. Peter H. Gibbon, *A Call to Heroism* (New York, NY: Grove/Atlantic: Atlantic Monthly Press, 2002), 182.
5. Francis Andersen, *Job: Tyndale OT Commentary Series* (London: Inter-Varsity Press 1976), 93. Used by permission of InterVarsity Press, P. O. Box 1400, Downers Grove, IL 60515. www.ivpress.com.
6. "20 Years is All It Takes" in an e-mail to Chuck Swindoll, 2002, www.crazydoodle.com/jokes/20years.html.
7. John E. Hartley, *The Book of Job* (NICOT) (Grand Rapids, MI: William B. Eerdmans Publishing Company, 1988), 85. Used by permission.
8. Warren Wiersbe, *Be Patient* (Colorado Springs, CO: Chariot Victor Publishing, A Division of Cook Communications, 1991), 21.
9. Eugene Peterson, "Introduction to Job," *The Message* (Colorado Springs, CO: NavPress, 2002), 840. Used by permission.
10. Joseph Bayly, *The Last Thing We Talk About* (Colorado Springs, CO: David C. Cook Publishing Co., A Division of Cook Communications, 1973), 55–56.

CHAPTER FIVE
THE MOURNFUL WAIL OF A MISERABLE MAN

1. Story of Chaplain Bill Bryan as told to Chuck Swindoll at Dallas Theological Seminary banquet. Used by permission.
2. Rosamund Stone Zander and Benjamin Zander, *The Art of Possibility* (Boston, MA: Harvard Business School Press, 2000), 44–45. Permission to reproduce granted by Harvard Business School Publishing.

3. C. H. Spurgeon, "The Minister's Fainting Fits" from *Lectures to My Students* (Grand Rapids, MI: Zondervan Publishing House, Ninth Impression, 1970), 155–156. Public domain.
4. Robert Alden, *The New American Commentary* (Broadman & Holman Publishers, 1993), 71. Used by permission.
5. John E. Hartley, *The Book of Job* (NICOT) (Grand Rapids, MI: William B. Eerdmans Publishing Company, 1988) 101. Used by permission.
6. Dennis Guernsey story. Used by permission.

CHAPTER SIX
RESPONDING TO BAD COUNSEL

1. Mark R. Littleton, "Where Job's Comforters Went Wrong" from *When God Seems Far Away* (Wheaton, IL: Harold Shaw, 1987), 79–88. Used by permission of Harold Shaw Publishers in *Sitting With Job*, edited by Roy B. Zuck (Grand Rapids, MI: Baker Book House, n.d.), 256.

CHAPTER SEVEN
CONTINUING THE VERBAL FISTFIGHT

1. William Henry Green, *Conflict and Triumph: The Argument of the Book of Job Unfolded* (Carlisle, PA: Banner of Truth Trust, 1999), 54–55. Used by permission, Banner of Truth: Carlisle, PA 17013.
2. H. L. Mencken, *The Divine Afflatus* (New York, NY: New York Evening Mail, 1917), 155.
3. "Oh To Be Six Again" (iRealms Internet 2003). www.irealms.co.za. Used by permission.
4. G. Campbell Morgan, *The Answers of Jesus to Job* (Westwood, NJ: Fleming H. Revell Company, 1964), 24–27. Used by permission.

CHAPTER EIGHT
WHEN REBUKE AND RESISTANCE COLLIDE

1. Warren Wiersbe, *Be Patient* (Colorado Springs, CO: Cook Communications, 1991), 46.

2. Lawrence J. Crabb, Jr., *The Pressure's Off* (Colorado Springs, CO: Waterbrook Press, 2002), 183. All rights reserved.

3. C. S. Lewis, *A Grief Observed* (New York, NY: Harper & Row, Publishers, 1961), 17–18. C. S. Lewis Pte. Ltd. 1961. Extract reprinted by permission.

CHAPTER NINE
GRACELESS WORDS FOR A GRIEVING MAN

1. "Going to Shout All Over God's Heaven," Negro spiritual. Public domain.

2. Denise Banderman, "GrAce" (Hannibal, MO: ChristianityToday.com, 2002) www.gospelcom.net/peggiesplace/tnt222.htm. Used by permission.

3. Lucy Mabery-Foster story as related by Chuck Swindoll. Used by permission.

4. John E. Hartley, *The Book of Job* (NICOT) (Grand Rapids, MI: William B. Eerdmans Publishing Company, 1988) 257. Used by permission.

5. C. S. Lewis, *A Grief Observed* (New York, NY: Harper & Row, Publishers, 1961), 9. C. S. Lewis Pte. Ltd. Extract reprinted by permission.

6. "Going to Shout All Over God's Heaven," Negro spiritual. Public domain.

7. Philip Yancey, *Disappointment with God* (Grand Rapids, MI: Zondervan Publishing House, 1988) 203–204. Used by permission of The Zondervan Corporation.

8. "Amazing Grace," John Newton. Public domain.

CHAPTER TEN
REASSURING WORDS FOR THE ASSAULTED AND ABUSED

1. Jeffrey A. Krames, *The Rumsfeld Way: Leadership Wisdom of a Battle-Hardened Maverick* (New York, NY: McGraw-Hill, 2002), 123.

2. *Ibid*, p.123.

3. *The Economist*, 25 St. James's Street, London SW1A 1HG, United Kingdom.

4. "The Builder," Author unknown.

5. Abraham Lincoln, "The Gettysburg Address," November 19, 1863. Public domain.
6. "The Ticket," a story told of Albert Einstein by Dr. Billy Graham in a speech made in Charlotte, North Carolina and reprinted as part of Dr. Graham's speech in *The Leadership Journal,* Spring 2003. Source of original story unknown.

CHAPTER ELEVEN
RESPONDING WISELY WHEN FALSELY ACCUSED

1. "The Saint" http://www.jokecenter.com/jokes/Religion/6755.htm-14k. Anonymous.
2. J. Oswald Sanders, *Spiritual Leadership* (Chicago, IL: Moody Publishers, 1994), 111. Used by permission.
3. Colonel Blacker, *Oliver's Advice,* 1834 quoted by John Bartlett (1820–1905), *Familiar Quotations, 10th ed.* 1919. Public domain.
4. Source unknown. Public domain.
5. "What Good News Do We Have for This Guy" story. Source unknown.
6. Abraham Lincoln in a letter to Secretary Stanton dated July 18, 1864, in which he refused to dismiss the Montgomery Blair, Postmaster General as quoted by John Bartlett (1820–1905), *Familiar Quotations, 10th ed.,* 1919. Public domain.
7. Story based on the experiences of Dr. Joel Filartiga and his son Joelita in Paraguay in 1976, htt://www.pbs.org/wnet/justice/law_background_filartiga.html.

CHAPTER TWELVE
HOW TO HANDLE CRITICISM WITH CLASS

1. Ernest Hemingway (1899–1961). Definition of "guts" in an interview with Dorothy Parker, *New Yorker* (Nov. 30, 1929). From *The Columbia World of Quotations* (New York, NY: 1996).
2. Martin Luther (1483–1546). Public domain.

3. Donald T. Phillips, *Lincoln on Leadership: Executive Strategies for Tough Times* (New York, NY: Warner Books, 1992), 66–67.
4. Steven F. Hayward, *Churchill on Leadership: Executive Success in the Face of Adversity* (Rocklin, CA: Forum, an Prima Publishing, 1997), 121–122. Used by permission of Prima Publishing, a division of Random House, Inc.
5. David Roper, *Elijah, A Man Like Us* (Grand Rapids, MI: Discovery House Publishers, 1998), 126–127. Used by permission of Discovery House Publishers, Box 3566, Grand Rapids, Michigan 49501. All rights reserved.
6. Warren Wiersbe, *Be Patient* (Colorado Springs, CO: Cook Communications, 1991), 91.
7. Stephen Charnock (1628–1680). Public domain.
8. "Someone with Skin On" story. Source unknown.
9. David Roper, *Elijah, Man Like Us* (Grand Rapids, MI 1998), 88–89, quoting Saint John of the Cross. Used by permission of Discovery House Publishers, Box 3566, Grand Rapids, Michigan 49501. All rights reserved.
10. Blaise Paschal (1623–1662). Public domain.
11. John E. Hartley, *The Book of Job* (NICOT) (Grand Rapids, MI: William B. Eerdmans Publishing Company, 1988) 354. Used by permission.
12. David Roper, *Elijah, A Man Like Us* (Grand Rapids, MI: Discovery House Publishers, 1998), 116–117. Used by permission of Discovery House Publishers, Box 3566, Grand Rapids, Michigan 49501. All rights reserved.

CHAPTER THIRTEEN
THE FUTILITY OF UNSCREWING THE INSCRUTABLE

1. Charles R. Swindoll, *The Finishing Touch: Becoming God's Masterpiece* (Nashville, TN: Word Publishing, 1994) 276–277. Used by permission.
2. Souce unknown.
3. A. W. Tozer, *The Knowledge of the Holy: The attributes of God: Their Meaning in the Christian Life* (New York, NY: Harper Collins/Harper & Brothers, 1961), 16, 18.
4. Teacher in the 21st Century, http://www.pipforschools.com/teacher_21st_century.html. Source unknown.

5. W. Tozer, *The Knowledge of the Holy: The attributes of God: Their Meaning in the Christian Life* (New York, NY: Harper Collins/Harper & Brothers, 1961), 10–12
6. Source unknown.

CHAPTER FOURTEEN
A RECOMMITMENT TO THINGS THAT MATTER

1. John Piper, *Brothers We Are Not Professionals* (Nashville, TN: Broadman & Holman Publishers, 2002), ix. Used by permission.
2. Charles Haddon Spurgeon (1834–1892), source unknown. Public domain.
3. Gary L. Bauer, "End of Day"—9/11/2002. Used by permission
4. James Russell Lowell (1819–1891), "The Present Crisis," from John Bartlett, *Familiar Quotations, Fifteenth Edition, 6ᵗʰ Printing* (Boston, MA: Little, Brown, and Company, 1937), 567. Public domain.
5. Homer Stewart's personal testimony. Used by permission.
6. Eugene H. Peterson, "Introduction to Job," from *The Message* (Colorado Springs, CO: NavPress, 2002) 841–842. Used by permission.

CHAPTER FIFTEEN
THE PASSIONATE TESTIMONY OF AN INNOCENT MAN

1. David Gergen, *Eyewitness to Power*, quoting Senator Alan Simpson (1931), (New York, NY: Touchstone, 2000). Public domain.
2. Roy B. Zuck, *Job* (Chicago, IL: Moody Publishers, 1978), 133. Used by permission.
3. Charles Wesley (1707–1788), "And Can It Be?" Public domain.

CHAPTER SIXTEEN
ANOTHER LONG-WINDED MONOLOGUE

1. David Atkinson, *The Message of Job: Suffering and Grace,* "The Bible Speaks Today Series" (Downers Grove, IL: Inter-Varsity Press, 1991), 122. Used by permission of InterVarsity Press, P. O. Box 1400, Downers Grove, IL 60515. www.ivpress.com.
2. John E. Hartley, *The Book of Job* (NICOT) (Grand Rapids, MI: William B. Eerdmans Publishing Company, 1988) 446–447. Used by permission.
3. "Since God is Taking My Picture" story. Source unknown.
4. Robert Grant (1778–1838), "O Worship the King" (Nashville, TN: Word Music, 1997). Public domain.
5. Donald Grey Barnhouse, *Let Me Illustrate: More Than 400 Stories, Anecdotes, and Illustrations* (Grand Rapids, MI: Fleming H. Revell/ division of Baker Book House, 1994), 132–133.

CHAPTER SEVENTEEN
A PENETRATING REPROOF FROM THE ALMIGHTY

1. Frank E. Gaebelein (editor), "Job," *The Expositor's Bible Commentary,* Volume 7 (Grand Rapids, MI: The Zondervan Corporation, 1985) 462.
2. David Atkinson, *The Message of Job: Suffering and Grace,* "The Bible Speaks Today Series"(Downers Grove, IL: Inter-Varsity Press, 1991), 145–147. Used by permission of InterVarsity Press, P. O. Box 1400, Downers Grove, IL 60515. www.ivpress.com.
3. Ibid., 147. Used by permission.
4. Robert Alden, *Job,* The New American Commentary (Nashville, TN: Broadman & Holman Publishers, 1993), 71. Used by permission.
5. Arthur Bennett, ed 1975. "Man A Nothing," *The Valley of Vision: A Collection of Puritan Prayers & Devotions* (Carlisle, PA: The Banner of Truth Trust, 1975) 91. Used by permission of Banner of Truth, Carlisle, PA 17013.
6. Gary Inrig, *True North* (Grand Rapids, MI: Discovery House Publishers, 2002), 142–143. Used by permission of Discovery House Publishers, Box 3566, Grand Rapids MI 49501. All rights reserved.

CHAPTER EIGHTEEN
FULL REPENTANCE FOR ALL THE RIGHT REASONS

1. *Best Lawyer Story*, Alteredbeast Forums, Author unknown. http://www.alteredbeast.org/vb/showthread.php?t=508.
2. John E. Hartley, *The Book of Job* (NICOT) (Grand Rapids, MI: William B. Eerdmans Publishing Company, 1988) 537. Used by permission.

CHAPTER NINETEEN
FINALLY . . . JUSTICE ROLLS DOWN

1. Frederick W. Faber (1814–1863), "There's a Wideness in God's Mercy" 1854. Public domain.
2. William R. Newell (1868–1956), "At Calvary" 1895. Public domain.

CHAPTER TWENTY

1. Oliver Wheeler, quoted by Glen Wheeler, *1010 Illustrations, Poems and Quotes* (Cincinnati, OH: Standard Publishing, 1967), 14.
2. Douglas MacArthur, on his 75th Birthday, quoted by Glen Wheeler, *1010 Illustrations, Poems and Quotes* (Cincinnati, OH: Standard Publishing, 1967), 15.
3. Charles R. Swindoll, *Tale of the Tardy Oxcart* (Nashville, TN: Word Publishing, 1998), 28.
4. "17th Century Nun's Prayer." Source Unknown.

CHAPTER TWENTY-ONE
WHAT JOB TEACHES US ABOUT OURSELVES

1. "How Do You Decide Who to Marry?" www.ozjokes.com. Author unknown.
2. Rosamund Stone Zander and Benjamin Zander, *The Art of Possibility* (Boston, MA: Harvard Business School Publishing Corporation, 2000),

118–119. Reprinted by permission of Harvard Business School Press. All rights reserved.

3. Francis Andersen, *Job: Tyndale OT Commentary Series* (London, IL: Inter-Varsity Press 1976), 93–94. Used by permission of InterVarsity Press, P. O. Box 1400, Downers Grove, IL 60515. www.ivpress.com.

4. David Roper, *Growing Slowly Wise: Building a Faith that Works* (Grand Rapids, MI: Discovery House Publishers, 2000), 26–27. Used by permission of Discovery House Publishers, Box 3566, Grand Rapids MI 49501. All rights reserved.

CHAPTER TWENTY-TWO
WHAT JOB TEACHES US ABOUT OUR GOD

1. "Couple from Minnesota." Author unknown.

2. A. W. Tozer, *The Knowledge of the Holy: The attributes of God: Their Meaning in the Christian Life* (New York, NY: Harper Collins/Harper & Brothers, 1961), 73.

3. Philip Yancey, *Disappointment With God* (Grand Rapids, MI: Zondervan Publishing House, 1988), 189–191. Used by permission of The Zondervan Corporation.

4. Ken Gire, *The Reflective Life: Becoming More Spiritually Sensitive to the Everyday Moments of Life* (Colorado Springs, CO: Chariot Victor Publishing, a Division of Cook Communications, 1998)

CONCLUSION

1. George MacDonald, *The Curate's Awakening* (Bloomington, MN: Bethany House Publishers, a division of Baker Book House Company, 1985) 60.

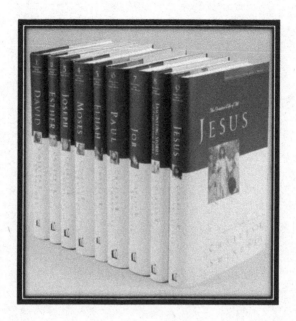

Ordinary People, Great Lives

The Great Lives from God's Word series explores ordinary men and women whose lives were empowered by God when they surrendered to Him. Learn from the great lives of our faith and how their stories can help us become who we were created to be.

This best-selling series from Charles Swindoll focuses on the lives of *David, Esther, Joseph, Moses, Elijah, Paul, Job,* and finally *Jesus,* the greatest life of all. Also available are *Fascinating Stories of Forgotten Lives* and the 365-day devotional *Great Days with the Great Lives.*

Visit your favorite bookseller to complete your collection.

INSIGHT FOR LIVING

THOMAS NELSON
Since 1798

JESUS

The Greatest Life of All

Jesus Christ. He is, without question, the most influential person in history. Millions of people claim the truths of the religion that bears His name.

But who exactly *is* Jesus? A popular religious teacher? An ancient martyr? Many today are unsure. Even scholars debate whether the Jesus of history is the Christ of faith. Now, more than ever, we need a clear understanding of the person and work of the man millions call *Savior*.

In this biographical study in the best-selling Great Lives from God's Word series, beloved pastor and Bible teacher Charles Swindoll introduces you to the carpenter from Nazareth as you have never seen Him before.

This fascinating biography, filled with biblical and historical insights, takes you on an unforgettable journey through the complex and provocative life of Jesus of Nazareth. His unique birth. His astonishing power. His controversial teaching. His shocking death. And His world-changing resurrection.

Refreshingly honest and deep, this in-depth profile reveals Jesus with great clarity and offers practical applications for your own life. Whether you're just curious about Jesus or a longtime follower of His life and teachings, you'll experience Him in a new way as you join Charles Swindoll in *Jesus: The Greatest Life of All*.

DAVID

A Man of Passion and Destiny

What does it mean to be someone "after God's own heart"? David, Old Testament shepherd, king, and psalmist, offers an answer in the shape of his own life.

In many ways he was a most extraordinary man—intelligent, handsome, abundantly gifted as a poet, musician, warrior, and administrator. Yet in other ways he was a most ordinary man—often gripped by destructive passion, rocked by family chaos and personal tragedy, and motivated by political expediency. How did David become the national hero of God's chosen people? Why is he the one character in the Bible described as "a man after God's own heart"? Charles Swindoll explores the many facets of David—from his teenage years and dysfunctional family life to his overwhelming passion for God.

David's life offers hope to all of us. It shows that God can do extraordinary things through ordinary men and women. And *David: A Man of Passion and Destiny* offers an insightful perspective on what it means to be truly spiritual, to become like David—men and women after God's own heart.

ESTHER

A Woman of Strength and Dignity

Everyone loves a transforming story. Rags to riches. Plain to beautiful. Weak to strong. Esther's story is that, and much more. It is a thought-provoking study of God's invisible hand, writing silently across the pages of human history. Perhaps most of all, it is an account of a godly woman with the courage, wisdom, and strength to block an evil plot, overthrow an arrogant killer, and replace terror with joy in thousands of Jewish homes.

In *Esther: A Woman of Strength and Dignity*, Charles Swindoll interweaves an ancient, real-life story with insight not only into the virtues of Queen Esther, but into how the qualities that formed and empowered her can be ours. We discover the practical process Esther must have gone through as she prepared herself for her life-and-death appearance in the king's throne room. And we enjoy watching the demise of the calculating and cruel Haman, who—like many biblical villains—died in the very trap he had set for someone else.

Through this captivating portrayal of Esther, not only do we encounter the grace, faith, and courage that identified her as a woman of God—we also discover how every Christian can live a transformation story.

PAUL

A Man of Grace and Grit

The apostle Paul. Converted terrorist, inspired author, amazing teacher, and patient mentor. This colossal figure strode boldly onto the stage of the first-century world and left an indelible signature of greatness never to be forgotten. His life? Magnificent! And his ministry? Impressive. While assigned sainthood by some today, by his own description he was "the chief of all sinners." No other person in the Bible, aside from Christ Himself, had a more profound influence on his world and ours than Paul.

He was a man of real grit, with a firmness of mind and spirit as well as unyielding courage in the face of personal hardship and danger. Tough, tenacious, and fiercely relentless, Paul pursued his divine mission with unflinching resolve. And God used him mightily to turn the world upside down for Christ in this generation.

But Paul's message and his style were also marked by gentle grace. This man, who tormented and killed the saints of God, understood and explained grace better than any of his contemporaries. Why? Because he never got over his own gratitude as a recipient of it. God's super-abounding grace transformed this once-violent aggressor into a humble-but-powerful spokesman for Christ. A man with that much grit desperately needed that much grace.

Perhaps that's why Paul's life is such a source of hope for us. If the chief of sinners can be forgiven and become God's chosen vessel, can He not forgive and use us as well? He can if we, too, become people of both grace and grit.

JOSEPH

A Man of Integrity and Forgiveness

In a world where faith is fading and integrity is rare, the life of Joseph shines like a brilliant star in the nighttime sky, showing us that following God brings hope even in the worst of circumstances. In *Joseph: A Man of Integrity and Forgiveness,* Charles Swindoll reveals a man buffeted with the same kinds of problems we face today—or worse. A man whose tenacious faith in God ultimately won him great honor and achievement.

No family today is more dysfunctional than Joseph's. No one faces greater temptation than what Potiphar's wife offered this man of faith. No faith is challenged more than Joseph's as he sat on death row in an Egyptian prison. Yet Joseph stood firm, modeling for us what is possible when ordinary people maintain their connections with God.

Swindoll traces the life of this intriguing man from the famous multi-colored coat, through the jealous rage that prompts his brothers to sell him into slavery, to his astounding rise to a position of national power. He follows Joseph through temptation and imprisonment to his ascension in Egyptian society after he explains the king's dreams, revealing a grim and threatening future and proposing a plan for saving the nation . . . and the brothers who deceived him.

It is a story that reads like an epic novel, filled with intrigue, tension, temptation, and torrential emotions. We are heartened today because although we face the same kinds of difficulties, Joseph's life also shows us we can triumph.

MOSES

A Man of Selfless Dedication

Moses. Was he the sleek-and-trim, fun-loving animated man in *The Prince of Egypt,* or the handsome, strong-hearted, superstar played by Charlton Heston in *The Ten Commandments?*

The most likely answer is "neither." The Bible gives a much more accurate picture of the Moses God used in such remarkable ways. Charles Swindoll paints a portrait of the biblical Moses in this fascinating look into the heart and mind of *Moses: A Man of Selfless Dedication.*

Swindoll gives us straight-from-the-shoulder facts based squarely on the truth revealed in God's Word. He also fills in the fine-line details of Moses' life with emotion and feeling, because Moses, like all of us, was a human being with faults and frailties. And finally, Swindoll helps us apply the lessons of Moses' life to our own daily dilemmas.

When you face your personal Red Sea test, will you be prepared? Your decision to go forward in life instead of retreating will be bolstered by your having studied the real Moses of the Bible—the Moses who tried to decline his assignment from God; the Moses who dazzled Pharaoh; the Moses who received the Ten Commandments; the Moses who was sometimes disobedient and weak; the Moses who was the greatest leader of God's people in all of history; the Moses of faith and selfless dedication to his God. If it's reality you're searching for, welcome to the world of Moses . . . and his God . . . as only Charles Swindoll can describe it.

ELIJAH

A Man of Heroism and Humility

Where are great leaders like Elijah today? Uncompromisingly strong, yet self-controlled? Disciplined, yet forgiving. Audaciously courageous, yet kind. Heroic in the heart of battle, yet humble in the aftermath. Rarely does someone model these invaluable traits more obviously than God's mighty prophet Elijah, whose calling was anything but calm and free from conflict.

Exploring the depths of Elijah's fascinating life as a prophet of God, Swindoll does not gloss over his human weaknesses. Rather, he presents an honest picture of this ordinary man who God transformed into His personal spokesman to confront idolatry and evil in the ancient world. It's a life worth emulating.

In a world that has lost its way and lacks godly, balanced leaders, we are more than ever in need of a few Elijah-like men and women who are not afraid to live courageously among their peers as they walk humbly with their God.

Charles Swindoll's wish is that *Elijah: A Man of Heroism and Humility* will help "establish deep within you a desire to stand strong for what is right as you bow low before Him who is worthy of your trust and obedience."

FASCINATING STORIES OF FORGOTTEN LIVES
Rediscovering Some Old Testament Characters

Would you rather be a person of significance or a person of prominence? Think carefully! The answer to that question will shape your entire future.

Charles Swindoll says, "Somehow life has taught us poorly. We're trained to think that the most significant people are star athletes, actors, and musicians—the ones we applaud, those whose autographs we seek, those who have worldly renown. They aren't. Not really. Most often, the people really worth noting are those who turn a 'nobody' into a 'somebody' but never receive credit."

What is forgotten far too often is this: *Success in God's kingdom and in the church depends upon faithful people the public rarely knows.*

The Old Testament contains numerous *Fascinating Stories of Forgotten Lives*—unsung heroes whose actions, sacrifices, or battles failed to ascribe them worldly renown. These great lives, however, reveal *significant* people whom God honors in the pages of His Word and, therefore, deserve our serious attention and emulation.

- Adino took out eight hundred armed, skilled fighting men *with his sword.*
- Eleazar attacked the Philistines *by himself* for so long that his comrades had to pry his sword out of his grip.
- Shammah, while his companions ran like scared cats from their enemies, *stood his ground—alone—and was victorious.*

And yet, did you recall any of their names? They're not on the rolls of the rich and famous. Still, they are *significant.* As Swindoll examines little-remembered Bible characters and events, he will help you discover biblical principles and practical applications for living so that you can be who you are in God's estimation—a person of true significance.

GREAT DAYS WITH THE GREAT LIVES

Daily Insight from Great Lives of the Bible

"We desperately need role models worth following," says Charles Swindoll. "Authentic heroes. People of integrity. Great lives to inspire us to do better, to climb higher, to stand taller."

Great Days with the Great Lives is a collection of biographies taken from the Great Lives from God's Word series. Each day provides a Scripture reference and devotional thought based on the experience of some of the greatest heroes of the Bible—men and women whose authentic walk with God will teach us, encourage us, and warn us.

These profiles in character from one of America's most beloved teachers, Chuck Swindoll, offer us hope for the future. They show us that God can do extraordinary things through ordinary men and women like us. They teach us what it means to be genuinely spiritual people—people after God's own heart.

Join Charles Swindoll for a full year of *Great Days with the Great Lives*—an exploration into the hearts and lives of God's heroes who continue to instruct and inspire.